Jack the Ripper
British Intelligence Officer?

For John Molyneux

© Tom Slemen and Keith Andrews 2010
Published by The Bluecoat Press, Liverpool
Book design by Michael March, Liverpool
Cover design Nick Oram and Daniel Bickerton
Printed by Ashford Colour Print

ISBN 9781904438915

To Paul
Happy 35th
have a great Day
from
Tom Slemen

Jack the Ripper

British Intelligence Officer?

Tom Slemen

with Keith Andrews

THE BLUECOAT PRESS

LIST OF ILLUSTRATIONS

The body of Mary Ann Nichols is discovered in Bucks Row. ... 22

Crest of the Royal Sussex Regiment. ... 33

Louis Diemschutz, found the body of Liz Stride. ... 61

Matthew Packer, fruiterer. ... 70

John Kelly – common law husband of Catharine Eddowes. ... 88

Map of Mitre Square. ... 99

Watkins discovers Eddowes' body in Mitre Square. ... 104

Position of Eddowes' body in Mitre Square. ... 105

Strange markings the Ripper inscribed on the face of Eddowes. ... 111

The message with every word spelt correctly – except Jews. ... 117

Sir Charles Warren. ... 123

Claude Reigner Conder in Palestine. ... 124

Baden Powell's sketch of a butterfly, and plans of fort hidden within. 133

The glyphs inscribed on the face of Kate Eddowes, and the glyph table. 135

Michael Davitt. ... 139

Timothy Kelly, one of the Phoenix Park murderers aged 20. ... 141

Aftermath of the Phoenix Park double murder 1882. ... 143

Liverpool Irishman Frank Byrne and his wife Mary. ... 144

George Lusk. ... 145

Joe Barnett, lover of Marie Jeanette Kelly. ... 183

13 Millers Court, off Dorset Street. ... 189

John McCarthy, landlord of Marie Jeanette Kelly. ... 190

Mohawk Minstrels at the Elephant and Castle, 1888. ... 203

Marie Jeanette Kelly's body on her bed. ... 218

Marie Jeanette Kelly on her deathbed. ... 221

Cord tied around Kelly's right calf. ... 232

Prime Minister Lord Salisbury. ... 277

MP Charles Stewart Parnell. ... 278

Josiah Conder in Japanse attire. ... 297

Kitchener as a young cadet at Woolwich. ... 331

Conder's watercolour of a womb. ... 335

Conder's watercolour of a woman. ... 336

Sir Charles Warren in his eighties. ... 365

CONTENTS

FOREWORD by Richard Whittington-Egan 4

1 JACK THE MYTH 8

2 POLLY NICHOLS 15

3 ANNIE CHAPMAN 29

4 ELIZABETH STRIDE 54

5 CATHARINE EDDOWES 85

6 THE LUSK KIDNEY 140

7 THE UNKNOWN VICTIM 159

8 MARIE JEANETTE KELLY 181

9 NATION ON A KNIFE-EDGE 254

10 TOWARDS A SOLUTION 292

AFTERWORD What if we are wrong? 366

INDEX 368

FOREWORD

Richard Whittington-Egan

"Of making many books there is no end." That is certainly true of volumes concerning Jack the Ripper. And much study of the many Ripperine theories that they weave, ranging across the entire spectrum of fantasy, ingenious to ingenuous, is indeed as *Ecclesiastes XII.12* proclaims, "a weariness of the flesh".

But there is, I am happy to be able to report, no weariness about Tom Slemen and Keith Andrews' book. Meticulously researched, it is sharply written, thoroughly readable, and totally fresh in the mystery-solving direction which it takes.

The tale that the authors have to tell, begins, of necessity, with a lengthy scene-setting recital of the crimes. They are clearly and cleanly delineated and the narrative angle cleverly concentrates on the illumination of the circumstances and personality of the victim in each case. The reader is transported into the legendary East End London world of the 1880s, where pea-soupers, swirls of raw fog from the river, set haloes about the gas-lamps, as they drift past shrouded, shuttered, tight-curtained, houses. Down these deserted mean streets and menacing dark-as-pitch alleys, stalks, phantasmagoric, the Ripper.

In the course of their century's search, the Ripper hunters have delved into all manner of places and have come up with all manner of nominations – Jack the Royal Prince (Albert Victor), Jack the Prime Minister (William Ewart Gladstone), Jack the Barrister (Montague John Druitt), Jack the Doctor (William Withey Gull), Jack the Uxoricide (William Henry Bury), Jack the Venenatious Publican (Severin Klosowski / George Chapman), Jack the Putative Diarist (James Maybrick), Jacqueline (the speculative unnamed midwife, not to mention such candidates as the mysterious Dr Stanley (proposed by Leonard Matters) and Dr Alexander Pedachenko (proposed by Donald McCormick), both nominees virtually as insubstantial as the innominate slayer.

Insubstantial or otherwise, Jack the Ripper is deeply embedded in our culture and we seem to labour under an aversion to calling him Mr Nemo. We have a kind of instinctive need to hang a meaningful, nominal label about his neck. This has led to absurdities – false conundrums, over-confident pseudo identifications, and literally shelves of books written by self-purblinded authors with obsessional fixations in regard to one cherished suspect. And the trouble is that each new nominee accretes a retinue of enthusiastic supporters.

Optimists have punted the 'cold case' notion that a possible solution might be sought in the resurrection of Kelly's mangled remains from her grave in St Patrick's Roman Catholic Cemetery, Leytonstone, and a scrutinising of them for her slaughterer's DNA. Perhaps some may still linger there, perhaps not, but, even if it did, it would yield no answer, for nowhere could be found the killer's DNA with which to match it.

There is a hard core of Ripperologists who believe that the identity of the Whitechapel killer will never be revealed. They feel, and not without good reason, that

5

since, even among the hierarchical personages of Scotland Yard, the headquarters of the City of London Police, and the Home Office, as well as among those actually out tramping the killing ground, there was total disagreement whenever the naming of a guilty party was mooted, the naming of names one hundred and twenty-two years later, is unlikely to import conviction.

Slemen and Andrews' suggested identification is a responsible one, at least meriting serious consideration. Becomingly modest, they refreshingly make no extravagant claims for their case, but leave the reader in no doubt as to their firm belief that their candidate truly fits the bill. Their hypothesis is that the Ripper had been a military intelligence agent in Ireland and the Middle East, a trained killer who had worked for the War Office and been chosen for the Whitechapel job by a Whitehall cabal. If you read carefully, you will find early textual nuances which anticipate this conclusion. It would not, however, be fair if I were to reveal the link between the authors' prime suspect and his victims.

Born a mere thirty-six years after Jack's last wielding of his knife, and while in all probability he was still alive, I have been studying the Ripper affair for the last seventy-five. I am aware of all those whose names have been put forward for the blood-stained wreath. But I have not been persuaded that the real Jack figures amongst any of them. Slemen and Andrews' submission is undeniably plausible, but my tenancy in the tower of unknowing is not yet at an end.

But, as Sherlock Holmes remarked to Watson, "the game's afoot", and this is surely all good fun, and harmless to boot, although I fear that fierce partisanship and its concomitant presbyopic tendency are antagonistic to rationality. One must allow, too, that undue solemnity can be just as destructive as insouciance or ridiculous hypothesising. Slemen and Andrews' offering is, however, without question an extremely significant addition to the shelf of worthwhile studies of the great East End enigma.

1

JACK THE MYTH

In 1888 an extraordinary killer nicknamed Jack the Ripper carried out a series of unique murders in the East End of London. Criminologists, social historians, armchair detectives, science fiction novelists, screenwriters, 'Ripperologists' and even occultists have all speculated on the identity of 'Jack', yet none of their explanations has ever fitted the facts of the Whitechapel Murders case. For many years in my youth I imagined the Ripper as a shadowy tall top-hatted opera-cloaked man who carried a Gladstone bag of surgical instruments in his gloved hand as he prowled the fogbound streets of Victorian London – someone like the late Ralph Bates, a gifted British actor who once portrayed a Ripperesque villain in the classically kitsch Hammer House of Horror film *Dr Jekyll and Sister Hyde* (1971). The premise of this film involved Dr Jekyll's discovery of a rejuvenating serum, derived from female hormones. In order to obtain these hormones he removed the pituitary glands, with a knife and scalpel, from the prostitutes of East London, carrying out this grisly work as his transsexual alter ego, Sister Hyde.

The archetypal folklore image of Jack had already become firmly entrenched in the collective consciousness of the public many years before, due to a celluloid milestone of suspense known as *The Lodger* (1926). This film, based on a stage version of the novel, *The Lodger,* by Marie Belloc

Lowndes, was directed by a young Alfred Hitchcock, with Ivor Novello – a major silver-screen heart-throb of the day – starring as a possible Ripper-style serial killer. The unsettling psychological Hitchcockian chiaroscuro imagery, stylistic outré effects and suspenseful scenarios conjured up by the director and his accomplice, the imaginative scenarist Elliot Stannard, formed a permanent association between Jack the Ripper and fog, shadows and dual personality. These unfounded associations were reiterated in further films featuring thinly veneered interpretations of the Ripper mystery, such as *Dr Jekyll and Mr Hyde* (1932), which featured Frederic March's Oscar-winning performance of the split-personality character.

Nine years later, the Robert Louis Stevenson classic was filmed once more, this time with Spencer Tracy in the title role. One of the most memorable moments of this latter film is the scene preceding Jekyll's full transformation into Hyde, with Tracy attempting to whistle an opera aria that his coarse 'other self' keeps changing into George Grossmith's song, 'See Me Dance the Polka'. Then we come upon the laughable low-budget *Jack the Ripper* (1959), a thoroughly fictionalised version of the 1888 slayings. Two later films were also entitled 'Jack the Ripper', and they have not fared much better than the lame 1959 attempt to bring the Whitechapel Murders to the screen. The first flick, made in 1979, starred Klaus Kinski as a Ripper who disposed of his victims' bodies by dumping them in the Thames, unlike the real murderer – who left five of the six women he killed on the spot where they were slain. The next was the 1988 made-for-television mini-series *Jack the Ripper* starring Michael Caine as Inspector Abberline, one of the chief detectives assigned to track down the Ripper. Transmitted on ITV in the United Kingdom on the 100th anniversary of the Ripper murders, David Wickes' *Jack the Ripper* had been causing a storm of controversy in the British Press because the director of the film had alleged that his film would reveal, once and for all, the identity of the Ripper. Prince Charles allegedly telephoned the director of the film to discover if his ancestor the Duke of Clarence had been the culprit. Like everyone else, His Royal Highness had to wait for the ludicrous ending of the film, where the Ripper is improbably shown to be Sir William Gull, the stroke-ridden 72-year-old physician to Queen Victoria! The same old man is later depicted as being the Ripper in *From Hell* (2001).

Michael Caine's Abberline was portrayed as an alcoholic trying to stay on the wagon in the 1988 film, but in *From Hell* Johnny Depp plays Abberline as an opium-addicted psychic. The real Inspector Abberline was a clean-living man, with the appearance and demeanour of a middle-aged bank manager. He was neither an alcoholic, a drug addict, nor a medium, and he is only one example of writers distorting the lives of the people who were part of the Whitechapel Murders story. *From Hell* and the David Wickes television movie, along with the stylish 1979 film, *Murder By Decree*, are based on the long-discredited book *Jack the Ripper: The Final Solution* by the late Stephen Knight. The claims of Knight's book are that Jack the Ripper was not one man, but three – an 'Unholy Trinity' comprised of a Royal physician, an impressionist painter and a coachman. I will be taking a closer look at Knight's conjecture in a later chapter.

In 1886, Robert Louis Stevenson's *Strange Case of Dr. Jekyll and Mr. Hyde* was published, and quickly captured the imagination of the reading public with its intriguing concept of a devil and saint cohabiting inside every one of us. In the novel, Dr Jekyll is a philanthropic physician, preoccupied with the task of polarising the good and evil of human personality. Once the evil part of a person is isolated and contained, it may be removed or destroyed, Jekyll believes, and the age-old problem of latent evil in human nature would be solved once and for all. Unfortunately, the drug Jekyll uses to explore the dark side of his own self physically and mentally transforms him into the repulsive Mr Hyde – the literal antithesis of Jekyll. Redemption comes in the form of an antidote that reverses the shocking transformation, but Hyde gradually becomes the dominant force in the equation, and carries out a murder. Jekyll loses control over the transformations, and ends up committing suicide because he is unable to obtain an essential ingredient for the antidote mixture. The book is exceptional in that it not only entertains, but explores problems of ethics and psychology.

If there was a chemical 'cure' for what we term 'evil' in human behaviour, would it be morally right to administer it? Wouldn't that bypass our free will? That question was addressed again 76 years later in another novel, entitled *A Clockwork Orange*, by Anthony Burgess. Today, we know only too well about the duality of the mind, and of the monsters and angels that can co-exist within the human psyche. Heinrich Himmler, leader of the SS, and head of the Gestapo, was a timid man who fainted when one hundred Jewish men and women were shot to death in his honour on the Russian front. The appalling spectacle caused Himmler to call for the introduction of poison gas as "a more humane means" of execution. Himmler had been a shy and inoffensive chicken farmer before World War Two, but ended up creating extermination camps, and coordinated the systematic killing of six million Jews, as

11

well as Communists, Poles and Roma people. Yet he felt faint at the sight of blood.

Himmler's duality of mind is a textbook example of the issues Stevenson used as the basis of his novel. Himmler, like Dr Jekyll, and most people with extreme dual personalities, was doomed to downfall. I do not believe that the Whitechapel Murderer was of that psychological type. After killing a number of women in a specific area of the East End he was heard from no more. Most serial killers working in a defined area are ultimately caught through escalating blood-lust or simply carelessness. The Ripper did not, in my opinion, commit suicide, and had no need to. The police admitted years after the murders ceased that they were really no wiser as to the identity of Jack the Ripper than they were in that terrible Autumn of 1888.

In May 1887 a dramatised version of *Jekyll and Hyde* opened in Boston. Thomas Russell Sullivan adapted the book for the stage and tailored the parts of the doctor and his alter ego for the American actor Richard Mansfield. Sullivan made several changes to the original storyline and introduced a love interest. What's more, jealousy was now the motive for Hyde's behaviour. In 1888 the Sullivan play opened at Henry Irving's Lyceum Theatre in London after a very successful run in America. Richard Mansfield played both Jekyll and Hyde, and this was seen as a somewhat novel approach, as two separate actors had previously been used to portray the two characters. The technique that 34-year-old Mansfield used to portray the act of transformation was sensational. Today, sophisticated computers are routinely used in films to 'morph' people and objects to create the illusion of a physical change taking place before our eyes, but back in Victorian times, working only by the green gloom of limelight, Mansfield turned himself into

Hyde on a stage devoid of any hi-tech gimmickry. He stood behind a fine gauze curtain, and slowly underwent a grotesque metamorphosis. No prosthetic fittings were used; the effect was the work of Mansfield's sheer acting genius, and it took the audience by storm. Screams filled the air and many members of the audience fainted. One critic later wrote of the onstage transformation: 'The changes made by this artist were startling in the extreme – one moment the benevolent doctor, his very presence a benediction, the next instant a fiend that would shame Dante's inferno.'

Hard-boiled theatre critic Clement Scott of the *Daily Telegraph* found himself thoroughly terrified and sickened by the murder scene at the end of the first act, describing it as: 'the most powerful and horrible thing ever seen on the modern stage.'

Of course, as one sensation was treading the boards of the Lyceum, another one was thought to be stalking the streets of the East End. His name was Jack the Ripper. It didn't take long for someone to connect the two. People wondered if Jack was also a Doctor leading a double life. Had the Jekyll and Hyde play inspired the mysterious murderer? Was the Ripper an insane physician who hid a murderous mind behind the respectable face of a West End doctor? There were even rumours that Richard Mansfield himself had been questioned by Scotland Yard detectives working on the Ripper case, because they thought his portrayal of Hyde had been 'too good to be mere play-acting'.

On Wednesday, 3 October 1888, the *Daily Telegraph's* 'Letters from the Public' column included a letter from a reader who suggested that 'the perpetrator [of the Whitechapel Murders] is a being whose diseased brain has been inflamed by witnessing the performance of the drama *Dr. Jekyll and Mr. Hyde* – which I understand is now wisely

13

withdrawn from the stage. If there is anything in this, let the detectives consider how Mr. Hyde would have acted – for there may be a system in the demonic actions of a madman in following the pattern set before him.'

The notion that the Whitechapel Murderer was a respectable man by day and a psychopathic monster by night was a popular idea that caught on, and it has never quite left the field of Ripperology. However, by the end of this book, I will attempt to show that Jack the Ripper was not a crazed doctor with a split personality, nor a group of Masons conspiring to protect the Monarchy. I will explore a possibility that has never been considered by any Ripperologist before: that 'Jack' was a renowned though belligerent academic, who dedicated his life to the service of his country and the defence of Queen Victoria's realm.

First, let us look at the murders of Jack the Ripper.

2

POLLY NICHOLS

Jack the Ripper killed six women within the space of around 87 days during the autumn months of 1888. One of these victims was never identified, and possibly met her death on, or after, 24 August 1888, not in the slums of Whitechapel, but in a respectable district of London's West End, and I will describe this mysterious murder later in the book.

The first victim of the Ripper was Mary Ann Nichols, a destitute woman of 43 years of age who was residing at a lodging house at 56 Flower and Dean Street in the Spitalfields district of London's East End. Mary Ann, known to her friends as Polly, was born in London's Dean Street, off Fetter Lane, in 1845, the daughter of humble locksmith Edward Walker. On Sunday 26 August 1888, Polly may have celebrated her forty-third birthday with a glass of gin and a rueful reminiscence on the past events of her troubled life. She may have cast her mind back to a certain Saturday in the January of 1864 when she was married to a printer's machinist named William Nichols at St Bride's Church on Fleet Street. Back in those days, Polly had been an attractive and petite young woman in her mid-twenties, trying her utmost to make the marriage work. She would give birth to five of William's children, and the Nichols family could have been such a happy one if William had only been faithful to her, but alas, the marriage began to deteriorate in earnest when Mary Ann was pregnant with her fourth child in 1876 and husband William had a passionate affair with Rosetta Walls, the nurse attending his wife.

By 1880 the marriage of William and Mary Ann had well and truly ended, without hope of reconciliation, and after the separation came Mary Ann's descent into the slums. The heartbreaking memories of a previous life with a husband and family, and the cruel spectre of the life they might have had, haunted the waking and dreaming mind of Polly Nichols for eight long years. Gin could sometimes alleviate the painful echoes of the past but alcoholism was the price to pay, and thus began Polly's downfall. She lost touch with her cheating husband and took shelter in the workhouses and doss-houses of the East End.

In 1888, Polly made one last desperate attempt to turn the tide of her life. Fresh from the workhouse, she managed to secure the position of a domestic servant in the employ of Samuel and Sarah Cowdry at a sizeable house in Wandsworth. It looked like a summer of hope for her, with the promise of brighter days ahead at long last. In May, Polly sat down and wrote a letter to her father:

Dear Father,
I just write to say you will be glad to know that I am
settled in my new place, and going on all right up to
now. My people went out yesterday, and have not
returned, so I am left in charge. It is a grand place
inside, with trees and gardens back and front. All has
been newly done up. They are teetotallers and religious,
so I ought to get on. They are very nice people, and I
have not too much to do. I hope you are all right and the
boy has work. So good-bye for the present.

From yours truly,

Polly

Answer me soon, please, and let me know how you are.

Polly's father Edward was pleased to receive the letter from his wayward daughter, and was probably relieved to hear that she was still alive. He wrote back to her but did not receive a reply. On 12 July Polly Nichols decided to abscond from the house of Mr and Mrs Cowdry after stealing clothing valued at three pounds and ten shillings. She fled from Wandsworth and arrived in Spitalfields a few days later, where she took up lodgings at 18 Thrawl Street, sharing a room with four equally unfortunate down-at-heel women. On Friday, 24 August 1888, Polly moved into a common lodging house on Flower and Dean Street known as the White House, just a street away from her previous 'residence'. With the other wrecks of humanity at the White House, Polly lived a hand to mouth existence each day, and her only belongings in the world were a fragment of looking glass, a white handkerchief and a comb.

Most books on the Ripper state that Polly was a prostitute, but friends of hers – people like Jane Oram (a name that is possibly a mishearing of Polly's friend, Ellen Holland) stated that Nichols was not a 'fast woman'. Obtaining doss-house rent money was not a priority with Polly on the last day of her life, according to the witnesses who saw her shortly before her mysterious death. In the early hours of Friday 31 August 1888, at half-past midnight, Polly was seen leaving the Frying Pan public house on the corner of Spitalfields' Brick Lane and Thrawl Street. The small bonneted woman went into her former residence, 18 Thrawl

Street, but around 1.20am, the deputy of the lodging house told her to leave the kitchen because she couldn't produce the four pence necessary for a bed for the night. Polly headed for the door and asked the deputy to save a bed for her, as she'd soon be back with the money. 'I'll soon get my doss money,' she promised, and pointed to the black bonnet perched on her greying head. 'See what a jolly bonnet I've got now,' she said, drawing attention to a new-looking black straw hat trimmed with black velvet that no one had seen on her before. Where it came from is still a mystery.

Five hours earlier a fire had broken out in the East End at the Shadwell Dry Dock, and it was still ablaze. The autumnal skies over London had already been of an unusual crimson hue at sunset, and now the low oppressive clouds of the night sky over Whitechapel were tinged with the orange glare from the dock blaze. Many people in the East End went down to the docks to watch the blaze, which was almost impossible to extinguish because barrels of brandy and gin had caught fire in the South Quay warehouses, and huge yellow and blue tongues of flame were leaping into the smoke-filled air. On an otherwise monotonous cold night, the raging inferno at the Shadwell Dry Docks was a magnet for loafers and impoverished sensation seekers. The men of the London Fire Brigade in their burnished helmets and horse-drawn fire engines were cheered on by the Cockney crowds as they tore off in the direction of the dock gates, and on the river floating fire engines, capable of pumping fifteen hundred gallons of water per hour, were being drawn by tugs to the blazing wharfs. The acrid smell of the fire was hanging in the damp night air at 2.30am when Polly bumped into her friend Ellen Holland on the corner of Osborn Street and the Whitechapel Road, outside of a grocer's shop. Mrs Holland had just returned from watching the dock fire, and was on her way back to the doss house in 18 Thrawl Street where she had lodged with Polly. She was concerned about her friend's drunkenness; Polly was staggering and leaning against the wall and shutters of the shop to steady herself, and her speech was slurred. From the time when Polly left the Thrawl Street doss house at 1.30am, until the time when she was seen coming down Osborn Street by Mrs Holland one hour later, Polly Nichols seems to have been off the streets in someone's private residence, for not one person set eyes on her during that period. She was not seen soliciting in the streets, and she was not seen in any of the local public houses, yet she had been drinking somewhere with someone.

At that time, there was a very mysterious individual knocking about Whitechapel and Spitalfields named Ted Stanley, who lodged – on and off – at Charles Argent's boarding house at 1 Osborn Place, Osborn Street – the street where Polly was seen staggering in the last hours of her life. Ted Stanley was a man of about 47, but looked a lot younger than his years, possibly because his life as a soldier in the army kept him in shape, and yet this same man seemed to have had a romantic involvement with a contemporary of Polly's named Annie Chapman, a 47-year-old woman living at Crossingham's Lodging House at 35 Dorset Street, just a few minutes' walk from Flower and Dean and Thrawl Streets, where Polly had lodged. Polly had been lodging in the White House on Flower and Dean Street, and that street ran into Osborn Place, where the enigmatic Mr Stanley was living. Stanley professed to be a bricklayer's labourer, but was nicknamed 'The Pensioner' by those who knew him, because he was thought to be a pensioned-off soldier. Stanley denied he was a pensioner, but later curiously admitted he was a soldier with the

Southern Division of the 2nd Brigade of the Hampshire Militia. Annie Chapman was only forty-seven, but due to ill health and hardship she looked much older. She was thickset, five-foot tall, plain-faced and barrel-nosed. People wondered why an athletic handsome man like Ted Stanley should share a bed with an unattractive middle-aged woman like Annie from Saturday to Monday at the Dorset Street doss house. Annie Chapman would later be brutally killed by the same murderer who took the life of Polly Nichols.

Police would later check out the whereabouts of Ted Stanley for 31 August 1888 and discover that the bricklayer's labourer/soldier was on duty at the military installation complex known as Fort Elson, Gosport.

Returning to Polly Nichols on that fateful morning on the Whitechapel Road, she admitted to Ellen Holland: "I have had my lodging house money three times today, and I have spent it."

Mrs Holland tried intently to persuade her intoxicated friend to come back to the lodging house with her, rather than roam the night looking for a customer. Polly Nichols assured her that she would soon be back at Thrawl Street after she had earned her doss house money from a client. As Polly staggered eastwards up the road, the Whitechapel Church clock chimed half-past two, and Mrs Holland returned to Thrawl Street full of concern for her friend. She would later identify Polly's body at the mortuary.

Just under an hour later, at 3.20am, 39-year-old carman, Charles Cross, left his home at 22 Doveton Street in Bethnal Green and walked to his place of employment – Pickfords in Broad Street. To get there Cross had to walk down Buck's Row, a narrow, poorly lit street half a mile from the corner where Polly Nichols had last been seen. As Cross walked down the northern side of Buck's Row, he noticed a dark shape laying across the entrance to a stable yard, opposite Essex Wharf. He imagined the object to be a bundle of tarpaulin sheeting that might have fallen off a cart entering the stable yard. It was hard for Cross to discern just what the shadowy object was in the stygian gloom of Buck's Row, until he was halfway across the road. Then he saw that it was a woman lying across the entrance to Brown's stable yard. She lay on her back with her skirts pushed up almost to her stomach, and her left hand touched the closed doors of the stable yard. Next to the same hand was a small black bonnet trimmed with black velvet. Cross wasn't sure if the woman had been raped and left unconscious by the attack, or whether she was dead.

Footsteps approached in the darkness. It was another carman, also from Bethnal Green, on his way to work, coming in Cross's direction. The man, in his late twenties, was Robert Paul, and he eyed Cross with suspicion as he approached. Cross drew his attention to the woman lying across the gateway of the stable yard, saying, "Come and look at this woman here".

Cross felt the woman's hands which were cold and limp. He believed her to be dead, but Robert Paul thought he could detect a faint breathing movement when he felt the woman's breast. "I think she's breathing, but very little if she is," he said. He asked Cross to help him prop her up against the doors of the stable yard in an effort to revive her, but Cross politely refused, probably because he thought the woman was dead, and besides, he couldn't afford to be too late for work. The two carmen attempted to make the woman decent. Her skirts had been pushed up to the waist, so the men rolled them down, and then continued on their way. If either of them met a policeman on their way to work they would certainly notify him of the woman in Buck's Row.

The body of Mary Ann Nichols is discovered in Bucks Row.

As it happened, on the corner of Hanbury Street and Old Montague Street, they met PC Jonas Mizen, and they told him about the woman in the gateway of Brown's Stable yard on Buck's Row. Mizen proceeded there immediately, and was not too surprised to see his colleague PC John Neil already on the scene. After all, Buck's Row was Neil's beat. PC Neil was sweeping the feeble beam of his bull's-eye lantern over the woman, and already he had seen that her throat had been severed. Her lifeless eyes were wide open and blood was still oozing from a deep wound in her throat. Less than thirty minutes before, PC Neil had passed the very spot where Nichols now lay, and had checked the doors to Brown's stable yard and found them to be securely locked. At that time he had seen and heard no one in Buck's Row. Neil detected a distinct warmness in the woman's right arm, above the elbow, and as he wondered if her life really was extinct, he heard a faint noise at the eastern end of Buck's Row. He turned to see a colleague – PC John Thain – who had been walking up Brady Street from the Whitechapel Road on his beat. PC Neil shone his bull's-eye lantern at him, and when PC Thain was within hailing distance, Neil cried out that there was a woman lying on the ground with her throat cut. "Run at once for Doctor Llewellyn!" he shouted, and Thain hurried off to the doctor's residence at 152 Whitechapel Road.

In the meantime, PC Mizen, the constable who had been alerted by the carmen Cross and Paul, arrived upon the scene, and PC Neil told him to get an ambulance cart and assistance from Bethnal Green Police Station. PC Neil then took the opportunity to look at the immediate environment of the possible murder for fresh clues left by the assailant, but he could see no splashes or trails of blood anywhere in the vicinity, nor could he see any wheel imprints in the muddy road, which meant that no carts, carriages or hansom cabs had recently travelled up Buck's Row.

Across the road from the stable yard was Essex Wharf warehouse, and when PC Neil rang the bell there, Walter Purkiss, the live-in manager, came to the second-floor landing window and peered out. Purkiss opened the window, and PC Neil drew his attention to the woman on the ground across the road. Neil asked him if he had heard any sounds of a disturbance or altercation in the street earlier on. Purkiss said he hadn't and nor had his wife. The couple had gone to bed at 11pm, but Mrs Purkiss had been awake for most of the night, yet she had not even heard the slightest sound of a scuffle. Walter Purkiss had also had a poor night's sleep, yet he had heard absolutely nothing. Therein lies the most baffling aspect of Jack the Ripper's first murder – killing in silence. When Sergeant Kirby arrived upon the scene and knocked up the people living in a cottage adjoining the site of the murder, they told him that they had heard nothing suspicious during the night. A widow, Mrs Emma Green, and her daughter had been in the front first-floor bedroom of the cottage at Number 2 Buck's Row since 11pm, but mother and daughter had heard nothing. Mrs Green's two sons lived in the same dwelling but they too had heard nothing suspicious. Mrs Green had been suffering from a bout of insomnia, and had hardly slept that night, but the only thing she had heard was the police sergeant knocking on her door. From her window she could see the corpse of Polly Nichols lying in front of the stable yard gates next door.

Just fifty yards away from the body, a constable had been on duty at the gate of the Great Eastern Railway yard, and when he was subsequently questioned by a fellow policeman, he said that he had not heard anything remotely suspicious in the area of Buck's Row that morning. The police continued to seek out more potential witnesses to the mystifying murder that morning, but the people they talked to, despite their close proximity to the murder scene, had not heard a sound or seen anyone about around the time of the murder, which a doctor later estimated to be around 3.10 to 3.20am, so it seemed as if a silent and invisible killer was at large. One woman thought she had heard something relevant that morning, but I will look at her story in a later chapter. Night watchman Patrick Mulshaw, an employee of the Whitechapel District Board of Works, was seventy yards away from the murder scene in the next street, watching over the sewage works at his coke-filled brazier, and although he admitted he had dozed off several times during his lonely watches of the night, he insisted he had definitely been awake between three and four in the morning. He saw

24

and heard nobody in the vicinity, but did say a man passed him around the time the body was discovered. The passer-by allegedly said to Mulshaw, "Watchman, old man, I believe somebody is murdered down the street."

Three horse-slaughter men had been at work in the same street as the watchman during the time of the murder, and at the beginning of the investigation, police regarded them with some suspicion because of the violent nature of their work. The men were James Mumford, Henry Tomkins and Charles Brittain, and they had worked at the 'knacker's' yard of Harrison, Barber & Co from between 8 and 9pm on the Thursday, until 4.20am on the Friday morning of the murder. The three men were separated and thoroughly interrogated by detectives, and not only did their alibis of being at work in the yard at the time of the murder match, PC Thain said he remembered Mumford, Tomkins and Brittain being in the yard when he was on his way to fetch Dr Llewellyn.

When Dr Rees Llewellyn inspected Polly's corpse by the light of several bull's-eye lanterns trained on the body by policemen, he noted the deep cut across the throat, and after making a brief preliminary examination of the cadaver, he officially pronounced life extinct. Dr Llewellyn had found that Polly's wrists and hands were cold, yet the lower extremities of her body were quite warm, and experience of such subtle indications led the surgeon to opine that death had occurred no more than thirty minutes previously. Addressing the officers he said, "Move her to the mortuary. She is dead and I will make a further examination of her there."

As the policemen lifted the corpse on to the ambulance cart, they saw and felt the blood that had coursed from the neck wound and soaked the back of the worn ulster overcoat. At this point, the full extent of the appalling injuries Polly had sustained was not yet visible. Police constables Mizen and Neil, and Sergeant Kirby took the body to the mortuary in the Workhouse Infirmary on Old Montague Street, and Dr Llewellyn went home to catch up on some sleep before the post-mortem later in the morning. However, the surgeon's slumbers were soon interrupted when he was once again awakened by the law. Llewellyn was summoned to the mortuary by Police Inspector John Spratling. Intending to compile notes for the coroner, Spratling had gone along to the mortuary, and had been shocked to see that the abdomen of the dead woman had been savagely ripped open from as far as the breast bone to expose the intestines. The mutilations were only now visible because the body was laid out beneath the superior illumination of the mortuary gaslights.

Years of experience could not prepare Dr Rees Llewellyn for the disturbing sight he beheld when he glanced at the disembowelled corpse. Averting his gaze from the torn-open abdomen, he noted the two curious bruises on each side of the dead woman's face. He speculated that the bruising had been caused by the killer as he exerted pressure with his finger and thumb, in the act of steadying the head before the throat-slitting. The surgeon also noted that there were two incisions across the throat of varying lengths. One was over eight inches in length and ran around the neck to a point about three inches below the right jaw, whilst the second inch-long cut commenced on the left side of the neck just below the ear. The long cut was so deep, it had sliced through the two carotid arteries, the gullet and windpipe and had reached down to the vertebrae of the spinal column. The incisions, Dr Llewellyn decided, had been made with a moderately sharp strong-bladed knife, and the cuts through the throat had been made in a left-to-right direction.

The killer had either been very lucky in evading the two policemen who had beats that covered Buck's Row, or he was a stealthy professional killer who had murdered in such circumstances before. Light sleepers, watchmen, horse slaughterers and patrolling policemen had seen and heard no one about before, during, or immediately after the murder of Polly Nichols, and the killer would carry out his grisly deeds on five more women in London in silence, and under what seemed like some cloak of invisibility. In fact, the notorious occultist Aleister Crowley later claimed that the Ripper was literally invisible because he was a practising black magician.

News of the shocking murder soon spread throughout London, and various friends of the dead woman came forward on hearing the description of the victim, including the mention of a scar on her forehead, and the words 'Lambeth Workhouse' stamped on her petticoats. Ellen Holland was one, and so was Mary Ann Monk, a woman who had been an inmate of the Lambeth Workhouse with Nichols in May 1888. Once identified, Polly's estranged father, Edward Walker, came forward. With tears streaming down his cheeks, he viewed his daughter's ravaged body and said, "I don't think she had any enemies; she was too good for that."

That day, William Nichols and one of his sons were brought to the mortuary on Old Montague Street by Detective Inspector Frederick Abberline. Mr Nichols braced himself as the mortuary attendant removed the lid of the dilapidated coffin to reveal his wife's body, dressed in a burial shroud. Choked with emotion, William gazed down at the face of Polly, barely able to utter a single sentence. He struggled to say, "I forgive you, as you are, for what you have been to me."

Five days later, Polly Nichols was buried at Ilford Cemetery, and two days after the funeral, a second savage and sinister murder took place just three-quarters of a mile from the murder scene at Buck's Row.

3

ANNIE CHAPMAN

In the previous chapter I alluded to Annie Chapman and her mysterious relationship with a man who called himself Ted Stanley. More is to be said about this intriguing character later, but for now, let us look at facts concerning the second canonical victim of Jack the Ripper. Annie Chapman was born in Knightsbridge in 1841, the first of five children of Lifeguardsman, George Smith. Annie was 47 years old in 1888, but this ill woman's care-worn face made her look a lot older than her years. She was undernourished, and suffering from a terminal tubercular disease of the lungs and brain, caused by contracting tuberculosis from fellow lodgers in overcrowded doss houses. Despite Annie's serious health problems, she was attempting to make a living from selling matches, making artificial flowers, and doing crochet work. Perhaps if things became too bleak, then she would have no alternative but to attempt prostitution, but from the reports of Annie's unattractive appearance and the grave state of her health, it's unlikely that she could have made a living as a streetwalker.

Before her descent into the abyss of the East End, Annie had been married to a Newmarket-born coachman named John Chapman. On Mayday 1869, Annie married John, with her younger sister Emily Latitia as a witness. The newly-weds lived at 29 Montpelier Place in Brompton for a short while, then in 1870 they moved to Number 1

Brook Mews North in Bayswater. In 1873 they once again relocated to 17 South Bruton Mews, at the prestigious address of Berkeley Square. In 1881, the Chapmans moved to Windsor, where John was employed as a coachman for a farm bailiff named Josiah Weeks. According to the census of 1881, Annie and John were living at 'Apartments Over Stables, St Leonard's Hill, Clewer, Berkshire'. The first child of the couple, Emily Ruth, arrived less than a year after the marriage, in 1870, and in 1873 another daughter, Annie Georgina was born. Seven years later, John Chapman junior was born – physically handicapped. This was the first of a series of tragedies to befall the Chapmans. Emily Ruth died from meningitis at the age of twelve, and John Chapman junior was put in the care of a charitable school.

The marriage between Annie and John was in tatters by the early 1880s, but the causes of the marital breakdown are not known with any certainty. Annie left her husband and family around 1884, and returned to London, where she received a weekly allowance of ten shillings from her husband up until his death, from cirrhosis of the liver at Christmas 1886. The death of John Chapman was a bitter blow, and the cessation of the ten shillings' allowance left Annie without any financial support, but that year brought more heartache when the man Annie had been living with – a sieve-maker named John – decided to desert her. The cause of the abandonment is not clear. Perhaps he had sponged off Annie's allowance and decided to move on when the money stopped coming. All we know is that John 'Sivvy' as they called him, walked out of the sad life of Annie Chapman and moved to Notting Hill. At this time, Annie was living at a huge four-story lodging house at 30 Dorset Street. Roland Hill of Bethnal Green owned the property, which accommodated 117 people, and he had leased the building to John McCarthy, the man who was also the landlord of Jack the Ripper's final victim – Marie Jeanette Kelly. In 1888, there was a report in the People newspaper (18 November) which stated that Annie Chapman knew Marie Jeanette, although most Ripperologists today doubt that the two victims knew one another. Annie lived in the very street where Marie Jeanette came to live – Dorset Street – and both women surely must have at least known one another by sight, as they frequented the same pubs; the Horn of Plenty at one end of the street, and the Britannia at the other. Both women were also regulars at the pub around the corner on Commercial Street – the Ten Bells.

The death of a husband, the ending of the ten-shilling allowance, and the loss of lover John Sivvy came as tremendous blows to Annie Chapman, and her close friend, Amelia Palmer, later said of the traumatic events at the murder inquest: "Since the death of her husband, Annie seemed to give way altogether".

Annie Chapman's violent demise was as mysterious and inexplicable as the silent slaying of Polly Nichols. The events leading to what Ripperologist's term as 'the second canonical murder' unfolded at Crossingham's Lodging House at 35 Dorset Street, a doss house accommodating 300 people, located just 60 yards away from Miller's Court, where Marie Jeanette Kelly – the Ripper's last victim – lived. Annie had been a regular at Crossingham's Lodging House since around May 1888, and was on pleasant terms with Timothy Donovan, the deputy of Crossingham's.

At 5pm on Friday, 7 September, Amelia Palmer bumped into Annie on Dorset Street and asked her friend if she intended to go to Stratford (where Annie sold her crochet work and artificial flowers). Chapman looked much paler than usual, possibly because she was suffering from a form of tubercular meningitis, and she told Amelia she felt too ill to do anything. Ten minutes later, Amelia came back down the street and saw that Annie was still standing in the same spot, looking quite sick. Amelia tarried and gazed sympathetically at her friend, but Annie told her pragmatically, "It's no use giving way. I must pull myself together and get some money or I shall have no lodgings."

As Amelia walked on she saw Annie slowly shuffling on down Dorset Street. That night at 11.30pm, Annie entered Crossingham's and asked the Deputy, Donovan, if she could go into the kitchen. Having said she could, he then asked where she had been keeping herself all week. Annie said she'd been in the infirmary. Given her health problems, Donovan would probably have believed her, yet there is no record of her being in any hospital during that 'missing week'.

Around midnight, William Stevens, a painter and lodger at Crossingham's, was drinking a pint of beer with Annie Chapman in the lodging house kitchen. Annie said she had just been to Vauxhall to see some friends (possibly a sister who lived in that district). She seemed to have obtained money from someone because she had sent a lodger out to fetch a pint of ale from the nearby pub, and later went out herself to get another drink. During this time spent in the kitchen, a trivial incident is reported to have taken place by Stevens, and it was to later provide a headache for the police. As Annie was handling a small cardboard box containing pills (possibly tablets she had received in a casual ward) it came to pieces, so she suddenly stooped down, and from the dirty floor of the communal kitchen, she picked up a scrap of paper to wrap the two pills in. Just why a woman as fastidiously clean as Annie Chapman did not use her clean handkerchief or muslin cloths to enclose the pills is a moot point. Anyhow,

Crest of the Royal Sussex Regiment.

according to William Stevens, the piece of discarded paper from the floor was a portion of a mysterious envelope. There was no postage stamp on it, but it did bear two stamped postmarks in red and black. The red postal stamp read: 'London, Aug. 23 1888' but the letters of the black postal marks were too indistinct to be legible. However, on the back of the envelope fragment, embossed in blue, were the two words: 'Sussex Regiment', and above them was the regiment's crest. There was also a partial address. Someone had written the letter 'M' and beneath it, the number '2'. Below this number were the two letters 'Sp', which some conjectured to be the first letters of 'Spitalfields'.

Around a quarter to two that fateful morning, John Evans, the night watchman of the lodging house, was sent down from the upstairs office to collect Annie's lodging money, but Annie said she didn't have enough, and went upstairs to the office to see Timothy Donovan, the deputy. "Tim, I haven't sufficient money for my bed," she explained, "but don't let it. It shan't be long before I'm in."

Donovan shook his head wearily and told her: "You can find money for your beer and you can't find money for your bed!"

According to Evans and Donovan, Annie Chapman stood for a while in the doorway, seemingly deep in thought, then said, "Never mind, Tim, I shall soon be back. Don't let the bed."

The bed was numbered 29, the very bed Annie usually slept in, and it was still vacant. John Evans saw Annie off the premises, and saw her walk down Dorset Street and turn into the court named Little Paternoster Row on her way to Brushfield Street.

Over three hours passed, during which Annie Chapman seems to have vanished off the face of the earth, for she is seen nowhere in Spitalfields or Whitechapel by anyone during those hours. There was an insubstantial rumour that she was serving behind the counter of the Black Swan public house on Hanbury Street, but not a soul ever came forward to report a sighting of Annie during the mysterious three hours that elapsed between the time when she left the lodging house and the moment when her body was discovered.

The grisly discovery was made by a small elderly carman named John Davis who lived in a rented attic room of 29 Hanbury Street with his wife and three sons. Davis had gone to bed at 8pm but couldn't sleep. He heard his sons come home at various times in the evening, and he was awake when his eldest came in around 10.45pm. Davis was wide awake from three to five in the morning before he drifted off into a light sleep which lasted about thirty minutes. He rose from his bed as the Spitalfields Clock was striking a quarter to six. The morning light was already filtering through the weaver's window, and Davis was soon sipping a cup of tea made by his wife, readying himself for another hard day's work at Leadenhall Market. Davis went down the flights of stairs, then along a passageway that ran from the front door to the back door. That morning, he noticed that the front door was wide open against the wall, but thought nothing of it, as it was a common occurrence. People leaving Number 29 often left the door open, although the son of the woman who rented the first two floors of the building claimed that prostitutes had brought clients into the passageway in the past, and had even carried out sex acts on the stairs. Why prostitutes or their clients would leave the front door of the building wide open before or after the sex act was never explained. The back door at the other end of the passage, leading to the back yard of Number 29, was closed that morning. Mr Davis pushed it open, and reflexively glanced down into the yard. What he saw would haunt him for the remainder of his life. The body of a woman lay on the ground on its back, situated between the fence on the left and the stone steps leading down into the yard. She was horrifically mutilated, with a portion of her intestines placed over her right shoulder, along with pieces of skin, and a length of bowel leading from the strewn mess to her ripped-open abdomen. The woman's throat was also deeply cut and her lifeless face was turned towards the house.

John Davis turned away from the horror, ran down the passageway and out through the front doorway of the house, screaming for help. The traumatised old man startled a passer-by named Henry Holland (who was on his way to work), and also attracted the attention of James Kent and James Green, two packing-case makers, standing outside the Black Swan public house at 23 Hanbury Street. "Come and look in the back yard," Davis muttered to Mr Holland. He then looked towards the packing-case makers three doors away down the street. "Men!" Davis shrieked, "Come here! Here's a sight! A woman must have been murdered!"

Green, Kent and Holland followed Davis down the passageway and stood at the doorway, viewing Chapman's body, and all of them were so terrified at the grotesque spectacle, they wouldn't even venture down the steps into the yard. James Kent in particular was so affected at the sight of the murdered woman, he wandered off, looking for a policeman in a daze and, unable to find one, he went off to gulp down a brandy (perhaps at the nearby Black Swan pub), then brought a piece of canvas from his workshop to the yard of 29 Hanbury Street, where he covered the grossly mutilated corpse. Henry Holland had also gone in search of a policeman, but unfortunately when he spotted one at Spitalfields Market, the policeman told him he could not come to his assistance as he was on fixed-point duty and was under strict orders not to leave the spot. He advised Holland to find another policeman, and the box-maker was incensed by this bureaucracy. He had told the policeman that the murder in Hanbury Street looked very similar to the one that had taken place in Buck's Row, but the policeman remained dutifully rooted to the spot. Holland later lodged a complaint against him at Commercial Street Police Station.

Soon after the discovery of the body that morning, the news of the murder started to spread throughout the immediate neighbourhood, and at two minutes past six,

Inspector Joseph Chandler of the Whitechapel Division was on duty in Commercial Street, near to the corner of Hanbury Street, when he saw a group of men running towards him. "Another woman has been murdered!" shouted one of the men, and Chandler went with them to the scene of the crime. He found people milling about in the passageway of Number 29, but none of them would venture down into the backyard. The inspector saw the body of the deceased lying on the ground on her back. In his fifteen years of service he had seen nothing to equal its brutality and horror. Indeed, there is an apocryphal story about Chandler turning to drink because he was afterwards haunted by nightmares of the mutilated and disfigured body in the backyard. There may be some truth in the tale, because Chandler was demoted to the rank of sergeant in 1892 for being drunk on duty.

That cold morning in the backyard of 29 Hanbury Street, Chandler stooped near the corpse and saw that her left hand rested on her left breast, and that her legs were drawn up slightly. A heap of intestines and parts of the belly wall and pubes rested on the ground above the right shoulder. The woman's throat had been cut deeply from left to right and back again in a jagged manner, and the gaping wound went right around the neck, and was so deep, it seemed as if the killer had been trying to decapitate his victim. Chandler remained in the yard and sent for the divisional surgeon Dr George Bagster Phillips.

At half-past six the doctor arrived and at once surveyed the awful scene. He and Chandler noticed that the dead woman – subsequently identified as Annie Chapman – had been searched after death. Her pocket had been cut open with the knife, and the killer had placed the contents of the pocket in a neat pile at Chapman's feet. These items were a piece of coarse muslin, a pocket comb in a paper case, and a small-tooth comb. Phillips believed these objects had not been casually cast there by the murderer, but placed there by design. Phillips would later tell the inquest that: "They had apparently been placed there in order, that is to say, arranged there." At the other end of the body – close to the head – a portion of the mysterious envelope Annie had allegedly picked up from the kitchen floor of Crossingham's Lodging House was found, and indeed contained two pills which Annie had supposedly placed in it. Phillips saw there were several distinct bruises on the right side of the head and neck, and from the positions of the discolourations, Dr Phillips deduced that the killer had seized Chapman by the chin before the throat was severed. Similar bruises had been found on each side of the face of Mary Ann Nichols, and it had been the opinion of Dr Rees Llewellyn that the bruising had been caused by the murderer's finger and thumb exerting pressure as he held the head still prior to the throat-cutting. In all likelihood, from the evidence uncovered by Dr Phillips, the unknown killer had first strangled Annie Chapman, then cut her throat, and had then proceeded to cut open her pocket and methodically search through the contents. He may have then removed the three brass rings Annie had worn on the middle finger of her left hand. Dr Phillips had deduced this fact by observing the abrasion of the first phalanx of the ring finger, as well as the marking of rings on the proximal phalanx of the same middle finger. After this, the Whitechapel Murderer had cut open her abdomen and lifted the intestines out of the way until he came to her womb. Chapman's womb, the upper part of her vagina, and the greater part of her bladder, were removed by the killer's knife, which had a blade estimated to be some 8 inches in length.

The mysterious murderer had struck in the backyard of a house were seventeen people were living, and no one had heard a sound. Just like the Buck's Row killing, the Chapman murder had been carried out in silence, and on this occasion, the killer had been cool enough to search through his victim's pockets, neatly arrange her belongings at her feet, before placing the corner of that curious envelope at her head. The Ripper had also wrenched off Annie's rings, then left the scene of the crime unseen and unheard. In the opinion of Dr Phillips, the murderer's backyard operation had shown anatomical skill and a talent for working at speed. He later voiced this opinion at the Chapman inquest: "My own impression is that anatomical knowledge was only less displayed or indicated in consequence of haste."

Shortly after this intriguing statement was made, the doctor added: "I myself could not have performed all the injuries I saw on that woman, and effect them, without a struggle in under a quarter of an hour. If I had done it in a deliberate way, such would fall to the duties of a surgeon, it would probably have taken me the best part of an hour. The whole inference seems to me that the operation was performed to enable the perpetrator to obtain possession of these parts of the body.'

How long had Annie Chapman's corpse lain in the backyard when it was discovered by old Mr Davis? By noting the onset of rigor mortis in the body, Dr Phillips estimated that Chapman would have died at around half-past four that morning, and he did admit that the low temperatures of that cold morning – and the great loss of blood from the body – would blur his estimate considerably. So, according to Dr Phillips, Annie Chapman had been dead for about two hours when John Davis discovered the body.

Three witnesses later came forward to contradict the time of death estimated by Dr Phillips. The first witness was John Richardson of 2 John Street, the son of 66-year-old Mrs Amelia Richardson – the woman who rented out half of 29 Hanbury Street. John Richardson stated that he was a porter at Spitalfields Market, but that he also assisted his mother in the business of packing-case making. Between 4.40 and 4.45am, John called at 29 Hanbury Street to check the security of the cellar door in the backyard. This cellar door was located to the immediate right of the stone steps when viewed from the top of those steps. Chapman's body had been found in the niche between the left side of the steps and the wooden fence. According to John Richardson, several months before, the cellar – which was used as a packing-case workshop – had been broken into and a saw and a hammer had been stolen. Since then, Mr Richardson had made it his business to call at his mother's home on the mornings he was at the market to see if the cellar was securely locked. On the morning of the murder at around a quarter to five, John had arrived at 29 Hanbury Street to find the front street door closed. He lifted the latch, entered the house, went down the passageway which bent slightly midway towards the right, around the flight of ten steps, and continued to the backyard door, which was closed. According to Mr Richardson, his foot was hurting because his boot was pinching it, so he sat on the stone steps leading down to the yard, with his feet resting on the flags of the yard, and he took out a knife to trim a strip of leather from the offending boot. He cut off the piece of leather, tied up his boot, and then went back into the passageway of the house and out through the front door, closing it behind him. By the pale light of predawn, John had been able to see everything clearly in the yard, and was sure of two things.

The cellar had been secure, and no corpse had been lying in the niche between the fence to the left and the stone steps. Whether John Richardson had taken the strip of leather he'd cut from his boot with him is unknown, but when an inch-by-inch search of the yard was conducted by the police after the discovery of Chapman's body, no such piece of discarded leather was found. Wynne E Baxter, the coroner at the inquest into Chapman's death, seemed to regard John Richardson's version of events with some doubt, and remarked: "You do not seem to have taken much trouble to see that it [the cellar door] was all right."

Furthermore, the coroner ordered John Richardson to fetch the knife he had used to cut the strip of leather from the boot, and when the market porter returned to the court with the knife, which had a 5-inch blade, the coroner noted that the blade was dull and seemed incapable of cutting shoe leather. He then handed it over to the police. Why was Richardson carrying such a weapon? He couldn't say, and believed he had put it in his pocket 'by mistake' before setting off for work. The coroner noted that John Richardson had not mentioned cutting leather from his boot in the backyard when he informed Inspector Chandler about his movements that morning. John had also told the coroner that he had seen strangers in the passageway of 29 Hanbury Street many times "all hours of the night" and had moved them on, whereas Mrs Amelia Richardson, John's widowed mother, had told the coroner that she had never heard about any strange men and women using the passageway or the yard of Number 29 for immoral purposes. Mrs Richardson stated that she rented half of the house – the ground floor portion, the workshop and the yard. She lived in the first-floor front room, where she had been sleeping with her 14-year-old grandson on the morning of the murder. The front room on the ground floor was a cats' meat shop, and the back room on the ground floor was a kitchen, which also doubled as a place for 'prayer meetings'. Mrs Richardson told the court that an hour before her son had come to the house on the morning of the murder, a lodger named Mr Thompson had left the house at around 3.50am. As he passed the door of her room, Mrs Richardson had muttered, "Good morning" as she lay half asleep in bed. After that, she had heard no sounds of a disturbance in the backyard, nor had any of the other sixteen people living in the house.

It transpired that Annie Chapman had been a familiar face at 29 Hanbury Street. Mrs Richardson said she knew Annie as "the dark woman that used to come around with the cotton and crochet work". Mrs Richardson had even bought items off Annie on numerous occasions when she had told her that she was hard-up. Would Annie Chapman have taken a client into the backyard of a house where she had received such charitable treatment? Wouldn't it be disrespectful to carry out sex acts with strangers in the yard of the house she had visited in daylight hours for legitimate reasons? Something does not ring true about the idea of a woman as unattractive and unhealthy as Annie Chapman resorting to prostitution in the backyard of a house where she would be recognised by John Richardson or possibly even Mrs Richardson if she happened to look out of her window. There were countless other dark corners, alleyways and backyards Annie Chapman could have chosen where she ran no risk of being recognised.

The second person to contradict the time of Annie's death as estimated by Dr Phillips, was Mrs Elizabeth Long, who lived at Church Row, Bethnal Green. On the morning of the murder, at around 5am, Mrs Long left home, bound for Spitalfields Market. She walked down Brick Lane, and just before she turned right into Hanbury Street, she heard the clock of the Black Eagle Brewery striking the half hour. As Elizabeth walked down Hanbury Street on the right-hand side, she saw two figures on the pavement ahead, and they were standing outside 29 Hanbury Street, close to the shutters of the shop. One of the figures was a woman, and she was standing with her face turned towards Mrs Long. The other figure was of a man, and he was facing the other direction, thus presenting his back to Mrs Long. Wynne E Baxter, the coroner, questioned Elizabeth about this intriguing sighting of the couple who may have been Annie Chapman and her murderer. "Did you see the man's face?" Baxter asked.

"I did not and could not recognise him again," answered Mrs Long, but added that, "he was however, dark-complexioned, and was wearing a brown deerstalker hat. I think he was wearing a dark coat but cannot be sure."

"Was he a man or a boy?" asked Baxter.

"Oh, he was a man over forty, as far as I could tell. He seemed to be a little taller than the deceased. He looked to me like a foreigner, as well as I could make out," Elizabeth told the coroner.

"Was he a labourer, or what?" Baxter queried.

Mrs Long recalled that the stranger had what she called 'shabby genteel' appearance. She had overheard the man say to the woman 'Will you?' and the woman in reply had said 'Yes.'

At that point, Elizabeth Long had passed them, and, unfortunately, had not looked back to see the face of the man who may have been Jack the Ripper. Mrs Long was taken to the Workhouse Infirmary Mortuary, where she positively identified Annie Chapman as the woman she had seen with the stranger in the deerstalker outside 29 Hanbury Street on the morning of the murder.

Another important witness in the Chapman inquest was Albert Cadosch, a carpenter who lived at 27 Hanbury Street – next door to Number 29. Cadosch stated that he got up at around a quarter-past five on the morning of the murder and went into his backyard – most probably to use the outdoor toilet. At around 5.20am, Cadosch was going back inside his house, when he heard voices coming from the left – from behind the wooden fence which separated his yard from that of Number 29. The voices sounded near, but the only distinct word the carpenter could hear was "No". Cadosch then went into the house for about four minutes, and then he returned to the backyard. He heard a thudding sound, like something – or someone – falling against, or striking, the wooden fence.

Some students of the Ripper murders have speculated that Cadosch may have heard the sound of the back door of 29 Hanbury Street hitting the fence as the killer opened it fully, swinging it back until it struck the palings, but the carpenter would have seen next-door's back door hitting the fence from his viewpoint, because that door was elevated, being at the top of the stone steps. Cadosch did not attempt to look over the 5 foot 6 inch tall fence, and was not curious enough to perhaps squint through a gap in the wooden paling. Instead he went to work. Outside in Hanbury Street, he saw no one about, and curiously, Cadosch did not see Mrs Long. Cadosch said he occasionally heard people in the yard next door at that time in the morning. The coroner established that Cadosch had not returned to the yard that morning out of curiosity, but because of the effects of a recent operation (probably a urological one carried out at the London Hospital, Whitechapel Road) which necessitated a return to the outside toilet.

The jury at the inquest returned a verdict of 'Wilful murder against some person or persons unknown.'

The mysterious killer had struck and left not a bloodied sole-print at the scene of the crime, or as much as a crimson smudge on the handle of the backyard door. The attack had been so savage, yet soundless enough to remain undetectable to the seventeen inhabitants of 29 Hanbury Street. One moment the killer was methodically arranging the contents of Annie's pockets on the floor of the yard; the next moment he was ripping her abdomen open and lifting out her intestines so he could get to the womb he intended to excise. The timing was as paradoxical as the killer's behaviour. Dr Phillips, from his vast experience in such matters, stated that Annie had lain dead in that yard for two hours, which meant she had died no later than half-past four that morning, yet John Richardson stated under oath that he had visited the yard between a quarter-to and ten-to five, and he said he was sure no body had been present while he was there. Then we have Mrs Long, who says she definitely saw Annie Chapman standing on the pavement in front of 29 Hanbury Street with a man at 5.30am, even though Albert Cadosch stated that at that same time in the morning, he had heard noises coming from the backyard of Number 29. So who are we to believe?

William Stevens, the lodger who had been drinking with Chapman before she left Crossingham's Lodging House on the morning of the murder, had stated that the murder victim had merely found the portion of the envelope in the kitchen and had wrapped her pills in it. What would such an envelope – bearing the crest of the Sussex Regiment – be doing in the kitchen of a doss-house in Dorset Street – one of the most notorious streets in the East End? Inspector Chandler had the gumption to follow this lead through, and he travelled down to Farnborough, where the 1st Battalion of the Sussex Regiment was stationed at North Camp.

Chandler showed the fragment of the envelope to a Captain Young, Acting Adjutant. Young confirmed that the embossed emblem was the official crest of the Sussex Regiment, and he told Chandler that such envelopes could be purchased at the canteen, so any of his men could have bought it there. Enquiries were soon made among the soldiers at the camp, and they were asked if they corresponded with anybody in Spitalfields, or with any person whose address commenced with a '2' but none of the soldiers admitted to writing to any such person at the address given. Chandler checked the signatures of the soldiers on their pay-books but found that none of the writing styles matched the letters on the envelope. Inspector Chandler was determined to get to the bottom of the envelope mystery, and in the course of his enquiries he visited a Post Office close to the military barracks, in Farnborough's Lynchford Road, where, he learned, envelopes bearing the embossed crest of the Sussex Regiment were available to anybody. Postmasters Henry Sumner and James Thirkettle examined the portion of the Chapman envelope and deduced that it had been posted at their post office, but they could not say by whom.

Chandler gave up trying to find a solution to the enigmatic envelope puzzle when he heard the explanation offered by William Stevens; that Chapman had merely picked up the scrap of envelope from the kitchen floor by the fireplace to wrap her pills in it. The question remained all the same, despite Stevens story; how did the envelope from Lynchford Road in Farnborough end up in a squalid lodging house in Dorset Street, which had the reputation for being the most evil road in London? The envelope was addressed to a residence which was either numbered '2', or started with that number, and from the 'Sp' we can presume the address lay in Spitalfields. When we look at the numbers of the addresses on the street where the envelope originated, we will see that only so many of them begin with '2'. There were two Crossingham Lodging Houses on Dorset Street in 1888. Chapman was staying in the one on the northern side of the street, at Number 35, which of course, has no number 2 in it. The other Crossingham lodging house on the southern side of the street was numbered 16 to 19, and again, that address has no number 2 in it. This leaves us with several addresses in Dorset Street that begin with the number 2. The most intriguing of these addresses are Numbers 26 and 27, for they are the numbers of John McCarthy's Miller's Court property and his shop, respectively. Not one person ever came forward to say he had been the author of the letter posted from a post office close to the military barracks in Farnborough to Dorset Street, and the Spitalfields recipient of the letter never made himself known either.

Would the killer strike yet again? This possibility seemed likely, given the fact that he had already killed two women, for without a doubt, the same knife had killed Nichols and Chapman. Who on earth was this fiend and why was he committing these horrific crimes against women? People naturally needed to know. Wynne E Baxter, who concluded the Chapman inquest, stated in his summing-up that the killer evidently had the anatomical knowledge to remove human organs more accurately than a person who merely slaughtered animals. Up to this point, the anonymous murderer of Mary Ann Nicholls and Annie Chapman was known only as the Whitechapel Murderer, but that was all to change. Seventeen days after the murder of Annie Chapman, someone penned a taunting letter and sent it to the Central News Agency at 5 New Bridge Street, Ludgate Circus, in

London. The envelope bore a penny stamp and was postmarked 'London E.C. 3'. The disturbing missive was written in red ink and dated 25 September 1888, although it was not posted until 27 September. It contained a threat to kill more women, and was written by a person claiming to be the Whitechapel Murderer. The letter was signed 'Jack the Ripper' – a name that would go down in the annals of infamy. Now the 'monster' had a name. The letter read:

Dear Boss,
I keep on hearing the police have caught me but they won't
fix me just yet. I have laughed when they look so clever
and talk about being on the right track. That joke about
Leather apron gave me real fits. I am down on whores
and shant quit ripping them till I do get buckled. Grand
work the last job was, I gave the lady no time to squeal
How can they catch me now, I love my work and want to
start again. you will soon hear of me with my funny little
games. I saved some of the proper red stuff in a ginger
beer bottle over the last job to write with but it went thick
like glue and I cant use it. Red ink is fit enough I hope ha.
ha. The next job I do I shall clip the ladys ears off and
send to the police officers just for jolly wouldnt you. Keep
this letter back till I do a bit more work then give it out
straight. My knife's so nice and sharp I want to get to
work right away if I get a chance, good luck .
yours truly

Jack the Ripper
Dont mind me giving the trade name

Underneath this, written in red crayon at right angles to the text was this further postscript:

wasn't good enough to post this before I got all the red
ink off my hands curse it.
No luck yet. They say I'm a doctor now ha ha

The police initially regarded this letter as a hoax, but a day later, on 30 September, the Whitechapel Murderer carried out his infamous 'Double Event' when he killed two women at locations less than three quarters of a mile apart within forty-five minutes, and the fourth victim – Catharine Eddowes – was found to have a severe injury to the lobe and auricle of her right ear. In fact, a part of this sliced ear fell from Eddowes' clothes when her body was being undressed at the mortuary. 'The next job I do I shall clip the ladys ears off and send to the police officers just for jolly wouldn't you,' the letter had promised. Of course, the killer had not sent the ears to the police, so perhaps the ear-clipping remark and partially severed ear of Catharine Eddowes was just a dark coincidence. All the same, Scotland Yard officials had multiple facsimile copies of the 'Dear Boss' letter circulated at police stations, and the same letter was subsequently copied on to large posters, along with the facsimile of another supposed communication from the killer, a postcard signed 'Jack the Ripper' which ran as thus:

I was not codding dear old Boss when I gave you the tip,
you'll hear about Saucy Jacky's work tomorrow double
event this time number one squealed a bit couldn't finish
straight off. had not the time to get ears for police. thanks
for keeping last letter back till I got to work again.

Jack the Ripper

This second message, purporting to be from the Ripper is known as the Saucy Jacky postcard, and its sloppy handwriting bore little resemblance to the neater calligraphy of the Dear Boss missive. It was addressed to the Central News Agency, dated 1 October, written in crimson, and bore a smear of blood-like ink. The contents of the postcard contain three possible coincidences. The author mentions a 'double event' and also makes an intriguing reference about obtaining the ears of a victim, and, as stated before, the Whitechapel Murderer did indeed kill two women in one night on 30 September, the day before the Saucy Jacky postcard was received, and the killer did slice off part of the second victim's ear, although it was possible that the author of the postcard had been a journalist assigned to the Whitechapel Murders case who had learned about the double event and the injuries to Eddowes' ear in the course of his investigation into the crimes. Such an unscrupulous reporter, out to cause a sensation by fabricating bogus letters from the mysterious killer could have written the Dear Boss letters and Saucy Jacky postcard. What better way to boost the circulation of a newspaper than by providing an actual specimen of a letter written by Jack the Ripper himself? Some of the more cultured keen-eyed readers were intrigued by the mention of the phrase 'Saucy Jacky' in the postcard, because William Shakespeare uses a very similar phrase on the thirteenth line of his Sonnet 128:

And situation with those dancing chips,
Making dead wood more blest than living lips.
Since saucy jacks so happy are in this,
Give them thy fingers, me thy lips to kiss.

Shakespeare's sonnets are laced with ambiguities, and in this sonnet, 'Saucy jacks' has two meanings: the keys of a musical instrument such as a harpsichord, and also a risque reference to penises. Coincidences abound in the Whitechapel Murders case, and this Shakespearean connection may be down to chance, but it could equally be possible that the author of the Saucy Jacky postcard was a well-read man who had been inspired from a phrase in one of Shakespeare's sonnets. The police later took the view that the Dear Boss and Saucy Jacky postcard were the inventions of a Fleet Street journalist and his editor. Some thought it strange how the Ripper happened to send his first letter and postcard, not to *The Times*, or *The Telegraph* or *Star*, but the Central News Agency, which served the entire Press. A murderer would surely write to a specific newspaper, and not to a news agency.

Hundreds of letters, signed 'Jack the Ripper', 'the Butcher', and many more colourful and grotesque names, were sent to Scotland Yard and the offices of national and local newspapers across Britain, and several irresponsible authors of these fake letters were traced and arrested. At Bradford in October 1888, 21-year-old Maria Coroner was discovered to be the author of two such letters, both stating that Jack had arrived in Yorkshire. She was bound over for £20 and given a six-month suspended sentence. A Welsh housewife named Miriam Howells also wrote several Jack the Ripper letters and narrowly escaped imprisonment in December 1888.

In recent years, a certain author has attempted to obtain the mitochondrial DNA of the Whitechapel Murderer from the backs of envelopes and stamps from the many letters sent to the newspapers and Scotland Yard by various correspondents claiming to be Jack the Ripper. These letters, all over a hundred years old, had of course been handled and mauled by countless people, such as police officials, archivists and researchers, which meant that they were already contaminated by a variety of DNA sources. The forensic team hired by the said author failed to reach a positive conclusion that would link the author's suspect with the letters. Watermarks on some of the alleged Ripper letters were also matched with watermarks on the stationery used by the author's suspect, but again this is not proof that the suspect was Jack the Ripper. Here is a good analogy to illustrate the situation. Suppose the Yorkshire Ripper, Peter Sutcliffe, had never been brought to justice, and a hundred years from now, students of the crime decided to analyse the mitochondrial DNA contained in the letters and audio tapes sent to George Oldfield, Assistant Chief Constable of West Yorkshire Police, and the *Daily Mirror*. We would be falsely assuming that the three letters sent between March 1978 and March 1979, as well as the audio cassette recording sent to Oldfield in June 1979, were from the Yorkshire Ripper. The DNA on the envelopes containing the letters and audio tape would perhaps eventually be traced to one John Samuel Humble (also known as Wearside Jack), and not the actual Yorkshire Ripper Stuart Sutcliffe.

A 'Reign of Terror' is a seemingly cliched phrase often found in books on the Whitechapel Murderer, but Jack the Ripper crimes really did create a widespread panic, especially in Spitalfields. One particularly poignant example was that of John Sodeaux and his wife. On Sunday, 6 January 1889, 52-year-Sodeaux, a silk weaver of 65 Hanbury Street – the street where Chapman was murdered – decided to hang himself from the stair banisters of his home because of severe depression. He had decided to join his wife, who had committed suicide on 12 October 1888, because she was terrified of meeting Jack the Ripper. She too had hanged herself from the banisters of her home.

4

ELIZABETH STRIDE

Elizabeth Stride was a fairly attractive woman, with a pair of lively intelligent greyish-blue eyes, a head of dark brown curly hair, and a pale oval face. She was slimly built and 5 foot 2 inches in height. In 1888 she was 45 years old, but looked ten to fifteen years younger. Her background and life history were clouded by a colourful tale she had spun about a brush with death. Liz often told how she, her husband, and two children had been on a large pleasure steamer called the *Princess Alice* on 3 September 1878 when the boat collided with a steam collier called the *Bywell Castle* on the Thames. The incident Liz mentions did take place, and was one of the greatest disasters of the nineteenth century, with almost 700 passengers drowning. Stride claimed that her husband and two children perished in the *Princess Alice* sinking, while she saved herself by climbing a rope. However, the coroner, C J Carttar, who held the six-week inquiry into the *Princess Alice* disaster, routinely had an alphabetical list of the victims drawn up. There is not a single mention of anyone named Stride among the register of the drowned. There was but one instance of a father and his two children being drowned in the sinking, an accountant named William Edwin Bell, aged 38, and his two sons, aged 10 and 7 years respectively. It therefore seems quite possible that Elizabeth Stride was lying about her traumatic experience on the doomed pleasure steamer.

To discover the real background of the woman who would become the third canonical victim of Jack the Ripper (but the fourth in my opinion), we have to rely on registrations of births, marriages and deaths, and the depositions of Elizabeth Stride's friends and associates. People such as Elizabeth Tanner, the landlady of the lodging house were Liz lived in her final days, and Michael Kidney, an Irish-born army pensioner who lived with Liz as her common-law husband, and Sven Olsson, the clerk of the Swedish Church that Liz occasionally visited to apply for alms. From these people and various documents of birth, marriage and death, this is what we have gathered about the life of Elizabeth Stride.

She was born Elisabeth Gustafsdotter on the 27 November 1843, north of Gothenburg, Sweden. She lived on a farm with her parents Gustaf and Beata until her later teens, and at the age of 17, Elisabeth took out a certificate of altered residence and moved to Gothenburg, where she found employment as a domestic in the employ of a worker named Lars Fredrik Olofsson. By March 1865, Gothenburg police had Elisabeth in their records as a prostitute. At the age of 21, Elisabeth gave birth to a still-born girl.

Almost a year later, Elisabeth took out another certificate of altered residence and came to London, but just why she went to the capital is not known. According to Michael Kidney, the last partner of Elisabeth, she told him that she came to London as a servant in a family, and later worked in domestic service with a gentleman near Hyde Park. Elisabeth was anglicised to become Elizabeth, and by the summer of 1866, she was officially registered at the Swedish Church in Prince's Square, St George-in-the East, as an unmarried woman, but by March 1869, Elizabeth had married a carpenter named John Thomas Stride, and soon after the marriage the couple lived at East India Dock Road in the district of Poplar. An 1870 edition of Kelly's trade directory lists John Thomas Stride as the keeper of a coffee shop at Poplar's Upper North Street. A year later, Stride's business has relocated to 178 Poplar High Street, and the coffee shop is subsequently taken over by a Mr Dale in 1875. The Strides' marriage came under a lot of strain at this time, although no one is sure what caused the marital stress. There were rumours that Elizabeth's affair with a policeman produced a child and scandalised the married constable's family. There were also claims that Elizabeth had realised that she and John were incompatible and had turned to the bottle in despair. However, the tales of the tryst with the policeman and Liz's burgeoning alcoholism have nothing to back them up.

All we know as fact is that by 1882, Mrs Stride lodged, rather infrequently, at 32 Flower and Dean Street, a lodging house in Spitalfields, where she had now earned the Cockney-slang nickname of 'Long Liz' because of her surname. Around the same time, Liz had also stayed at addresses in Devonshire Street and Fashion Street, and in the final years of her life, she stayed with Michael Kidney for roughly three years at 38 Dorset Street, ten houses away from the small room where final Ripper victim Marie Jeanette Kelly was staying in 1888. Dorset Street seems to connect most of the Ripper's victims. Annie Chapman lived there, and had once stayed in a lodging house owned by John McCarthy, Marie Jeanette Kelly's landlord; in fact Chapman knew McCarthy well. Catharine Eddowes – the Ripper's fourth victim – once stayed in a shed at Miller's Court, where Marie Jeanette was later murdered.

As mentioned before, Elizabeth Stride lived at 38 Dorset

Street with Michael Kidney, but she would go off from time to time on her own, and many Ripperologists have interpreted Liz's sudden departures from Kidney as being the results of drunken quarrels. On just one occasion in the three years spent in Kidney's company, the Swede charged her common-law husband with assault at Thames Magistrates' Court, but she didn't even bother turning up to prosecute.

Where was Liz going during her mysterious visits? Well, she was a fluent Yiddish speaker, and she put her linguistic talent to use by working for the Jews of Whitechapel. What type of work was this? No one is too sure, but many students of the Whitechapel Murders believe Stride was probably casually employed as an occasional domestic servant and charwoman by the Jews. Five days before her murder, Elizabeth Stride suddenly left Michael Kidney, and told several friends she had walked out on him because of a tiff, but Kidney would later testify at the inquest to being on good terms with Stride in the final days of her life. This is to be expected of course, as Kidney did not want the police to regard him as a suspect with a motive for killing his partner. At the inquest into the death of Stride, the coroner asked Kidney why his partner had frequently left him for various periods, and Kidney stated: 'It was the drink that made her go away.'

The last few days of Stride's life are cloaked in mystery, and the scant information about her activities and whereabouts from witnesses are inconsistent and even suspect. According to Elizabeth Tanner, the deputy of the lodging house at 32 Flower and Dean Street, Stride had lodged on and off at her premises for six years, yet she knew virtually nothing about her beyond the fact that her nickname was Long Liz. Tanner did not even know Stride's surname. The widow Tanner said she had last seen Stride alive around 6.30pm on Saturday 29 September. At that time, Stride was drinking with her in the Queen's Head public house on the corner of Fashion Street and Commercial Street. On Saturday morning, Stride had cleaned two rooms for Mrs Tanner at the lodging house, and had been paid sixpence in return. Stride and Tanner later went to the Queen's Head pub to have a drink, then walked back together to the lodging house. Mrs Tanner then went to another part of the lodging house, and did not see Stride again until she was called upon to identify the woman's body at the mortuary. Two people said they had talked to Elizabeth Stride in the kitchen of Mrs Tanner's lodging house between six and seven o'clock that evening. Charles Preston, a barber who had been a lodger for eighteen months, said that Stride was dressed to go out, and had asked him for the loan of a clothes brush (which Preston couldn't find). Stride was wearing a black jacket trimmed with fur, and a striped silk handkerchief round her neck. "She did not tell me where she was going on Saturday evening," said Preston, "and never mentioned what time she was coming back."

Stride would later be found dead in the yard adjoining a Jewish Socialist Club with a red rose in her lapel, but Preston was quite sure that there had been no rose pinned to Stride's jacket when he had seen her on Saturday evening. At the inquest into Stride's death, Preston stated: "She has always given me to understand her name was Elizabeth Stride, and that her mother was still living in Sweden. I have heard her speaking fluently in a foreign language to people in the lodging house."

The other witness who spoke to Stride in the kitchen of the common lodging house was Catherine Lane, a charwoman who lodged at Tanner's with her dock labourer husband Patrick. She had known Stride for six or seven years. Catherine later told the coroner: "I spoke to the deceased on Thursday between 10 and 11 in the morning. She told me she had a few words with the man she was living with and left him. I saw her on Saturday afternoon when she was cleaning the deputy's rooms. I last saw her between 7 and 8 o'clock on Saturday evening. She was then in the kitchen, and had a long black jacket and black hat on."

"Did she tell you where she was going?" queried the coroner.

Catherine told him: "She did not. When she left the kitchen she gave me a piece of [green] velvet and asked me to mind it until she came back. The deputy would always mind things for the lodgers, and I do not know why she asked me to mind the velvet for her. The deceased showed me the piece of velvet on the previous day. I knew the deceased had sixpence when she left, as she showed me the money, but I cannot say if she had any more money besides that."

We must therefore assume that, in addition to the sixpence Tanner paid to Stride for cleaning the lodging house rooms, the deputy must have also paid for Stride's drink or two at the Queen's Head as the Swede still has sixpence on her when she leaves the lodging house kitchen around 7pm to 8pm, according to Catherine Lane.

Elizabeth Stride then leaves the Flower and Dean Street lodging house and steps into Limbo for five to six hours, for not another soul in Whitechapel seems to have seen her until the discovery of her body shortly before one o'clock on the following morning. This is a common denominator in all of the Ripper killings. In the hours running up to the murder, each victim seems to spend a period of unaccounted time off the streets, out of sight of anybody – except the killer – before being found disembowelled and mutilated. After Long Liz's last departure from the Flower and Dean lodging house, there are six alleged sightings of her, but for reasons that will shortly become apparent, the sightings are unreliable, and some are plainly pure invention. Mistaken eyewitness accounts, attention seekers, and downright liars out to make money from the press are nothing new to murder investigations in modern times, and in the bleak poverty-stricken streets of the East End, there was instant fame and, more importantly, money, to be gained by those who could involve themselves in the gripping mystery of the unfolding Whitechapel Murders case. Sensational left-wing Socialist newspapers like the *Star*, and even the more conservative dailies such as *The Times*, *Telegraph* and *Standard* were hungry for the smallest titbit on the faceless killer stalking Whitechapel and Spitalfields, and although reporters in those hard-pressed times could hardly be accused of chequebook journalism, they did pay for any copy to be had from potential witnesses to the crimes, and relatives and friends of the Ripper victims. People with the most tenuous connections to the Ripper's victims were quick in coming forward to the press-hounds for the financial rewards, and the journalists were not very discerning towards the tall tales these people related, because it filled the columns and gave the readership the impression that some progress, however slight, was being made in the detection and apprehension of the phantom-like killer.

At one o'clock on the Sunday morning of 30 September 1888, the body of Elizabeth Stride was discovered in Dutfield's Yard, a long pitch black enclosure that adjoined the International Working Men's Educational Club in Berner Street. The 27-year-old steward of the club, Louis Diemschutz, made the discovery as he tried to drive his

Louis Diemschutz, found the body of Liz Stride.

pony and two-wheeled costermonger's barrow into the yard. Besides being the club steward, Diemschutz was also a seller of cheap jewellery, including brass rings (of the type that Annie Chapman had acquired before her death) and he had been returning from the market at Westow Hill, Crystal Palace, where he sold his wares each Saturday. Diemschutz usually dropped off his unsold jewellery and any money he'd made at the club before stabling the pony in George Yard, Cable Street. Upon this occasion, the pony shied to the left as Diemschutz drove the barrow through the entrance of Dutfield's Yard. The animal halted, and stubbornly refused to proceed. "Come on," said Diemschutz to the animal, impatiently, "what's the matter?" He looked down into the mud and could just discern an object lying parallel to the club wall. Diemschutz prodded the dark shape on the floor with the handle of his whip then got down off the barrow to investigate further. He struck a match, but it was very windy that night, and a small gust blew out the flame. However, the brief illumination from the match was bright enough to show Diemschutz that the dark heap was the body of a woman. Whether she was dead or drunk, Diemschutz could not tell. He rushed into the club in search of his wife. Some Ripperologists have Diemschutz hurrying into the club to find his wife because he believes it may be her body lying in the yard. However, Diemschutz himself states that he went to look for his wife because she was of "a weak constitution, and I did not want to frighten her." Diemschutz states further in the press: 'I did not wait to see if she [Stride] was drunk or dead. I did not disturb it, but went at once into the club and asked where my missus was. I did this because I knew my wife had rather a weak constitution, and anything of that kind shocks her.'

Louis found his wife with a servant girl and several members of the club in the ground-floor dining room. "There is a woman lying in the yard but I cannot say whether she is drunk or dead!" he cried. He found a candle then returned to the yard with a young tailor's machinist named Isaacs Kozebrodski, and before the two young men could even reach the woman's body they could see the stream of blood coming from it down the yard as it oozed from its source: the long gash in the unknown female's throat. Mrs Diemschutz followed her husband and his friend as far as the kitchen door, which led out into the yard and was located less than twelve feet from the body. That running blood must have filled her with terror, because it meant that the murder was recently committed, and it also meant that the killer had audaciously gone about his gruesome work in the yard, just a matter of feet away from the door of the kitchen where she had been making coffee and tea for the club members singing upstairs. That kitchen door had been standing ajar. Mrs Diemschutz must have shuddered at the thought of the murderer lurking outside in the pitch-blackness, possibly watching her and the servant girl as they worked in the gas-lit kitchen.

Diemschutz and Kozebrodski saw that Stride was lying on her back, her face slightly turned towards the wall of the club, her eyes open and lifeless. Her right open hand rested on her chest, and there was a small smear of blood on the back of the hand, as if it had been made by the killer's blood-smeared finger as he positioned Liz's hand over her bosom. It's equally possible that this blood had unknowingly been transported from the stream of blood on the ground or from the neck wound to the right hand of the corpse by Diemschutz as he prodded the body in the darkness with his whip-handle. At this point, the two Jews did not notice the tissue-wrapped clutch of breath-sweetening cachous that were grasped in the dead woman's other hand.

Diemschutz and Kozebrodski rushed out of Dutfield's Yard in search of the law, shouting "Police!" Meanwhile, the news of the woman with the cut throat had spread to the members who had been singing merrily upstairs in the Socialists' Club. One of these members was Morris Eagle, a Russian Jew living in the Commercial Road, who also sold jewellery like his comrade Diemschutz. A fellow Socialist named Gilleman came bounding up the stairs and announced that there was a dead woman in the yard. Eagle hurried downstairs to the muddy yard and struck a match. Just twenty minutes before, Eagle had passed the very spot where Stride

People's Library. Published by the group „Knights of Liberty"
New York.

פֿאָלקם־ביבליאָטהעק. הערוסנעגעבען פֿון דער גרופּע ,,ריטטער דער
פֿרייהייט" אין ניו יאָרק.

GESETZ UND AUTORITAET

von

PETER KROPOTKIN.

פֿרײַ איבערזעצט און בעארבייטעט פֿון

פֿ. א. פֿראנק.

LONDON.
"Worker's Friend" Printing Office,
40, Berner Street, Commercial Road.
1889.

Worker's Friend literature.

had drawn her last breath. He had gone out of the club by the front door in Berner Street to escort a lady friend home at a quarter to midnight, and had returned to the club at twenty minutes to one. Finding the club's front door closed, he had entered the premises by the side door in the yard, and had not noticed a body lying in the mud. This narrowed down the time window within which Stride was killed.

Many other members of the club had passed through Dutfield's Yard in the minutes leading up to the mysteriously silent murder. William Wess, a writer and printer of what was then classed as subversive radical literature, came out of the club and walked down the yard to the office of the Der Arbeter Fraint (The Worker's Friend) Printing Press. Wess carried a bundle of papers detailing his Marxist ideology in his distinctive copperplate handwriting. These pages were taken into the office of the Worker's Friend Printing Press, where the editor Philip Krantz was working busily on a manuscript by gaslight. The office of the radical press consisted of two rooms. The room adjoining the club kitchen (but not connected to it) was where the compositor worked, and the room next to it was where Krantz worked his long hours. William Wess had a short conversation with the editor about the handwritten literature, then left the printing office and walked back up the yard.

At this point Wess casually noticed that the gates of Dutfield's Yard where wide open, though this did not strike him as unusual, as those gates were usually open at such a late time. Around a quarter past twelve, Wess went into the Socialist Club to call for his brother, and at half-past twelve he walked to his lodgings at 2 William Street, just a five-minute walk away. Like Eagle, Wess passed over the spot where Stride would later be found and saw nothing suspicious. Around the same time, an American printer and photographer named Joseph Lave came out of the Berner Street club to get a breath of fresh air. He walked into the street and observed that the district was quieter than it usually was at that time. Ten minutes later, Lave re-entered the club, and like the other witnesses, saw nobody suspicious prowling about.

Diemschutz and Kozebrodski failed to find a policeman that eventful morning, but their excited shouts of "Murder!" and "Police!" did attract the attention of a stout man who was standing outside the Bee Hive public house two streets away from Berner Street. Horse-keeper Edward

Spooner was standing with a young woman at the doorway of the corner pub when he saw Diemschutz and Kozebrodski rush past crying out about the murdered woman and trying their utmost to find a policeman. When the two wild-looking socialists saw that there was no policeman in sight on Grove Street, they came running back in Spooner's direction, and the horse-keeper stopped them and asked what the matter was. "A woman has been murdered," gasped Louis Diemschutz. The young lady with Spooner shuddered at the dreadful news. Spooner accompanied Diemschutz and Kozebrodski to the scene of the crime, and when the three men reached Dutfield's Yard, there were already 15 to 20 people standing around the corpse, and not one of them would touch the body. One onlooker struck a match, and Spooner knelt down and lifted Stride's chin slightly – to reveal the gaping wound in the sliced neck. Blood was still flowing from the throat and Stride's chin felt distinctly warm. Spooner noticed a red rose, backed with maidenhair fern, pinned to the lapel of Stride's jacket, and in her left hand he could see the tissue paper containing the aromatic cachous.

Five minutes elapsed before the police finally arrived. Morris Eagle and another member of the Socialist Club had dashed northwards up Berner Street in search of a policeman, as comrades Diemschutz and Kozebrodski had been desperately seeking one in the southern end of the street, and Eagle and his associate had found PC Henry Lamb 252H and another policeman on Commercial Road, one of the main thoroughfares of Whitechapel. The beat of PC Lamb took him down Commercial Road, and he had passed the top of Berner Street just minutes before.

At Dutfield's Yard, Lamb saw the gaggle of bystanders, mostly members of the Socialist Club, clustered around the body of Elizabeth Stride. The policeman fiddled with the notoriously troublesome bull's eye lantern. Once it was lit, he shone it at the mob then told the second constable who had arrived to go and fetch a doctor. Lamb also told Morris Eagle to go and report the murder at Leman Street Police Station. Lamb trained the feeble light of the lantern's flickering flame on the dead woman. The crowd crept forward out of macabre curiosity, and Lamb warned them: "Now now, get back or you might get blood on your clothing, and then you'll be in trouble." The semi-circle of bystanders didn't heed the warning in the slightest and inched forward, entranced by the faint spotlight sweeping over the appalling injuries to the woman's throat. PC Lamb blew on his whistle, and the shrill blast broke the morbid spell cast over the spectators by the corpse. Lamb put his hand on Stride's face and found it to be slightly warm. He felt her wrist but no pulse was detected. He noted the position of the woman's right hand on her breast, and silently speculated, by looking at the position of the body, that she had been peacefully laid down by the killer. Her clothes were not in the least rumpled.

At 1.10am, Dr Frederick William Blackwell was roused from his sleep by a policeman hammering on the door of his residence at 100 Commercial Road. The constable whom Lamb had sent had arrived. Blackwell's assistant, Edward Johnston told the groggy surgeon that his services were needed at 40 Berner Street, which was just around the corner from the doctor's home. Johnston accompanied the policeman to the scene of the latest Jack the Ripper murder as Dr Blackwell dressed. The bleeding from Stride's neck had stopped by the time Johnston had arrived in Dutfield's Yard. Minutes later, Dr Blackwell also arrived, took out his fob watch and beckoned to a policeman. It was so dark in the yard Blackwell had to inspect the watch dial with a constable's bull's eye lantern. The time was 1.16am. After consulting his watch, the surgeon made an on the spot examination of Stride by the light of the policeman's lantern. At the subsequent inquest, Blackwell detailed his findings:

"The deceased was lying on her left side obliquely across the passage, her face looking towards the right wall. Her legs were drawn up, her feet were close against the wall of the right side of the passage. Her head was resting against the carriage-wheel rut, the neck lying over the rut. Her feet were three yards from the gateway. Her dress was unfastened by the neck. The neck and chest were quite warm, as were also the legs, and the face was slightly warm. The hands were cold. The right hand was open and on the chest, and was smeared with blood. The left hand, lying on the ground, was partially closed, and contained a small packet of cachous wrapped in tissue paper. There were no rings nor marks of rings, on her hands. The appearance of the face was quite placid. The mouth was slightly open. The deceased had round her neck a check silk scarf, the bow of which was turned to the left and pulled very tight. In the neck there was a long incision which exactly corresponded with the lower border of the scarf. The border was slightly frayed, as if by a sharp knife. The incision in the neck commenced on the left side, two-and-a-half inches below the angle of the jaw, and almost in a direct line with it. It nearly severed the vessels on the left side, cut the windpipe completely in two, and terminated on the opposite side one-and-a-half inches below the angle of the right jaw, but without severing the vessels on that side. I did not ascertain if the bloody hand had been moved. The blood was running down the gutter into the drain. It was running in an opposite direction to the feet. There was a quantity of clotted blood just under the body."

Dr Blackwell was joined by Dr Phillips, the divisional police surgeon, around two that morning. By then, Chief Inspector West, Inspector Charles Pinhorn, and Superintendent Thomas Arnold – the right-hand man of Sir Charles Warren, Chief Commissioner of the Metropolitan Police – were in Dutfield's Yard. Superintendent Arnold was, like many policemen in Victorian times, an ex-soldier, having served in the Crimean War. He got on quite well with hardliner Sir Charles Warren, a man who had enjoyed an adventurous military career before his appointment as Chief Commissioner of the Met in 1886. After his two-year stint as a police chief, Warren would resume his life in the military.

Dr Phillips and Dr Blackwell could not offer credible explanations to illustrate how the murderer of Elizabeth Stride had managed to subdue his victim in such a way as to literally lay her down in the mud of Dutfield's Yard in a quiet manner. Dr Blackwell hypothesised that the killer had 'caught hold of Stride's silk scarf, and pulled her backwards before cutting her throat', whereas Dr Phillips conjectured that the murderer had seized Stride by her shoulders and 'placed her' on the ground. However, when the corpse was washed, two bluish discolourations were found just below the collarbones in front of the chest. The doctors agreed that these strange marks were not abrasions from the murder weapon, or bruising from punches – but pressure marks, left by the killer as he pressed specific points on the woman with considerable force – using both of his hands. It was as if the Ripper had rendered the woman unconscious by expertly applying pressure to nerve points at the base of her neck and clavicle area. He would then lay her down, push her head sideways so she faced the wall, then proceed to cut the throat. The arterial spurt of blood against the wall

69

Matthew Packer, fruiterer.

and the left side of Elizabeth Stride indicates this is what exactly happened that night.

The cachous in the tissue paper, gently clasped in Stride's left hand, seemed out of place. An analysis of Stride's stomach contents revealed that she had not eaten any such cachous. She had eaten cheese, potatoes and a starchy farinaceous foodstuff before her death, but Liz had not consumed a single breath-sweetening cachou, nor had she eaten grapes within many hours of her death. Two doors from the International Working Men's Club, at Number 44 Berner Street, there lived a colourful elderly man named Matthew Packer, who used the ground floor of his home to carry on his business as the local greengrocer and fruiterer. When house-to-house inquiries were made on Berner Street on the morning of the murder, at 9am, Sergeant Stephen White called at Packer's shop and quizzed him about his whereabouts and movements around the time of the Stride murder. In White's report, dated Thursday, 4 October, he writes:

About 9.a.m, I called at 44 Berner Street and saw Matthew Packer, fruiterer in a small way of business. I asked him what time he closed his shop on the previous night. He replied "Half-past twelve, in consequence of the rain it was no good for me to keep open." I asked him if he saw anything of a man or woman going into Dutfield's Yard, or saw anyone standing about the street at the time he was closing his shop. He replied "No, I saw no one standing about neither did I see anyone go up the yard. I never saw anything suspicious or heard the slightest noise. And knew nothing about the murder until I heard of it this morning."
I also saw Mrs Packer, Sarah Harrison and Harry Douglas residing in the same house but none of them could give the slightest information respecting the matter.

That should have been the end of the matter regarding Packer, but a couple of days after the statement was taken, two private inquiry agents from the West End – Messrs Le Grand and Batchelor – visited Berner Street. These two mysterious gentlemen of military bearing, both in their mid-thirties, had been hired after George Lusk, the head of the Mile End Vigilance Committee, had contacted their detective agency in The Strand. The Committee was allegedly dissatisfied with the police's handling of the Whitechapel murders case, and had set up a type of glorified

71

neighbourhood watch made up mainly from burly unemployed men armed with coshes who were assigned beats that commenced at midnight. Each one of these unofficial policemen was equipped with a whistle and a pair of sturdy boots and actually received small payment for his services.

Charles Le Grand was the head of the detective agency, living at 3 York Place, Baker Street, with an office at 283 The Strand. Le Grand was a pseudonym, and little is known about the 35-year-old detective's real background, beyond the fact that he had previously called himself Christian Nelson in 1877 – when he was sentenced to eight years' penal servitude for a series of serious thefts from shops. He served seven of those years – on the condition he periodically reported to the police for seven years for purposes of supervision. However, after May 1884, Christian Nelson vanished into obscurity until he reincarnated himself as Charles Le Grand in 1888. The year before, Le Grand had written a letter in violet ink, addressed to Sir Charles Warren, in which he complained about the unfair way he'd been treated by a policeman. In the letter, Le Grand ranted that he would burn down public buildings if his grievance was not taken seriously. This same dangerous fantasy-prone criminal carried an eight-chambered revolver, and was rumoured to be running a brothel, and this was one of the two men George Lusk was looking to for advice and guidance!

It is not known whether Le Grand's partner in the agency – J H Batchelor – also had a criminal record.

Le Grand and Batchelor visited Berner Street and interviewed Matthew Packer. The old man now had an intriguing tale to tell which he had not related to Sergeant Stephen White. He told Le Grand and Batchelor:

*On Saturday night [September 29] about 11 p.m., I
served a young man, aged about twenty-five to thirty,
about five feet and seven inches in height, with a long
black coat buttoned up, and a soft felt hat on – a kind of
Yankee hat – and he had broad shoulders. He had a
dark complexion. He was rather quick in speaking and
had a rough voice. He had a loud sharp way of
speaking, and had a quick commanding way with him.
He sounded educated. He looked to me like a clerk or
something of that sort. I am certain he wasn't what I
would call a working man or anything like us folks that
live around here. A woman came up with him from
Backchurch End [the lower end of Berner Street] and
she was dressed in a black frock and jacket, fur around
the bottom of the jacket, and she wore a black crape
bonnet. She was playing with a flower like a geranium –
white outside and red inside. After the couple had stood
there for a while, the man leaned forward to the serving
window of the shop and said, "I say old man, how do
you sell your grapes?"*

*I said to him: "Sixpence a pound the black 'uns, sir, and
fourpence a pound the white 'uns."*

*He turns to the woman and says: "Which will you have,
my dear, black or white? You shall have whichever you
like best."*

*The woman decided she'd have the black. So he said:
"Give us half a pound of the black ones, then."*

Packer put the bunch of black grapes into the brown paper
bag and handed them out of his window to the man. The
customer's soft hand placed the three pennies in the grape-
seller's rough palm. As the rain fell, the couple stood there
in front of Packer's shop, eating grapes, oblivious to the

inclement weather. The man and the woman with the geranium then moved about six yards along to edge of the pavement near the entrance to Dutfield's Yard, and they remained there for about a minute or so, then crossed the road. Packer peeped out of his window at the couple, then remarked to his wife, "Why, them people must be a couple of fools to stand out there in the rain eating grapes they bought here. They might just as well have had shelter!"

Just after midnight, the Packers closed and shuttered the window as the rain hammered down on Berner Street, and the odd couple was still standing on the pavement, facing the very place where Elizabeth Stride would soon meet her death.

Le Grand and Batchelor fell for Packer's tale, and two Jewish sisters at 14 Berner Street, just two of the street's residents visited by the West End detectives, even seemed to corroborate Packer's claims when they stated that they had both seen "a blood-stained grape stalk" that had survived the rainy murder night in Dutfield's Yard. The police had combed the yard looking for clues, yet Le Grand and Batchelor somehow found the grape stalk in the mud and muck! It wasn't long before newspapers got wind of this new 'development' and dispatched a reporter to the Berner Street fruiter.

Sergeant Stephen White – the man who had recently quizzed Matthew Packer – was shocked when he read the latter's story about the couple to whom he sold grapes. White's superiors were not amused, and ordered the sergeant to pay another visit to Packer immediately. White visited the grocer's shop but Mrs Packer told him that the 'detectives' had taken her husband to the mortuary to see if he could identify the murdered woman. White was furious at the activities of the amateur investigators. He made his way to the mortuary, and bumped into Matthew Packer and one of the detectives from the agency.

Packer recognised Sergeant White and slowed his pace. The last time he had met the policeman, he had told him that he had seen no one suspicious about on Berner Street on the night of the murder. Sergeant White scanned the well-dressed private inquiry agent in his dapper suit and bowler, then scowled at Packer. "Where have you been?" he asked.

Packer sheepishly avoided eye contact and turned to Batchelor. "This detective asked me to go and see if I could identify the woman."

"And have you done so?" White asked.

"Yes," Packer replied, "I believe she bought some grapes at my shop about twelve o'clock on Saturday."

Minutes later, Charles Le Grand walked along the street and asked his partner what the matter was. Sergeant White interposed before Batchelor could speak, and asked the men what they were doing with the witness. In an indignant manner, Le Grand announced that he and his partner were private detectives, upon which Sergeant White said, "May I see your credentials sir?"

Le Grand produced a card from a pocket book, but when White attempted to take hold of it, the detective pulled it away and refused to allow the policeman to inspect it. White attempted to wrench Packer from the questionable investigators, but Le Grand, using force and his persuasive powers that would shame a confidence trickster, managed to convince Packer to snub White and accompany them instead.

Sergeant White had no luck with the elderly yarn-spinner later that day when he once again visited the shop at 44 Berner Street. He collared Packer at the shop, and asked him how his memory had undergone such a creative improvement since the last occasion when he was interviewed. A carriage trundled up to the shop, and Le Grand and Batchelor alighted from the vehicle. They told Matthew Packer to come with them at once. Sergeant White's patience was now extremely strained by the interfering, dandily-dressed dilettantes, and he asked them what on earth was going on. Le Grand explained in a matter-of-fact way that he was taking Mr Packer to Scotland Yard to be interviewed by the most senior police official in the land: Sir Charles Warren.

Packer was indeed taken to Scotland Yard, where the Assistant Commissioner, Alexander Carmichael Bruce, wrote down what the grocer had to say, and he soon noticed many discrepancies in the account, compared with the story Packer had related to the *Evening News* and *Daily Telegraph* reporters, as well as Sergeant White, and Le Grand and Batchelor. Sir Charles Warren and the rest of the police were not at all impressed when Matthew Packer changed the details of his story on several further occasions. Packer's mention of the geranium held by Stride as she visited his shop was derived from an erroneous newspaper article on the murder where the red rose Stride had worn was described as a white flower with a red centre. Packer enjoyed his 15 minutes of fame and a short-lived surge in business. People bought grapes at his stall just so they could claim to have been served by the same man who had served the Ripper, eating the very same type of black grapes the Whitechapel Murderer ate. Customers from near and far asked Packer what the fiend had looked like, and the old man told them embroidered versions of his shaky police statements. As luck would have it, Matthew Packer would even meet Jack again! He later told disbelieving reporters that on 27 October, he had been standing at his barrow on a corner of Commercial Road and Greenfield Street, when the suspected murderer passed him, and shot "a most vicious look" at him. Packer sent someone to get a policeman at once, but the man in black reacted by leaping on to a Blackwall-bound tram. By this time the journalists of the *Evening News* and the *Daily Telegraph* had had quite enough of Packer, and on 13 November of that year, the old fantasist gave a pathetic account of how a man who had come into his shop to buy rabbits, knew for certain that his cousin was Jack the Ripper! After that the reporters of Fleet Street, and even the hacks of the sensationalist *Star* newspaper ignored Matthew Packer.

There had been other alleged sightings of Stride and her possible killer on the night Packer said he'd sold grapes to the man accompanying the woman with the geranium (who Packer identified as Stride). The other accounts given by five other witnesses paint a very confused picture of the murder victim's whereabouts shortly before her death. We will start with the most reliable of these witnesses – Mrs Fanny Mortimer, who lived at 36 Berner Street, two doors away from the International Working Men's Educational Club.

According to Dr Frederick Blackwell, Elizabeth Stride had been murdered at around 12.56am that morning, and from 12.30am to 1.00am, Mrs Fanny Mortimer was standing on the front doorstep of her home in Berner Street. To her right she could see a young man and his sweetheart on the corner of Berner and Fairclough Streets, outside the board school. Further to her right, Mrs Mortimer had a close view of the gates of Dutfield's Yard, and in the crucial half hour she spent on her doorstep, she saw no one enter or leave the yard of the International Working Men's Educational Club. How on earth then, did the killer make his escape from the yard? Louis Diemschutz was certain that no one had fled the yard as he approached from the Commercial Road end of Berner Street, and the sweethearts on the corner saw and heard no one suspicious in those four minutes before one o'clock when Elizabeth Stride was mysteriously incapacitated, laid down in silence, and killed. Most Ripperologists have stated that the killer must have fled into Berner Street somehow, and some have conjectured that the Ripper waited in the darkness of Dutfield's Yard until Diemschutz went into the club to get help. In those dramatic seconds, the murderer slipped in between Diemschutz's barrow and the open gate and hurried down Berner Street.

In reality, this would be a very risky manoeuvre. Upon leaving Dutfield's Yard, he would come to the attention of Mrs Mortimer, who would be standing just two houses away to his left. To his right, were the sweethearts on the corner. Just around the corner of the street, in Fairclough Street, people were still about, even at that late hour. A dock labourer named James Brown for example, who had just returned from a Chandler's shop. Mr Brown recalls seeing the couple on the corner near the board school, but can recall seeing no one else. Further down Berner Street, past the Fairclough Street junction, at Number 64, an indigo warehouse labourer named William Marshall was loafing on his doorstep at a quarter to midnight. In fact, Marshall later claimed he had seen Stride an hour before she died, going south – in the opposite direction of Dutfield's Yard. Marshall was taken to the mortuary to look at Elizabeth Stride's body, and he said she had definitely been the woman he had seen on the previous night.

Whether or not Stride was heading south down Berner Street an hour before her death is debatable, but we can see the dangers of being seen in Berner Street on the night of the murder are very evident. We have the nosy

Mrs Mortimer to the north of the club, the sweethearts across the road on the corner, people going to the chandlers on Fairclough Street, and a loafer on his doorstep at 64 Berner Street. Then we have a young man named Leon Goldstein (who curiously happens to be a member of the International Working Men's Education Club) who, shortly before 1am, came down Berner Street from the Commercial Road end. He was carrying a black shiny bag, and Mrs Mortimer noticed him immediately. She watched him glance up at the lit windows of the Socialists' Club, then cross over to the other side of the street. He turned the corner by the board school, where the two young lovers were standing. Goldstein heard and read about the Stride murder on the following day, and later went to Leman Street Police Station to identify himself. He told the police that he had come from a coffee house on Spectacle Alley and had been heading home to 22 Christian Street, which ran parallel to Berner Street. Goldstein explained that he was a traveller who dealt in cigarettes, and that the black shiny bag he had carried – described by Mrs Mortimer – had contained empty cigarette boxes. Little is known about Goldstein's background. He may have been related to the family firm of Goldstein & Son who tried to smuggle a ton of tobacco on to their Spitalfields premises in the previous September. The police and a Custom House official apprehended the would-be smugglers and they were arrested.

We are still not finished with the people passing through Berner Street, because two further witnesses each claimed there were two more people in the street in the minutes leading up to Stride's murder. Firstly, we have PC William Smith's tale. PC Smith's 25-minute beat took in Berner Street. He claimed he had been in the street at around 12.35am (twenty-one minutes before Stride's estimated time of death) and that he had passed a woman standing on the pavement on the side opposite the Socialists' Club. At that time she had been wearing a red rose in her coat. Smith stated that he had a good look at her face, and when he was shown Stride's body in the mortuary, he identified her as the woman he'd seen with the rose in her jacket. Smith said the woman was with a man, described as respectable-looking and sober, about five feet seven or eight inches in height, about 28 years of age, with a dark complexion and a small dark moustache. The man wore a dark, hard felt deerstalker hat, and the attire of a clerk; a white collar and tie, and a black diagonal cutaway coat. However, PC Smith then states that this smartly-dressed man was carrying a suspicious 18-inch-long parcel, wrapped up in newspaper. One would have thought that such a respectable man would have concealed a murder weapon (which seems to be what Smith is hinting at with his description of the newspaper parcel) in a presentable case. Fanny Mortimer did not see the couple, even though (if they ever existed) they would have been standing almost opposite her house.

Not one of the many members coming and going from the International Working Men's Educational Club reported the couple PC Smith alleges he passed either. Neither of the sweethearts on the corner by the board school wore a rose or carried a newspaper parcel, so was the couple seen by 26-year-old PC William Smith 452H an invention? It would seem so. Policemen are only human like the rest of us, and there are many cases on file of Victorian policemen covering up the occasional sly cigarette breaks or furtive sip of a watchman's whiskey during their mind-numbing monotonous beats. PC James Harvey, for example, who will feature in the next episode of the Ripper's crimes, was dismissed from his job in July 1889 for reasons that were never made clear, but there were rumours of him drinking on duty. On the one night PC Smith shirks from duty for a while, Jack the Ripper strikes on a street that forms part of his beat. At the inquest into Stride's murder, the coroner asks PC Smith's colleague – PC Henry Lamb 252H – two interesting questions: "There is a recess in the yard [next to the International Working Men's Educational Club], is there not? Did you go there?"

PC Lamb replies: "Yes, and I afterwards went there with Dr Phillips. I examined the dust-bin and dung-heap. I noticed there was a hoarding, but I do not recollect looking over it."

An ordnance survey map and a detailed parish map of St George in the East were consulted, and these maps showed how easy it would be for someone to escape from Dutfield's Yard, not from the Berner Street entrance, but from the arched underpass at the opposite end of the yard, where the lazy PC Lamb admitted he couldn't be bothered to look over a hoarding. On the map, the hoarding and a nearby covered shed, are accurately marked with an X – which means 'arched underpass'. A hoarding, similar to the one in Dutfield's Yard, will be scaled just a week after Stride's murder when a killer with the Ripper's skills deposits a torso on the building site of New Scotland Yard.

So, rather than risk being seen by loafers, nosy neighbours, loitering sweethearts, policemen on their beat, homeward-bound cigarette-dealers and the other nocturnal denizens in Berner Street, the killer only has to walk to the end of the yard and climb over a hoarding which measures five-and-a half-feet in height. He then walks through a yard that takes him into Backchurch Lane, and within minutes he follows the lane on to Commercial Road. From there, the

Ripper is well on his way to kill again, that same night, in his trademark style of almost supernatural silence.

Next we come to the curious tale of Israel Schwartz, a Hungarian Jew, who says he actually saw a man who could have been Jack the Ripper, fighting in the street with Stride, for everyone to see. However, Schwartz's Ripper bears no resemblance to PC Smith's Ripper, and the Hungarian also claims his Ripper had an accomplice. The original statement by Schwartz, made at Leman Street Police Station on 30 September 1888, has been lost and probably no longer survives. We have to look to Chief Inspector Swanson's notes of 19 October to glean what we can regarding Schwartz's story:

12.45am 30th [September] Israel Schwartz of 22 Ellen Street, Backchurch Lane, stated that at that hour on turning into Berner Street from Commercial Road and had got [sic] as far as the gateway where the murder was committed he saw a man stop and speak to a woman, who was standing in the gateway. The man tried to pull the woman into the street, but he turned her round and threw her down on the footway, and the woman screamed three times, but not very loudly. On crossing to the opposite side of the street, he saw a second man standing, lighting his pipe. The man who threw the woman down called out apparently to the man on the opposite side of the road: "Lipski!" and then Schwartz walked away, but finding that he was followed by the second man, he ran off as far as the railway arch but the man did not follow so far.

Schwartz cannot say whether the two men were together or known to each other. Upon being taken to the mortuary, Schwartz identified the body as that of the

woman he had seen and thus describes the first man who
threw the woman down: age about 30, height 5 ft
5inches, complexion fair, hair dark, small brown
moustache, full face, broad-shouldered; dress: dark
jacket and trousers, black cap with peak, had nothing in
his hands.
Second man: age 35, height 5 ft 11 inches, complexion
fresh, hair light brown, moustache brown; dress: dark
overcoat, old black hard felt hat with a wide brim. Had
a clay pipe in his hand.

Mrs Diemschutz, the wife of Louis, who later found Stride's body, had been at work with a servant in the kitchen of the club, with the kitchen door ajar, yet these two women had heard nothing, even though Stride was found within twelve feet from that door in the yard outside. Schwartz said Stride screamed three times, yet no one heard her, even from twelve feet away. Israel Schwartz was not produced as a witness at the Stride inquest. Was his colourful unsubstantiated tale a fabrication, dreamed up to earn money and fame from journalists who were hungry for a reported sighting of the Whitechapel Murderer? I think so. Often, the boring truth does not produce good copy in the columns of newspapers, whether they're the *Telegraph*, *The Times*, or the *Star*, and the truth is, nothing much happened on Berner Street in the final hour of Saturday night and the first hour of Sunday morning. It rained. A couple in love were blissful to the weather, but Matthew Packer decided the weather wasn't helping his business, and shut up shop at half-past midnight. Meanwhile, up the street at Number 36, 48-year-old Mrs Mortimer, stood on her step, while her 50-year-old husband William, a carman, probably dozed in his bed. The mother of three sons and two daughters,

Fanny Mortimer had her work cut out for her as all mothers have, and in an age with no radio or television, the comings and goings in the street were a form of entertainment. Who knows, perhaps she even had some affection for PC William Smith, the young man who passed her door regularly each night. She states that on more than one occasion in the past, there had been fights at the Socialists' Club two doors away, but on this rainy, windy night going into 30 September, she sees nothing to divert her mind from her everyday cares.

Meanwhile, in Dutfield's Yard, a man who will capture the macabre imagination of the world, and who will be hunted unsuccessfully for generations, is at work, closing in on Elizabeth Stride like a living shadow. Despite the wind and rain, Stride will be found warm and dry, because she has just left the kitchen of the International Working Men's Educational Club. Where else could she have come from? Elizabeth Stride, a woman who can speak fluent Yiddish, as well as her own native Swedish and English, had probably eaten her last meal at the club – cheese, potatoes and that starchy farinaceous foodstuff – the half-digested remnants of Bourekas perhaps?

A detective asked Diemschutz if he had known Stride, and the Socialist categorically denied he had ever set eyes on her before, yet in a subsequent interview with a newspaper, Diemschutz made a curious comment. He told the reporter how Stride was much better dressed than Annie Chapman; but how did he know this? Had Diemschutz known the previous victim of Jack the Ripper?

5

CATHARINE EDDOWES

The Sunday morning of 30 September 1888 had more gruesome surprises in store for the police. At 1.45am, forty-five minutes after the body of Elizabeth Stride was found in Dutfield's Yard, another victim of Jack the Ripper was discovered around three-quarters of a mile away to the west, in Mitre Square, just ten minutes' walking distance from the scene of the Stride murder. The second victim was Catharine Eddowes, a 46-year-old woman who had only been released from Bishopsgate Police Station at one o'clock that morning. Catharine had been arrested at 8.30pm on the previous day for being drunk and disorderly on the Aldgate High Street, just around the corner from the place where she would meet a savage death at the hands of a silent sinister killer. Bishopsgate Police Station was an eight-minute walk away from Mitre Square, one of the darkest and most secluded places in London after nightfall. Before the Ripper's previous victims had been killed, they had all gone missing for an hour or more, and no one could remember seeing them on the streets or in a public house with anyone. After Catharine Eddowes left Bishopsgate Police Station at 1am that Sunday, not one of the many people milling about the East End that weekend would recall seeing her. Not only does Catharine seem to have spent an unaccounted period of time with someone shortly before her murder, she also seems to have been in someone's company before she was arrested on the day before she met her death.

Let us go back in time to learn a little about Catharine's life, her last days alive, and how she came to lose her life in a pitch-black corner of Aldgate's Mitre Square.

Catharine Eddowes was born in 1842 at Wolverhampton, the daughter of George Eddowes, a tinplate worker, and his wife Catharine. In 1843 the family moved to London, and twelve years later, Catharine's mother died of tuberculosis. In December 1857, the father George Eddowes passed away, leaving young Catharine an orphan destined for the Bermondsey Workhouse. Fortunately Emma Eddowes, Catharine's 22-year-old sister, wrote to her Aunt Elizabeth in Wolverhampton, pleading with her to take 15-year-old Catharine under her wing. Aunt Elizabeth acquiesced and so the teenaged Catharine Eddowes had a lucky escape from the toil of the workhouse, but she didn't appreciate life in her new home and months later, she robbed money from her employer and ran away from home to live with an uncle – Thomas Eddowes – in Birmingham.

A few years afterwards, around 1861, Catharine went to live with an army man named Thomas Conway. She bore two of his children and then moved to London with him, where a third child was born. There is a real question mark hanging over Conway. I have ascertained that he was born near Kilgever, near County Mayo, Ireland, around 1835. The 1871 census lists him as living at 1 Queen Street, Southwark, London, with his occupation listed as a pedlar. He was 36 years old in 1871, which would make him 53 in 1888. Listed with Conway on the census are Catharine Conway, aged 28, with her occupation described as a laundress, and their two children, 7-year-old Catharine A Conway, who was born at Yarmouth, Norfolk, and 3-year-old Thomas Conway, born at

Westminster. We know that in 1873 Thomas Conway was drawing an army pension, because he had served in the 18th Royal Irish Regiment, but the odd thing is that he had enlisted into military service under the name of Thomas Quinn. Catharine was his common-law wife for twenty years, and was known during this time as Catharine Conway. Such was her loyalty to Thomas, she often maintained she was legally married to him and even had his initials – 'T C' – tattooed on her left forearm.

By the early 1880s, the 'marriage' was on the rocks. They moved to 71 Lower George Street in Chelsea, but then went their separate ways, and it's hard to discover why. According to Catharine's daughter Annie, the break-up was caused by her mother's excessive drinking and the way she constantly walked out on the family, but Catharine's sister said Conway's drunken behaviour and violent ways drove his common-law wife away. The truth of the matter was that Thomas Conway was a teetotaller, and Catharine had a drink problem – even her older sister Emma admitted that she drank excessively, but she also claimed that she had seen her face "frightfully disfigured" by Conway.

In 1881, a new love entered Catharine's life, and like Thomas Conway, he was also an Irishman. John Kelly was a labourer and jobbing market porter who had worked for twelve years in the employ of a fruit salesman named Albert Lander. It is not known with any certainty how Kelly came to lose his job, but it is thought that a bronchial condition and a kidney ailment caused his general health to deteriorate until he became unemployable. Eddowes at this time was said to be working for the Jews, but in what capacity, no one is entirely sure. Some researchers into the Whitechapel Murders have assumed she was a cleaner or charwoman for the Jews. Catharine met John at Cooney's –

John Kelly – common law husband of Catharine Eddowes.

a common Whitechapel lodging house at 55 Flower and Dean Street – a street up from Thrawl Street, where the first canonical Ripper victim, Mary Ann Nichols, had lived. The couple proved very compatible, and were inseparable for the next seven years until Catharine met her death. During those final seven years, Kelly and Eddowes never left the lodging house, except to go hop-picking in the country, a popular way to earn a little extra money for many thousands of East Enders in those days. The hop farmers hired casual labour in the autumn months, and so, early in September 1888, John and Catharine (now affectionately called Kate by her partner) travelled nearly 35 miles to go hop-picking in Hunton, near Maidstone in Kent. Kelly later told the *Star* newspaper:

> *We went hopping together mostly every year. We went down*
> *this year as usual. We didn't get on any too well, and*
> *started to hoof it home. We came along in company with*
> *another man and woman who had worked in the same*
> *fields, but who parted with us to go to Chatham when we*
> *turned off towards Maidstone. The woman said to Kate, "I*
> *have got a pawn ticket for a flannel shirt. I wish you'd take*
> *it, since you're going up to town. It is only in for nine-*
> *pence, and it may fit your old man." So Kate took it and*
> *we trudged along. It was in at Jones's (the pawnbrokers),*
> *Church Street, in the name of Emily Burrell.*

John Kelly also said that he and Kate had slept in the same barn as Emily Burrell and her unknown male companion. This couple subsequently parted with Kelly and Eddowes and went north to Chatham, home to the Royal School of Military Engineering – the British Army's Centre of Excellence for Military Engineering training. This was and still is the famous regimental headquarters of the Royal Engineers. Lieutenant General Sir Charles Warren, who was then the Chief Commissioner of the Metropolitan Police Force, not only began what would prove to be a spectacular military career at the Royal School of Military Engineering in Chatham in the 1850s, but returned there many times – from 1880 to 1884 as an Instructor of Surveying. In 1886, Warren became the Chief Commissioner of the Metropolitan Police, succeeding Sir Edmund Henderson.

In September 1888, as Kelly and Eddowes were hop-picking, Thomas Callan and Michael Harkins, two Fenians – known as the Jubilee plotters – were languishing in nearby

Chatham Jail. Here is their story. On the sunny morning of Tuesday, 21 June, 1887, bunting and flags decorated the streets of London, and royalists were out in their millions. Queen Victoria was celebrating her Golden Jubilee with a grand procession through London, through thoroughfares crowded with loyal subjects. The procession would culminate in a Service of Thanksgiving at Westminster Abbey. The occasion was something of a propaganda exercise, to present a rosy picture of a content Royalist Britain in her finest hour to the steadily emerging sections of a discontented society that were promoting revolutionary forms of socialism and even anarchism. These were very dangerous years for the monarchy, and an uprising amongst the working class was expected any day. At 11.15 am on that 50th Jubilee morning, the Royal Procession left Buckingham Palace, escorted by the Indian Cavalry, with guardsmen lining the route shoulder to shoulder. An army of plain clothed detectives carrying pistols had infiltrated the flag-wavers, and Sir Charles Warren himself had given specific military orders for the safe conduct of the Queen from Buckingham Palace to Westminster Abbey. Forty-nine years before, the monarch had entered Westminster Abbey for her coronation in June 1838. On Jubilee Day 1887, she entered the Abbey for the second time in her life, unaware of the complex machinations of a huge conspiracy orchestrated by her own intelligence service. Meanwhile, up at Liverpool, three Irish-American dynamiters arrived from New York on the SS City of Chester; their mission – to put enough dynamite in the crypt of Westminster Abbey to blow the monarch, the Royal Family and the Cabinet to kingdom come. Unfortunately for the three Fenians, they had arrived too late – the procession was already underway, but this didn't dissuade them from making another attempt at striking at the heart of the British Empire, and so they travelled on to London – unaware that they were being followed by British Intelligence agents and Special Irish Branch officers. Those three 'dynamitards' were kept under surveillance for five months, and during that time they blew the covers of most of the Fenian agents in Britain. The three so-called 'Jubilee Plotters' were later arrested and charged with conspiring to blow up Queen Victoria, members of the Royal Family and the Tory Cabinet at Westminster Abbey. The three Fenians knew they had been framed of course, as they hadn't even been able to plant the dynamite under the vaults of Westminster Abbey, because of their late arrival at Liverpool Docks. The whole 'black operation' masterminded by the Prime Minister Lord Salisbury and his 'cabal' had been a resounding success. The whole charade served to shatter the Irish republican terrorist network in mainland Britain and to associate the despicable Jubilee Plot in the minds of the public with the constitutionalist Irish leader Charles Stewart Parnell; in other words, the fake Jubilee Plot was also a smear campaign against Parnell's Home Rule struggle.

The two men who supposedly intended to detonate the Jubilee bomb – Thomas Callan and Michael Harkins – were sent specifically to a jail in Chatham to be interrogated and tortured.

Conditions for treason prisoners in Chatham Jail were barbaric, with constant harassment of the prisoner and systematic disturbance of his sleep. It was also a punishable offence to speak to another prisoner. Half of those jailed there died or became hopelessly insane before release. An 1890 report on prison conditions at Chatham Jail, categorically denying any ill-treatment of Fenian prisoners, can only be described as a whitewash.

Emily Burrell, who altruistically gave Kate Eddowes a pawn ticket for a flannel shirt, and her unidentified male companion, left the couple and went to Chatham, never to be seen or heard from again. Within days Kate Eddowes would die at the hands of Jack the Ripper. When police would find Burrell's pawn ticket on Kate's body, they would visit the pawnshop of Joseph Jones and discover that the mysterious Emily Burrell of Chatham had given her address to the Spitalfields pawnbroker as 52 White's Row, on 31 August – the very day Mary Ann Nichol's had been murdered by the Ripper. Wasn't that an odd coincidence? No one named Emily Burrell lived at 52 White's Row – the street next to Dorset Street, where Jack would kill his final victim in five weeks' time. No one in White's Row had heard of Emily Burrell, and to this day she has not been traced in any census as living in either Spitalfields or Chatham. When Kate Eddowes became the next victim of Jack the Ripper, the details of Emily Burrell's name and address were reported in every newspaper in the land, yet neither she nor her partner ever came forward, at a time when people who had the most tenuous links to the Ripper's victims were coming out the woodwork to earn a little money from the press-hounds. There is another connection with Eddowes and Dorset Street, the neighbouring street to White's Row. According to several newspaper reports of the time, when Kate and John couldn't afford the eight-pence fee for a double bed at Cooney's lodging house, they usually went to the Workhouse in Shoe Lane, Mile End – but sometimes Kate Eddowes slept in a shed – at 26 Dorset Street – where Marie Jeanette Kelly lived with Joe Barnett.

So, then, Kate Eddowes and Irishman John Kelly returned to London after stopping off at the High Street in

Maidstone, where the latter purchased a pair of boots at the shop of one Arthur Pash. From a nearby shop, called Edmett & Son, Kate bought a black jacket, trimmed around the collar and cuffs with imitation fur. The boots and the coat were, perhaps, purchased with the little money the couple had earned from hop-picking, although the hop season of 1888 was a very bad one. By the time the they reached London on the Thursday afternoon 27 September 1888, they were, as Kelly later stated to a newsman, 'both done up for cash.' They were flat broke and needed to find cash quickly if they wanted to stay together at Cooney's lodging house.

That night, Eddowes and Kelly slept in the casual ward at Shoe Lane, and on Friday morning they woke up destitute, but somehow, Kelly managed to earn sixpence from a short-lived job. The price for a double bed for the night at Cooney's was eight pence, and a single cost four pence, so Kelly urged his partner to sleep at Cooney's in a single bed. "Here, Kate," Kelly said, selflessly, offering her four pence, "you go to the lodging house and I'll go and stay at Mile End casual ward."

"No, John," Kate replied, pushing back the offer in his hand, "you take the fourpence and go to the lodging house, and I will go to the casual ward."

Kelly shook his head and insisted on her staying at Cooney's but Kate refused his gesture and she had it her way; she went to the casual ward at Shoe Lane and spent the night there. Kelly stayed at Cooney's. The superintendent of the casual ward at Shoe Lane later came forward after the murder of Kate Eddowes with an incredible tale. He said that on the Friday preceding her murder Kate had turned up at the casual ward. He knew her quite well as she was a regular visitor to the ward, and so he asked her where she had been, as he hadn't seen her for about a month. "I've been hopping down in Kent," she told him, then enigmatically added, "I have come back to earn the reward offered for the apprehension of the Whitechapel murderer; I think I know him."

The superintendent didn't know whether Kate was joking, but if she was it was in bad taste, given the widespread panic Jack the Ripper had caused since his last two murders. "Mind he doesn't murder you too," remarked the superintendent light-heartedly.

"Oh, no fear of that," said Kate, confidently.

Did Kate Eddowes return from hop-picking because she had met Jack the Ripper in Kent?

On the morning of Saturday, 29 September 1888, things looked bleak for Eddowes and Kelly. Her common-law husband decided he would have to pawn his new boots – or 'pop them' as they said in those days. "We'll pop the boots and have a bite to eat," Kelly told Kate.

"Oh no, don't do that, John," she protested. She was so proud of John, and didn't like the idea of him walking the streets of Whitechapel barefoot; it was demeaning and undignified, but Kelly insisted it was the only quick way to make some money. Many students of the Jack the Ripper murders have portrayed Catharine Eddowes as a common prostitute, but there is no evidence whatsoever which points to her being a streetwalker. She worked for the Jews, and was described as quite a scholarly woman. Five days after Eddowes was murdered, on 5 October 1888, a reporter from the *Evening Express* paid a visit to Cooney's lodging house and interviewed several of the lodgers. Most of them had known Eddowes, and all of them had nothing but praise for her. All of the lodgers interviewed made complimentary comments that were typical of the tributes describing Eddowes:

"Ah, she was a good sort, I know," said one man, "and often gave me the price of my kip when I was short of a night."

"Yes, she was a good sort," agreed a burly looking matron standing by, "and I wish she were here now a-putting down her teapot, as she used to do, along with us."

Kate's friends in Flower and Dean Street strongly resented the idea that she was a woman of immoral character, and claimed that she was as true as any wife could be to Kelly. "Kate was a decent woman," said one of the females, "and worked for the Jews; that's how she got her living; she never did any harm in her life." And this apparently was the general opinion entertained of the unfortunate woman's character.

Kate Eddowes took John's new boots to the pawn shop of Joseph Jones at 31 Church Street. She told Mr Jones her name was Jane Kelly, and gave a Dorset Street address. Mr Jones recorded her details in his book as John Kelly waited at the door of the pawnshop in his bare feet. Kate received two shillings and sixpence for the boots, and with a portion of this meagre amount the couple bought tea, food and sugar. What was left was spent on a breakfast at the communal kitchen in Cooney's in Flower and Dean Street. This last breakfast the couple would ever have, took place, according to Fred Wilkinson, the deputy of the lodging house, between 10.00am and 11.00am. The couple then went drinking, and by lunchtime they were completely broke again.

According to Kelly, he was about to try his luck in the markets for any possible jobs to be had, despite being barefooted, when Eddowes hit on the idea of scrounging some money from her married daughter Annie Phillips in Bermondsey. Now, this story of Kelly's seems a bit suspect, because Kate had no idea where Annie lived. Annie hadn't seen her mother in two years and had moved home several times, leaving no forwarding address so her mother couldn't find her. She did this because in the past, her mother had persistently scrounged money from her. Furthermore, Kelly would later lie about the way in which he came to learn of Kate's violent death, so we must treat whatever he states with a little suspicion.

If Kate wasn't going to see her daughter across the Thames, where on earth was she going to find some money that afternoon? Had she really discovered who Jack the Ripper was in the Kent countryside? Surely she would have gone straight to the police with John Kelly. No, instead, she falls into that now familiar pattern of the previous Ripper victims – she vanishes for a while, and is seen by no one for six-and-a-half hours. According to John Kelly, he and Kate parted company in Houndsditch – which lies in the opposite direction of Bermondsey – at around two o'clock that Saturday afternoon. Kate promised to be back at Cooney's no later than 4.00pm, as John had told her he was worried about her safety with the mysterious murderer being at large. Kate's last words to him were: "Don't fear for me. I'll take care of myself and I shan't fall into *his* hands."

Kate Eddowes never found her daughter that afternoon. Annie Phillips would later come forward at the inquest into her mother's death and state categorically that she had not seen her mother that Saturday, and had not set eyes on her in over two years. Where did Kate go, then? She doesn't seem to have gone that far from Houndsditch, because at 8.30 that Saturday evening, she reappeared on the streets in a drunk and disorderly state outside 29 Aldgate High Street. A crowd had gathered around her, attracting the attention of PC Louis Robinson. He immediately went to investigate and discovered Eddowes lying drunk but conscious on the pavement. At this time, 29 Aldgate High Street was the premises of 50-year-old furniture dealer Henry Phillips. Could he have been related to the same family of Phillips that Kate's daughter, Annie had married into? It's a tantalising question that remains to be answered, however, neither Mr Phillips, nor anyone else for that matter, would later come forward to throw some light on the whereabouts of Kate Eddowes in the six-and-a-half hours she had spent, supposedly looking for Annie Phillips.

How had this penniless woman ended up insensibly drunk on the Aldgate High Street? Who had she been drinking with? No one recalled seeing her in any of the local public houses. PC Robinson summoned a PC George Simmonds for help, and the two policemen hauled Kate to her feet and walked her to Bishopsgate Police Station. Sergeant James Byfield saw Kate being brought into the station, supported between the two constables at 8.45pm. She reeked of drink. Byfield said, "What's your name?"

In a slurred voice, Kate Eddowes replied, "Nothing."

Seeing that the woman was incapable of standing up and a danger to herself, Byfield had her put in a cell to sober up. At 9.45pm that evening, PC George Henry Hutt, the gaoler of Bishopsgate Street Station, came on duty. He visited Eddowes several times until, at 12.55am, he decided she was sober enough to be released, but of course before he could discharge the prisoner, he would have to take her name and address. Hutt escorted Eddowes to the office to take down her details. Kate claimed she was Mary Ann Kelly, of 6 Fashion Street. She also asked PC Hutt what time it was.

"Too late for you to get any more drink," he told her sternly.

"Well, what time is it?" she asked again.

"It's just on one," Hutt told her.

"I shall get a damned fine hiding when I get home then," she replied.

"And serve you right," Hutt said, self-righteously. "You have no right to get drunk."

The policeman directed her to the passageway via a swinging door, and at the end of the corridor Kate came to the exit door which led on to the cold rainy autumn street. She pushed instead of pulling for a few moments.

"Please pull it to!" said Hutt.

Kate did so and before she embarked on that terrible short journey to meet her barbaric fate, she called out cheekily, "All right, good night, old cock."

Being an observant policeman, PC Hutt noticed that Kate turned left – towards Houndsditch – which lay in the opposite direction to Flower and Dean Street and Cooney's lodging house.

Minutes before Eddowes would leave the police station, Elizabeth Stride – three quarters of a mile away in Berner Street – was being seized by the throat by Jack the Ripper, who then choked her into unconsciousness – or perhaps, as I have suggested in the previous chapter, rendered her unconscious by applying expert pressure on the nerve points of her neck and clavicle area. The bruise marks on Stride certainly indicate that this is what he did before cutting her throat.

Forty minutes after Eddowes left Bishopsgate Police Station, at around 1.40am, PC James Harvey was on his beat in Duke Street, a street dominated by the Great Synagogue. At the side of the synagogue was a dimly-lit narrow covered entry called Church Passage, which led into one of the darkest and quietest places in London at that time in the morning – Mitre Square. PC Harvey did not enter the

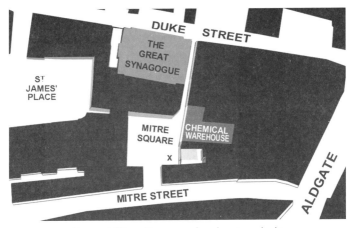

Map of Mitre Square, showing proximity
of Eddowes' body to the chemical warehouse.

square, he merely looked into it, and seeing nobody about and hearing nothing suspicious, he retraced his steps back up Church Passage and resumed his beat.

The square lay just within the eastern boundary of the City of London, in the Portsoken Ward, adjoining the district of Aldgate. There were three entrances to Mitre Square; a wide, well-illuminated carriageway from Mitre Street, the aforementioned Church Passage, which led from Duke Street, and a narrow covered entry that ran into St James's Place (which was also known as the Orange Market). Mitre Square was once the site of the Priory of the Holy Trinity, where it is alleged a murder took place in 1530. Brother Martin, the so-called 'mad monk', supposedly stabbed a woman praying at the altar through the heart. This incident is probably fictitious. A female would certainly not have been allowed into the priory to pray. In December 1865, *The Times* reports that a calamitous blaze broke out at 7 Mitre Square and quickly engulfed the premises of Messrs Cohen and Lavy, cigarette manufacturers. The inferno – which took the life of Mr Lavy and a William Hayman – was thought to have been caused by an obscure highly combustible compound known as 'Chinese Fire'. Mr Cohen had saved his own life by leaping through a window.

In 1885, 5 Mitre Square was a safe-house for Fenian dynamite bombers, and the most infamous members of these terrorists were John Gilbert Cunningham and Harry Burton, who bombed the Tower of London. Inspector Frederick Abberline – one of the major detectives who would be assigned to the Whitechapel Murders case – gave evidence against the Fenian bombers, and had visited Burton's room at Mitre Square before the arrest. At the trial, the terrorists talked about their search for a suitable trunk to house a bomb, and considered an American trunk or portmanteau. The bombers were always on the lookout for an innocent-looking box or case to house their bombs, and there is a curious incident regarding a wooden case which once again leads us back to Mitre Square. Eighteen days before the 'Double Event' killings of Stride and Eddowes, on 12 September 1888, a small article in *The Times* stated:

At the Guildhall, before Alderman Sir Andrew Lusk,
Alexander Birke, Great Garden-chambers, Whitechapel,
shoemaker, was charged with stealing from an enclosure
in front of 4 Mitre Street, Aldgate, an empty wooden
case, the property of Messrs Kearley and Tonge [of Mitre
Square]. Evidence was given by a person named Morris.
The alderman said an old, empty champagne case was
worthless, or nearly so; moreover, there was no actual
proof that the accused took it. Witness: But the value of
the thing has nothing to do with it. I have known a

person convicted for stealing a turnip.
Sir Andrew Lusk: Probably; but I never did convict for
stealing a turnip, and never will. Witness: The prisoner
has been convicted before. Harris (the gaoler): I do not
know him.
The Alderman: The man is not known. No proof has
been given that he stole the box; and if he had, the value
is nothing! He has been in prison all night, and I now
discharge him.
The decision was received with applause, which was
instantly suppressed.

What a storm in a teacup over the alleged theft of an old
champagne case from Mitre Square – but such a case had
been used by the Fenians to house their bombs before.
What is interesting about the article is that the Draconian
Mr Morris who was giving the evidence against Alexander
Birke was none other than George Morris, the night
watchman at the warehouse mentioned in the article –
Kearley and Tonge. Morris, a man in his mid-fifties, had
been a policeman in his younger days, and had retired from
the Met six years before, in 1882. He was on duty at Kearley
and Tonge on the night of September 29-30, and often had
the door of the warehouse ajar, so that he was able to hear
the footsteps of a policeman named Edward Watkins
walking by on his beat every twelve to fourteen minutes.
According to the East London Advertiser of 6 October 1888,
at 1.30am, on the morning of 30 September 1888, PC
Watkins called at the warehouse and handed a can of tea to
Morris and told him to have it hot by the time he came
around again on his beat. Watkins then continued his beat
around Mitre Square, and seeing no one was about, he
resumed his patrol of the neighbourhood. Ten minutes later,

PC Harvey, a policeman of twelve years' experience, came down Church Passage from Duke Street and looked in on the square. He saw nobody and heard nothing, and so he turned around, walked back up Church Passage, turned right into Duke Street then on to Aldgate. Not every policeman carried a watch in those days, and Harvey estimated the time of his visit to Mitre Square by the Aldgate Post Office Clock.

Incidentally, unknown to PC Harvey and the other policemen in the area, a robbery was going on at the Post Office in the High Street, Aldgate, as Jack the Ripper was at large in the neighbourhood on the night of the Double Event. A 24-year-old Bloomsbury man named Francis Robarti was later arrested for the robbery. He stole £250 in stamps and £50 in cash from the Post Office, and was subsequently sentenced to two months' imprisonment with hard labour.

The beat system of the Victorian policeman was ingenious. The beats interlocked in such a way, that if a constable was late at a certain point on his beat where he usually saw a colleague, it was obvious that something was amiss. PC Harvey would have seen and nodded or talked to PC Watkins at a certain point on his beat, and when one studies the modus operandi of Jack the Ripper, it becomes clear that he has a working knowledge of these police beats. It's as if the killer had carefully studied the beats of the patrolling policemen so he knew how much time he had to carry out his grisly and silent work. Furthermore, most of the victims were killed and apparently left at locations where they were bound to be discovered within minutes of their deaths. In the intricate network of patrolling policemen on interlocking beats (many of which, were deliberately reversed at the time of the Whitechapel murders in the hope of confusing the culprit) a mad murderer striking randomly would be sure to come unstuck. That is why many killers who imitated Jack after the Ripper murders ended were caught. Those who kill out of bloodlust in a random fashion are usually caught because of a lack of foresight and planning. The Son of Sam, the Yorkshire Ripper, and many other serial killers were caught after making blunders which led to their arrest.

In modern times, the Zodiac killer, who terrorised Northern California in the 1960s, evaded arrest because he seemed to plan out his murders, and from the ciphers he devised to communicate with the baffled police, he was a man of above average intelligence with a good knowledge of literature, chemistry, mathematics, electronics, firearms and geometry. Of course, had Zodiac carried out his crimes in an area as small as Whitechapel – as opposed to the hundreds of square miles of his killing grounds in Northern California – he would, in all probability, have been captured. The five accepted, canonical murders of Jack the Ripper took place over 71 days, whereas Zodiac was at large for many years, and some criminologists even believe that he was not responsible for all of the murders accredited to him. Zodiac, with all of his planning, was seen on numerous occasions, allowing police artists to create a photo-fit of his face. Furthermore, several victims of Zodiac survived, whereas Jack the Ripper left no survivors in his wake, and was so stealthy, no one saw or heard him. Those who claimed to have seen Jack gave descriptions that never matched.

Let us now return to that Victorian Sunday morning in Mitre Square. PC Watkins has left the square at 1.30am, and ten minutes after this, PC Harvey has looked in on the square and seen nobody loitering about. The square is empty. The door to the Kearley and Tonge warehouse is ajar, and the night watchman Morris – who can hear anyone

Watkins discovers Eddowes' body in Mitre Square.

entering the square – hears nothing. At 3 Mitre Square, the Pearse family are sound asleep, and the head of this family is ironically a policeman in his forties named Richard Pearse, who may have been 'installed' at this address to keep a watch on Fenians in the square. Richard Pearse and his wife Grace have long retired to bed, and the couple and their children are all sleeping soundly.

At 1.44am, PC Watkins entered the square again from Mitre Street, and turned right to face the darkest corner with only the faint illumination of his Bull's Eye belt lantern showing the way. He slowed his gait as he saw something on the ground. It turned out to be the corpse of Kate Eddowes, lying on its back in a pool of blood, horrifically mutilated. The feet of the dead woman pointed towards the centre of the square. In the seventeen years Watkins had served as a policeman, he had never seen a

Position of Eddowes' body in Mitre Square.

sight as gruesome as this. Realising that the woman was probably another victim of the Whitechapel murderer that he had heard and read so much about, Watkins raced over to the Kearley and Tonge warehouse and alerted the night watchman George Morris. To the door, which was ajar, he shouted, "For God's sake mate, come out and assist me!"

Morris emerged from the building with a lamp and said, "What's the matter?"

"Another woman has been cut to pieces," Watkins told him excitedly, pointing to the dark corner. The two men went to view the body by the combined light of the night watchman's lamp and the Bull's Eye lantern. To a *Star* newspaper man, who would later ask Watkins to describe Eddowes' corpse, the policeman stated: "She was ripped up like a pig at the market."

The *Daily News* featured a more detailed account from Watkins:

> *I came round to Mitre Square again at 1.45am, and entering the square from Mitre Street, on the right-hand side, I turned sharp round to the right, and flashing my light, I saw the body in front of me. The clothes were pushed right up to her breast, and the stomach was laid bare, with a dreadful gash from the pit of the stomach to the breast. On examining the body I found the entrails cut out and laid round the throat, which had an awful gash in it, extending from ear to ear. In fact, the head was nearly severed from the body. Blood was everywhere to be seen. It was difficult to discern the injuries to the face for the quantity of blood which covered it.*
> *The murderer had inserted the knife just under the left eye, and drawing it under the nose, cut the nose completely from the face, at the same time inflicting a dreadful gash down the right cheek to the angle of the jawbone. The nose was laid over on the cheek. A more dreadful sight I never saw; it quite knocked me over.*

Morris the watchman ran off for assistance, and bumped into PC Harvey, who was patrolling Aldgate on his beat. Harvey in turn summoned PC Holland from the south side of Aldgate and the two policemen went at once to the assistance of PC Watkins in Mitre Square. PC Holland subsequently went to fetch Dr George William Sequeira from 34 Jewry Street, Aldgate. Sequeira, the first doctor to examine Eddowes, arrived at 1.55am, and around this time, the news of the murder in Mitre Square reached the ears of Inspector Edward Collard at Bishopsgate police station.

Before heading to Mitre Square, Collard sent a constable to fetch Dr Frederick Gordon Brown at 17 Finsbury Circus in the City. Dr Brown, incidentally, in addition to being a City Police surgeon, was also a prominent Freemason, and at one time he was the Grand Officer of the Grand Lodge of England. Dr Wynne Baxter, the coroner who presided over the inquests on Mary Ann Nichols, Annie Chapman and Elizabeth Stride, was also a Freemason (of South Saxon Lodge). Sir Charles Warren, the Metropolitan Police Commissioner, had been a Freemason from the age of nineteen. Now, at the age of forty-eight, he was one of the highest-ranking Freemasons in the world, who had founded numerous lodges across the globe, including the Quatuor Coronati Lodge, the premier lodge of Masonic research. Sir Charles founded the Quatuor Coronati Lodge with eight other brethren, amongst them novelist and historian Sir Walter Besant – the brother-in-law of Annie Besant, the radical Socialist reformer and Marxist who worked in the East End and inspired the successful Match Girls' Strike of 1888. Sir Walter Besant, a close friend of Sir Charles Warren, and, as mentioned, a member of the same Masonic lodge, was a secretary of the Palestine Exploration Fund, which was then based at 1 Adam Street, Adelphi, London – quite close to the Victoria Embankment. Sir Walter also had an East End connection; he not only wrote about the misery and poverty of the people of East London, his 1882 book, *All Sorts and Conditions of Men*, a stirring story about East End life, was a truthful and sympathetic portrayal of the poor, and it inspired the construction of The People's Palace – an educational institution on Mile End Road, an academic establishment worthy of the West End. This East End polytechnic, which had a library, concert and reading room, gymnasium, baths, art gallery, and classrooms to hold 5000 pupils, was opened in May 1887 by Queen Victoria.

In a round about but nevertheless factual way, I have illustrated how, through his Masonic friends, Sir Charles Warren was interconnected with the doctors and police surgeons on the ground during the Ripper murders, and have shown how just one of his close friends, Sir Walter Besant, worked closely with the people of the East End. Some authors of books on the Whitechapel Murders have taken the Masonic element rather too far. Much has been made of the Eddowes murder taking place in Mitre Square; the mitre and the square are symbolic tools of Freemasons, and we will see later in this chapter how part of Eddowes' apron had been torn away by the killer after she was murdered. The apron, of course, is an item worn by Freemasons, and is derived from the working apron of the original stonemasons from which Freemasonry stems. Buck's Row, the scene of the first Ripper murder, has no Masonic history or relevance attached to it, nor does Hanbury Street, where Annie Chapman was killed, have any arcane Masonic nexus. Berner Street, where Elizabeth Stride was murdered, is not in any way connected to Freemasonry either. The long arm of coincidence misleads in many a murder case, and has been the pitfall of many an ambitious author out to crack the greatest whodunit in history. I believe that Kate Eddowes was not taken or lured to Mitre Square as part of some complicated Masonic conspiracy; I believe that she went there to meet someone as part of a prearranged rendezvous, and was intercepted instead by Jack the Ripper.

At the inquest into the mysterious death of Kate Eddowes, Dr Frederick Gordon Brown described what he found that morning in Mitre Square:

The body was on its back – head turned to the left shoulder – the arms by the side of the body as if they had fallen there, both palms upwards – the fingers slightly bent, a thimble was lying off the finger on the right side. The clothes drawn up above the abdomen, the thighs were naked, left leg extended in a line with the body, the abdomen was exposed, right leg bent at the thigh and knee. The bonnet was at the back of the head – great disfigurement of face, the throat cut across, below the cut was a neckerchief. The upper part of the dress was pulled open a little way. The abdomen was all exposed. The intestines were drawn out to a large extent and placed over the right shoulder – they were smeared over with some feculent matter. A piece [of intestine] of about 2 feet [in length] was quite detached from the body and placed between the body and the left arm, apparently by design. The lobe and auricle of the right ear was cut obliquely through. There was a quantity of clotted blood on the pavement on the left side of the neck, round the shoulder and upper part of the arm, and fluid blood-coloured serum which had flowed under the neck to the right shoulder – the pavement sloping in that direction. Body was quite warm – no death stiffening had taken place. She must have been dead most likely within the half hour. We looked for superficial bruises and saw none – no blood on the skin of the abdomen or secretion of any kind on the thighs – no spurting of blood on the bricks or pavement found. No marks of blood below the middle of the body – several buttons were found in the clotted blood after the body was removed. There was no blood on the front of the clothes. There were no traces of a recent connection [i.e. the killer had not had sex with the victim]. When the body arrived at Golden Lane [Mortuary] some of the blood was dispersed through the removal of the body to the mortuary. The clothes were taken off carefully from the body, [and] a piece of deceased ear dropped from the clothing.

The face was very much mutilated. There was a cut one-quarter of an inch through the lower left eyelid dividing the structures completely through the upper eyelid on that side, there was a scratch through the skin on the left upper eyelid – near to the angle of the nose the right eyelid was cut through to about half an inch. There was a deep cut over the bridge of the nose extending from left border of the nasal bone down near to the angle of the jaw on the right side, across the cheek – this cut went into the bone and divided all the structures of the cheek except the mucous membrane of the mouth. The tip of the nose was quite detached from the nose by an oblique cut from the bottom of the nasal bone to where the wings of the nose join on to the face. A cut from this divided the upper lip and extended through the substance of the gum over the right upper lateral incisor tooth.

There was on each side of cheek a cut which peeled up the skin forming a triangular flap about an inch and a half. There was a little mud on the left cheek – 2 slight abrasions of the epithelium under the left ear. The throat was cut across to the extent of about 6 or 7 inches. A superficial cut commenced about an inch and a half below the lobe and about two-and-a-half inches behind the left ear and extended across the throat to about 3 inches below the lobe of the right ear.

We examined the abdomen, the front walls were laid open from the breast bone to the pubes. The cut commenced opposite the ensiform cartilage.

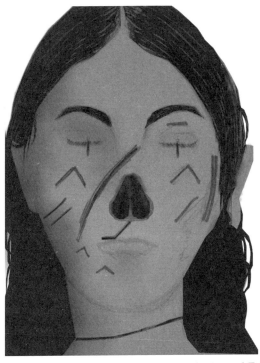

Strange markings the Ripper inscribed on the face of Eddowes.

Dr Brown also discovered that the left kidney and most of the womb were missing from the corpse of Kate Eddowes. The curious inverted V-shaped marks carefully inscribed under the eyes of Eddowes, the slicing off of her nose, the slashing of her right ear, the appalling injuries inflicted to her abdomen, the excision of a kidney, and the removal of the womb, would obviously have taken quite some time, and as we know the window of time within which the Ripper was working, we can say he was a phenomenally fast operator. As we have seen, PC Harvey had looked in on the

111

square at 1.40am, and had seen nothing – but is it possible that he had not noticed the body of Eddowes lying in the darkest corner of Mitre Square? It is possible. PC Watkins had left the square at 1.30am, and at 1.44am he returned from his beat to find the body of Eddowes. Dr Brown opined that the killer could not have performed his grisly work in less than five minutes, whereas Dr Sequeira estimated that the injuries to Eddowes could have been inflicted in around three minutes. The killer of Kate Eddowes had, in that dark corner of Mitre Square, somehow located the kidney of his victim and removed it. The human kidney is covered by a membrane, buried in fat and hard to locate, and yet Jack the Ripper had excised it quickly, along with the womb, which is as big as an average-sized orange. Jack had apparently been rooting through the pockets of his victim, just as he had with Annie Chapman.

Inspector Edward Collard of the City Police, inspected Eddowes's corpse in Mitre Square at around 2.03am, and at the inquest he stated that three small black buttons, of the type used for women's boots, a thimble, and a small mustard tin containing two pawn tickets (one for John Kelly's boots and the other for the flannel shirt, given to Eddowes by 'Emily Burrell'), were found just to the left of the body. Also to the left of the body, between it and the left arm, the Ripper had placed a 2-foot-long piece of intestine. This section of intestine had been straightened and laid out to look like some macabre semblance of a military man's swagger stick. Amongst the possessions carried by Eddowes, a printed handbill was found, featuring the name of Frank Cater, a 25-year-old cheesemonger (and possibly grocer) of 400 Bethnal Green Road. Frank and Lydia Cater lived at that address with their sons, three-year-old Frank junior and two-year-old Christopher. *The Times* misreported

Cater's address as 405 Bethnal Green Road, and the police made a rather half-hearted search for him that was not successful. To this day, it is not known why Kate Eddowes was carrying a printed handbill which promoted the business of Frank Cater, and curiously, the cheesemonger never came forward to throw any light on the mystery, despite his name being mentioned in most of the newspaper articles covering the Eddowes murder. John Kelly, the common-law husband of Kate Eddowes, did not comment on the matter either. In fact, I'm surprised Kelly didn't go directly to Bethnal Green Road in an effort to locate and question the mysterious Frank Cater. Cater seems to have been a dishonest man, according to reports in *Reynold's Magazine* and *Lloyds Newspaper*, dated 1 November and 8 November 1891 respectively, Cater was fined 14 pounds, 31 shillings and sixpence for trying to pass off half a pound of margarine as butter to a customer at his shop in Bethnal Green Road.

A reporter from the *Evening News* visited John Kelly at Cooney's Lodging House, Flower and Dean Street, days after the murder of his partner Eddowes. Kelly is described as suicidal, and when the reporter asks him if he thinks the murderer will ever be captured, he optimistically answers: "It's my belief it won't be long before he's taken, and a very good job too."

On 3 October, Kelly states in an article in the *Star* how he came to learn of his common-law wife's death:

When she did not come home at night I didn't worry, for I thought her daughter had asked her to stay over Sunday with her. So on Sunday morning I wandered round in the crowds that had been gathered by the talk about the two fresh murders. I stood and looked at the

113

*very spot where my poor old gal had lain with her body
cut to pieces and I never knew it. I never thought of her
connection with it, for I thought she was safe at her
daughter's. Yesterday morning [Tuesday 2 October] I
began to be worried a bit, but I did not guess the truth
until after I had come back from another bad day in the
market. I came in here [Cooney's Lodging House] and
asked for Kate, she had not been in. I sat down on that
bench by the table and carelessly picked up the Star
paper. I read down the page a bit, and my eye caught the
name of 'Burrell'. It looked familiar, but I didn't think
where I had seen it until I came to the word
'pawnticket'. Then it came all over me all at once. The
tin box, the two pawntickets, the one for the flannel shirt,
and the other for my boots. But could Kate have lost
them? I read a little further. 'The woman had the letters
T.C., in India ink, on her arm.' Man, you could have
knocked me down with a feather! It was my Kate, and
no other. I don't know how I braced up to go to the
police, but I did. They took me down to see the body, and
I knew it was her. I knew it before I saw it, and I knew
her for all the way she was cut. I told the police all I
have told you, and I suppose I will tell it again to the
Coroner. I never knew if she went to her daughters at all.
I only wish to God she had, for we had lived together a
long while and never had a quarrel.*

This version of events, as reported in the newspaper, does
not ring true at all, as at the inquest into the death of
Eddowes, John Kelly admitted that he had learned of the
incarceration of Kate at Bishopsgate police station from a
woman on the Saturday night. Kelly stated that he couldn't
remember what time it was when he heard about Kate's

arrest, but the woman (never identified by Kelly) had told him she had seen Eddowes between two policemen as they escorted her through Houndsditch to the police station. Kelly didn't make any inquiries at the station to see if his common-law wife had indeed been arrested for being drunk and disorderly (despite her having no money to buy drink), and he told the coroner that, because he knew she was being held in custody, he was confident she'd return to him on the Sunday morning.

Dr Frederick Gordon Brown's examination of the corpse of Kate Eddowes determined that partly digested farinaceous food had escaped from the sliced end of the stomach. Traces of farinaceous food were also found in the stomach of Elizabeth Stride, the other canonical victim of Jack the Ripper who had been killed around forty-five minutes before Eddowes. Like Stride, Eddowes had also been quietly laid down on the ground by Jack the Ripper – then killed. The six-inch blade of the knife had cut through the neck to the bone of the spine. Both Eddowes and Stride had earned a little money by running errands for the Jews. Kelly himself, in the aftermath of the murders, also worked for the Jews, running errands for them, as well as doing odd jobs at Spitalfields Market.

At 2.20am on the morning of the double murder, PC Alfred Long was walking down Goulston Street, a quarter of a mile from Mitre Square. He passed a grim tenement building principally inhabited by Jews, known as the Wentworth Model Dwellings. He passed the entrance which led to numbers 108 to 119 of the dwellings, and seems to have noticed nothing out of the ordinary. PC Long had been drafted in from Whitehall Division, and had served in the Metropolitan Police force for four years. Before that he had spent twelve years in the 9th Queen's

Royal Lancers, a cavalry regiment. Long had been drafted into Whitechapel like many other policemen to augment the existing force during the Ripper scare, and on this night, the first night of a beat he had never walked before, he was not yet aware of the murder of Kate Eddowes. When PC Long came down Goulston Street again on his beat, at 2.55am, he passed the aforementioned entrance to the Wentworth Dwellings tenements, and this time he noticed something light on the floor of the common stairway. It was a piece of white cloth, and it was bloodstained and wet. On the black brick jamb of the doorway, above the apron, someone had neatly written five lines of twelve small words in white chalk. For over a century, these words have been analysed and pondered upon by criminologists and lay persons alike, but not one person has ever made any sense of the graffito, which stated:

The Juwes are
The men that
Will not
be Blamed
for nothing

The message was written in neat handwriting with every word spelt correctly – except Jews, which was spelt Juwes. PC Long believed the apron had not been there when he had last passed that entrance to the Wentworth Model Dwellings, but he couldn't be sure about the enigmatic graffito; it was possible that he had walked by without noticing it.

The white cloth found by PC Long turned out to be a piece of the apron Kate Eddowes had been wearing when she was killed in Mitre Square. The killer had evidently cut

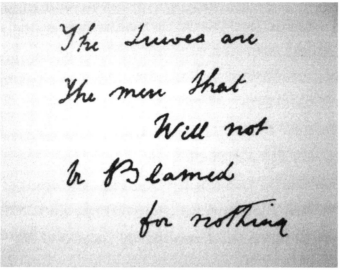

*The message was written in neat handwriting with every word
spelt correctly – except Jews, which was spelt Juwes.*

the piece of fabric from the apron and possibly used it to
wipe his hands and the knife – or so some of the police
reasoned. Jack the Ripper had not done this with his three
previous victims, and it's likely that he only took a portion
of the apron with him so he could use it to draw attention to
that doorway in the Wentworth Model Dwellings, where he
also chalked his baffling five-liner. Some criminologists
have queried whether the Ripper wrote the graffito at all,
but at the inquest, the coroner asked Daniel Halse, a
detective officer with the City Police, if the writing on the
wall had the appearance of recently being done, and Halse,
one of the first policeman to see the message, was
convinced the writing was fresh. It couldn't have been there
long, as one of the Jewish residents of the tenement would
have surely wiped the seemingly anti-Semitic message off
the wall.

At last, the Ripper had left a clue. Scotland Yard and the newspapers were in receipt of many dozens of letters purporting to be from the Whitechapel Murderer, yet most of them – if not all of them – were undoubtedly hoaxes, but here on a wall in Goulston Street, the killer himself had actually written a message. Now all the police had to do was to photograph the chalked message and print facsimiles of it to circulate in newspapers. Someone would perhaps recognise the handwriting. Why did Jack the Ripper, in the words of one policeman, "… fool around chalking things on walls when his life was imperilled by every minute he loitered?"

Well, if the Ripper specifically chose that particular doorway to write his mystifying message and throw down the blood-soaked apron, could there be any connection with the tenants living at 108 to 119 Wentworth Street Dwellings and the site of the other murder in Berner Street – the Jewish Socialists' Club? There is a tenuous though obvious link. They were both places frequented by Jews, of course, but if we probe a little deeper we will find another connection.

On Saturday 16 March, 1889, Israel Sunshine, of 119 Wentworth Street Dwellings – where the bloody apron was deposited and the chalked message was written – became involved in a melee with one Louis Diemschutz, the 27-year-old unlicensed hawker of cheap jewellery and live-in steward of the International Workingman's Educational Club, who found the body of Elizabeth Stride the same morning that Eddowes was killed. The scene of the fracas was 40 Berner Street, adjacent to Dutfield's Yard, where Stride was found with her throat cut. Young Israel Sunshine, a Jewish Socialist in his late teens, had, like Louis Diemschutz, come to Whitechapel from Russia. A wave of anti-Jewish pogroms had swept Russia in 1881, after the Jews were wrongly blamed for the assassination of Tsar

Alexander II. The Tsar had in fact been killed by a group of radicals known as the People's Will. The People's Will had contacted the Russian government and demanded a constitution, the right to free elections, and an end to censorship. Their demands were not met, so the terrorist faction attacked the Tsar and killed him (after several unsuccessful attempts) with a bomb. When the blame for the Tsar's assassination fell upon the Jews, there were pogroms in 166 Russian towns. Thousands of Jewish homes were destroyed, Jewish men, women and children were killed and injured, and the new Tsar, Alexander III, also blamed the Jews of Russia for wide-scale rioting that broke out, so in May 1882, he introduced the so-called Temporary Regulations – laws that banned Jews from all towns of less than ten thousand people, even within the Pale of Settlement – the western border region of Imperial Russia, which allowed permanent residence of Jews. This policy of racial discrimination was the major impetus for mass emigration, and between 1880 and 1920, over two million Jews fled from Russia. A majority of these Jews went to the United States, but many came to London's East End. In 1875, General Charles Warren – later to become the Metropolitan Police Commissioner during the Whitechapel Murders – was greatly concerned with the 'problem' of Jewish migration. That year, General Warren put forward an idea formulated by himself and his colleagues Claude Reignier Conder and Horatio Herbert Kitchener – all soldiers in the Royal Engineers. In a book entitled The Land of Promise (London, 1875), Warren wrote:

> *Give Palestine a good government and increase the commercial life of the people and they may increase tenfold and yet there is room. The soil is so rich, the*

119

climate so varied, that within ordinary limits it may be
said that the more people it contains, the more it may
accept. Its productiveness will increase in proportion to
labour bestowed on the soil until a population of 15
million may be accommodated there.

British support for a 'Jewish Restoration' – the setting up of a permanent homeland for the Jews had many prominent supporters. Sir Charles Warren, Field-Marshall Kitchener, and the archaeologist and soldier Colonel Claude Reignier Conder have been mentioned. Lord Palmerston, the man who led a Royal Commission to consider the defences of the United Kingdom in 1859, was also a staunch supporter of Jewish settlement in the Holy Land. Palmerston was also instrumental in the construction of Gosport's Fort Elson – the fortification in which Ted Stanley, Annie Chapman's shadowy 'lover', was stationed at between 6 August and 1 September 1888. I have described in a previous chapter on Annie Chapman how Stanley wove what seemed to be an unnecessary web of lies by pretending to be a pensioned soldier to Annie and other people he knew in Whitechapel, when in fact he was on active service and part of the 2nd Brigade Southern Division of the Hants Militia, stationed at Fort Elson. Why he was travelling back and forth between Fort Elson and the East End is unknown, but there is a real possibility that he was a military spy for the British Government, keeping watch on the Anarchists and Fenians of the East End.

Another personage of note who was committed to a grand plan for repatriating the Jews to the Holy Land was Lord Lindsay (Alexander William Crawford Lindsay). In 1847, Lord Lindsay wrote:

The soil of Palestine still enjoys her Sabbaths, and only waits for the return of her banished children, and the application of industry, commensurate with her agricultural capabilities, to burst once more into universal luxuriance, and be all that she ever was in the days of Solomon.

Lord Lindsay's son, James Ludovic Lindsay, KT, VD, DL, JP, LLD, FRS, VPSA (1847-1913), has a curious connection to the Whitechapel Murders. He became the 26th Earl of Crawford upon the death of his father in December 1880. Crawford was a great collector of books and also had a longstanding interest in the occult. Crawford was also interested in Fenianism and the Whitechapel Murders, and in the late 1880s he corresponded with Sir Robert Anderson, the Assistant Commissioner of the Metropolitan Police and the officer in charge of the investigation into the Whitechapel Murders from 6 October 1888 until the case was closed in 1892. Years after the death of the Earl of Crawford, the following scrap of undated correspondence was found amongst his papers:

2 CAVENDISH SQUARE
W.

My Dear Anderson,
I send you this line to ask you to see and hear the bearer, whose name is unknown to me. She has or thinks she has a knowledge of the author of the Whitechapel murders. The author is supposed to be nearly related to her, and she is in great fear lest any suspicions should attach to her and place her and her family in peril.

I have advised her to place the whole story before you,
without giving you any names, so that you may form an
opinion as to its being worth while to investigate.

Very sincerely yours,

Crawford

The woman referred to in the letter remains a mystery. She was never identified, and in all probability was just one of the many people in London who suspected someone or other of being Jack the Ripper. The popular image of the Ripper at the height of the murders was that of an insane doctor, and the police were besieged with tip-offs from people from every class in society who harboured suspicions about anyone who seemed even remotely eccentric. Sir Robert Anderson, to whom the letter is addressed, was a devout Christian, a Lay Preacher, a learned scholar of the Biblical scriptures, and former head of an intelligence department that investigated Fenians and Anarchists. He was a good friend of colleague Sir Charles Warren, a man who was also a serious student of the Old and New Testament. Long before Warren had been given the job as the Commissioner of the Metropolitan Police, he had been a Captain in the Royal Engineers, and between 1867 and 1870, he had achieved international fame as the renowned excavator of Jerusalem. Warren had been commissioned by the Palestine Exploration Fund in London to make excavations at the Temple Mount, Jerusalem, in 1867, at a time when the Ottoman Turks were administering the Holy City.

Warren was a strong-minded individual, and he was determined to excavate a tunnel through the Mount, and during the tunnelling work, the sledgehammers and chisels

Sir Charles Warren.

made enough noise to reverberate through the walls of the Al-Aqsa Mosque, where the prayers of the faithful were rudely disturbed. Warren and his labourers were stoned and further excavations were forbidden by the governor of the city, Mehmed Emin Aali Pasha. Somehow, Warren convinced the Ottomans to allow him to resume his tunnelling and he made many archaeological discoveries as a result. Warren's work in the Middle East expanded our knowledge of the topography of ancient Jerusalem and the archaeology of the Temple Mount. Sir Robert Anderson was also a fan of Warren's close friend, Lieutenant Claude Reignier Conder, and in Anderson's essay 'Christ and Criticism', he calls Conder 'a very high authority' and indeed, Conder was one of the greatest and most controversial Biblical archaeologists of his day. Together, he

123

Claude Reigner Conder in Palestine.

and Warren wrote the *Jerusalem* volume in the *Survey of Western Palestine* series of publications, a book which was reprinted many times and earned them both widespread fame. Copies of the publication were dispatched to the Universities of Cambridge and Oxford, as well as the British Museum. Warren even had part of the excavated ruins of the Temple Mount named after him. To this day, one of the major entrances to the Temple – still paved with original Herodian stones – is referred to as Warren's Gate.

As an eminent Biblical archaeologist and Orientalist, Warren had a thorough knowledge of ancient languages, and was able to decipher many ancient inscriptions found on stones and monuments unearthed throughout the Middle East. A case in point is the Moabite Stone, a black slab of basalt, measuring three-and-a-half feet in length and two-and-a-half feet in width, discovered at Dhiban, east of the Jordan River, in 1868. Warren was instrumental in the discovery of the Moabite Stone, a victory monument erected by Mesha, king of Moab in 850 BC. Warren not only read the inscriptions of the stone, he was well versed in all the branches of the so-called Altaic languages, which includes 66 languages spoken by around 348 million people worldwide. Most of these languages are spoken in and around Central and north-east Asia, and the name 'Altaic' is derived from the Alti Mountains in Central Asia. The language is thought to have been spread by nomadic horsemen who lived on the plains near the Alti Mountains. One group migrated to the Korean Peninsula and the islands of Japan, and another group settled in Europe. The most westerly member of the Altaic family is Turkish, but there is also a Mongolian branch of the language, and a Tungusic branch, which is made up of Manchu, Evenki, Lamut, Nanai and Sibo.

Sir Charles Warren and his close friend Lieutenant Claude Reignier Conder were masters of the Altaic languages, and they were both familiar with Manchu. Conder was one of the greatest experts on the Altaic languages in the world, and he was also an expert on Hittite. Altaic and Hittite were the languages of the Levant, and Conder wrote many books on the origins of these languages. Conder found it curious that the cuneiform version of the word 'Hittite' was 'Khittae' and wondered if there was some etymological connection between 'Khittae' and 'Cathay' and 'Catai' – two ancient names of China. Both these words originated with the name 'Khitan' an even older Chinese word for a tribe that once ruled northern China around the time of Marco Polo's visit. It was Polo who first called China Cathay in the thirteenth century AD.

Conder believed that when the Hittite empire crumbled in 1180 BC, many of the Hittites (mentioned in Genesis as the sons of Heth) fled eastwards – to China. He observed how the early Chinese dressed in a similar fashion to the Hittites, right down to their turned-up shoes. The Hittites wore pigtails, and so did the early Chinese. What's more, the Hittites mastered the art of extracting iron ore to smelt and cast, and so did the Chinese around that time. Both cultures were well known for the domestication of the horse and their formidable skills in equitation.

Conder researched deeper into the similarities between the Hittites and the Chinese, and discovered that many words and numbers in the Manchu language seemed to have connection with Babylonian and even English language. The most intriguing of these words was 'juwe'. In Manchu, juwe means 'two' and in English, we have words like 'dual' and 'duo' which pertain to two. On 13 March 1909, 21 years after the Whitechapel Murders, Claude Reignier Conder gave a lecture at Caxton Hall in London, entitled 'The Origin of the Chinese' and the talk was presided over by none other than Sir Charles Warren. During the lecture, Conder discussed the similarities between the various languages of the world and Manchu – an Altaic language – and in the course of the lecture, he chalked the word 'juwe' upon a blackboard and then chalked the word 'two' in English followed by the French word for two – 'deux'.

This of course, brings us back to that cryptic five-liner, chalked by Jack the Ripper on the night of the two murders:

The Juwes are
The men that
Will not
be Blamed
for nothing

At around 5.15am, Sir Charles Warren personally visited the doorway in the Wentworth Model Dwellings where this message had been chalked, and after reading the twelve chalked words, he ordered them to be erased. Warren feared that mention of the word Juwes would stir up anti-Semitic feelings in Whitechapel, and he later defended his decision to erase the graffito in a letter to the Home Secretary Henry Matthews:

Sir,
In reply to your letter of the 5th instant, I enclose a
report of the circumstances of the Mitre Square Murder
so far as they have come under the notice of the
Metropolitan Police, and I now give an account
regarding the erasing of the writing on the wall in
Goulston Street which I have already partially explained
to Mr. Matthews verbally.
On the 30th September on hearing of the Berner Street
murder, after visiting Commercial Street Station, I
arrived at Leman Street Station shortly before 5am and
ascertained from the Superintendent Arnold all that was
known there relative to the two murders.
The most pressing question at that moment was some
writing on the wall in Goulston Street evidently written
with the intention of inflaming the public mind against
the Jews, and which Mr. Arnold with a view to prevent

127

serious disorder proposed to obliterate, and had sent
down an Inspector with a sponge for that purpose,
telling him to await his arrival.
I considered it desirable that I should decide the matter
myself, as it was one involving so great a responsibility
whether any action was taken or not.

I accordingly went down to Goulston Street at once
before going to the scene of the murder: it was just getting
light, the public would be in the streets in a few minutes,
in a neighbourhood very much crowded on Sunday
mornings by Jewish vendors and Christian purchasers
from all parts of London.
There were several Police around the spot when I
arrived, both Metropolitan and City.
The writing was on the jamb of the open archway or
doorway visible in the street and could not be covered up
without danger of the covering being torn off at once.
A discussion took place whether the writing could be left
covered up or otherwise or whether any portion of it could
be left for an hour until it could be photographed; but after
taking into consideration the excited state of the population
in London generally at the time, the strong feeling which
had been excited against the Jews, and the fact that in a
short time there would be a large concourse of the people in
the streets, and having before me the Report that if it was
left there the house was likely to be wrecked (in which from
my own observation I entirely concurred) I considered it
desirable to obliterate the writing at once, having taken a
copy of which I enclose a duplicate.
After having been to the scene of the murder, I went on to the
City Police Office and informed the Chief Superintendent of
the reason why the writing had been obliterated.

I may mention that so great was the feeling with regard to the Jews that on the 13th ulto. the Acting Chief Rabbi wrote to me on the subject of the spelling of the word "Juewes" [sic] on account of a newspaper asserting that this was Jewish spelling in the Yiddish dialect. He added "in the present state of excitement it is dangerous to the safety of the poor Jews in the East [End] to allow such an assertion to remain uncontradicted. My community keenly appreciates your humane and vigilant action during this critical time."

It may be realised therefore if the safety of the Jews in Whitechapel could be considered to be jeopardised 13 days after the murder by the question of the spelling of the word Jews, what might have happened to the Jews in that quarter had that writing been left intact.

I do not hesitate myself to say that if that writing had been left there would have been an onslaught upon the Jews, property would have been wrecked, and lives would probably have been lost; and I was much gratified with the promptitude with which Superintendent Arnold was prepared to act in the matter if I had not been there. I have no doubt myself whatever that one of the principal objects of the Reward offered by Mr. Montagu was to shew to the world that the Jews were desirous of having the Hanbury Street Murder cleared up, and thus to divert from them the very strong feeling which was then growing up.

I am,
Sir,
Your most obedient Servant,
C. Warren

The other detectives thought Warren's decision to erase the only real clue left by the Ripper was insane. Surely the chalked message could have been photographed first? Despite Warren's in-depth knowledge of the Altaic and Manchu languages, he later writes to Sir Godfrey Lushington, the permanent under-secretary of the Home Office, telling him that he can't make sense of the word 'Juwes':

The idiom does not appear to me to be either English, French or German, but it might possibly be that of an Irishman speaking a foreign language. It might be the idiom of Spain or Italy.

On 26 February, 1887, just a little over a year before the Whitechapel Murders, James Glaisher, Chairman of the Executive Committee of the Palestine Exploration Fund in London, wrote a letter to Editor of *The Times*, praising Captain Claude Reignier Conder for his amazing decipherment of Hittite Hieroglyphics:

Sir, – It is with great pleasure that I announce, through the columns of The Times, a discovery, the news of which I have this day received from Captain Claude Conder, R.E., the discoverer. It is no less than the reading of the mysterious Hittite inscriptions which have baffled every attempt to decipher them since their discovery in the year 1872. They were first found by Burckhardt in the year 1808. You will observe that Captain Conder at present gives the world only a portion of the results of his discovery. He has, however, read the whole of the inscriptions and all the gems and seals bearing Hittite legends. He has placed in the hands of Sir Charles Wilson and Sir Charles Warren documents showing how

he has arrived at this discovery, and he has in
preparation a memoir which will be published, together
with complete readings, by the Palestine Exploration
Fund without any delay. In anticipation of his memoir,
I have only to say that the questions raised and the
points illustrated by this discovery promise to equal in
interest those of the cuneiform inscriptions, or the
hieroglyphics. One point only I will here mention, that it
throws great light on the early chapters of the book of
Genesis, and explains certain names in ancient history
which have hitherto been impossible to explain.

From what Captain Conder has told me, I think we
may hope to produce his memoir before the end of next
month. Meantime, there are reasons why the language in
which the inscriptions are written and the manner in
which the discovery was arrived at should be kept back
until the memoir is completed and the whole story can be
told at length.

I must add a word of congratulation to Captain Conder,
whose patient researches into this subject for the last four
years have been at length so brilliantly rewarded.

I remain, Sir, your obedient servant,
JAMES GLAISHER, Chairman of the
Executive Committee.
Palestine Exploration Fund, 1, Adam-street,
Adelphi, W.C.

Captain Conder had indeed made a breakthrough in the decipherment of the Hittite inscriptions, and he placed his findings, in his own words: "in the hands of two well-known Orientalists, Sir Charles Wilson and Sir Charles Warren."

If Jack the Ripper left a possible clue in his chalked message on the wall, what was he trying to say? The five-liner seems to be conveying a message to someone in the know – but about what? Well, the bloodstained portion of apron on the ground and the message on the doorway make it clear that the message is referring to someone at that address, 108 to 119 Wentworth Model Dwellings. Most criminologists have assumed that the writer of the graffito was uneducated, as he had seemingly misspelled the word Jews and had composed a sentence with a double negative, but who would write in such consistent well-formed calligraphy and misspell a simple 3-letter word (Jew), yet spell 'blamed' and 'nothing' correctly? The chalked message seems to be a cipher. Warren himself certainly had a working knowledge of such ciphers, and was also something of a wordsmith himself, as he used to issue orders to his officers in rhyming couplets. One of these, written before the 'Bloody Sunday' incident in 1887, ran thus:

The Commissioner has observed there are signs of wear,
On the Landseer Lions in Trafalgar Square,
Unauthorised persons are not to climb,
On the Landseer Lions at any time.

A boyhood friend and military colleague of Warren, Sir Robert Baden Powell, writes in his book *My Adventures As A Spy*, about military information being encoded in many forms, including hieroglyphic and even Hindustani ciphers, to prevent it being read if it fell into enemy hands. Lieutenant-General Baden-Powell is now synonymous with the Scouting Movement, but he served for a number of years in the British Secret Intelligence Service. In 1890, Baden-Powell went on a reconnaissance mission in Dalmatia, disguised as an eccentric butterfly collector! Baden-Powell writes of this outrageous mission:

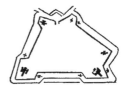

Baden Powell's sketch of a butterfly,
and plans of fort hidden within.

I went armed with most effective weapons for the
purpose, which have served me well in many a similar
campaign. I took a sketchbook, in which there were
numerous pictures – some finished, others only partly
done – of butterflies of every degree and rank, from a
"Red Admiral" to a "Painted Lady".
Carrying this book and a colour-box, and a butterfly net
in my hand, I was above all suspicion to anyone who
met me on the lonely mountain side, even in the
neighbourhood of the forts.
I was hunting butterflies, and it was always a good
introduction with which to go to anyone who was
watching me with suspicion. Quite frankly, with my
sketch-book in hand, I would ask innocently whether he
had seen such-and-such a butterfly in the neighbourhood,
as I was anxious to catch one. Ninety-nine out of a
hundred did not know one butterfly from another – any
more than I do – so one was on fairly safe ground in
that way, and they thoroughly sympathised with the mad
Englishman who was hunting these insects.
They did not look sufficiently closely into the sketches of
butterflies to notice that the delicately drawn veins of the
wings were exact representations, in plan, of their own
fort, and that the spots on the wings denoted the number
and position of guns and their different calibres.

133

So, sensitive military information can be encoded into innocent-looking drawings of butterflies, and even translated into abstruse ciphers that use hieroglyphics and words from foreign languages such as Hindustani. The message chalked by Jack the Ripper on the morning of what would later be referred to as the Double Event – the killing of Eddowes and Stride – was personally read by Sir Charles Warren, then erased by him, even though many of the detectives at the scene of the graffito urged the Commissioner to have the strange message photographed before erasure. The writing on the wall obviously meant something to Warren, given his extensive knowledge of ciphers, the Altaic language, Manchu, and the location of the message – a tenement inhabited principally by Jews. Furthermore, the 'glyphs' inscribed on the face of Kate Eddowes by Jack the Ripper look suspiciously like Moabite inscriptions – and, as we know, Sir Charles Warren could easily read such glyphs – but what did they spell out on the face of the murder victim?

Frederick William Foster, an architect and surveyor, went to amazing lengths to record as much information about the victim and the scene of the crime, supposedly for the coroner. Not only did Foster make two detailed sketches of Kate Eddowes and her injuries (with one drawing based on an on-the-spot sketch made by Dr Brown of the body), he also drew a number of highly detailed drawings of Mitre Square itself at different scales, as well as meticulous plans of the streets surrounding the square. No such attention was given to Nichols or Chapman. No sketches of Buck's Row or the backyard of Hanbury Street were drawn up by a surveyor for the benefit of the coroner – so why all the fuss over the demise of Eddowes? In April

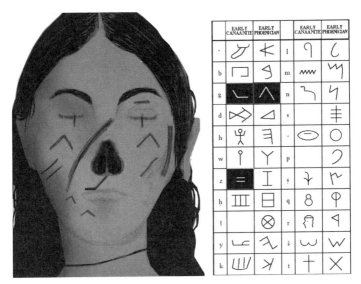

	EARLY CANAANITE	EARLY PHOENICIAN		EARLY CANAANITE	EARLY PHOENICIAN
'			l		
b			m		
g			n		
d			s		
h			'		
w			p		
z			ṣ		
ḥ			q		
ṭ			r		
y			š		
k			t		

The glyphs inscribed on the face of Kate Eddowes,
and the glyph table.

1889, Foster would be enlisted by the police to make a scale drawing of a public house parlour where a shooting had taken place, in what turned out to be a manslaughter case, but the plan of that single room – with a scale of an inch to a foot – was nowhere near as detailed as the comprehensive plans he drew up in the Eddowes murder.

The first murder of the morning had been, as we have seen, in Dutfield's Yard, Berner Street, the yard used by Louis Diemschutz, the steward of the International Workingman's Educational Club standing adjacent to the yard. Stride was found clutching a tissue containing aromatic breath sweeteners known as cachous, yet we know that she had not been eating these, as no traces of them were found in her stomach during the post mortem, so the killer had placed them in her hand. Is it possible that the killer did this so Diemschutz's pony would be drawn to the

135

strong sweet scent of the cachous as it entered the almost pitch-black yard? Discovery of the body would then be certain. Perhaps the killer thought the body would be overlooked because of the abysmal lighting conditions in the yard, but the sweet-smelling cachous would attract the attentions of the pony drawing Diemschutz's barrow. Ironically, in the event, the pony veered away from the body, possibly because the scent of Elizabeth Stride's blood swamped out the sweet smell of the aromatic cachous. What is certain is that Stride was killed in the yard of a Socialists' Club, where a steward would later be involved in assaulting a person who lived at 108-119 Wentworth Model Dwelling, where the apron of Eddowes was deposited and a chalked message was left on the jamb of the doorway. Then we have yet another link between the Socialists' Club and Mitre Square, where Eddowes met her silent, gruesome fate. On 22 March, 1889, the *Jewish Chronicle* reported how printed handbills (of the type Eddowes carried advertising Frank Cater) were distributed around Whitechapel by the Jews of the International Workingman's Educational Club. The handbills read:

SYNAGOGUE PARADE

A procession of Jewish unemployed and sweaters' victims will be held on Saturday, March 16, 1889, and will proceed to the Great Synagogue, where the Chief Rabbi will deliver a sermon to the unemployed and sweaters' victims. The procession will start at half-past twelve from 40, Berner Street [the International Workingman's Educational Club], Commercial Road, E. We demand work to buy bread, and the hours of labour to be eight per day. Come in large numbers, and bring your friends with you.

The article in the *Jewish Chronicle* also tells how Phillip Krantz, Editor of the Jewish Weekly radical newspaper, *The Worker's Friend* (*Der Arbeter Fraint*) had meetings with the Rabbis of the Synagogue, which is very close to Mitre Square. The first meeting, with the Delegate Chief Rabbi, Hermann Marcus Adler, was a failure, with Adler telling Krantz that the Great Synagogue was a place for worship and not political demonstrations. Krantz was undeterred, however, and he later returned to the synagogue and was admitted, along with his Socialist comrades and many Jews, most of them new arrivals from Russia. They had marched from the Berner Street club with a band playing the 'La Marseillaise'. Police kept a keen eye on the demonstration, and it is significant that policemen – including, for example, the likes of City Detective, Superintendent Alfred Foster – were keeping the Jews from Berner Street under very close surveillance.

At the synagogue, the Socialists and Anarchists from the Berner Street club got ready to address such things as the right to an 8-hour working day, the right to work to buy bread, the need to organise a strong body of workers to strike against the Capitalist rulers, and an end to sweatshop working conditions with men, women and children working 18-hours a day. However, Krantz and his comrades learned that Rabbi Adler was not in attendance, and so the crowds of discontented 'subversives' left the synagogue and went to Mile End Road to hold an 'indignation meeting'.

The Socialists' Club in Berner Street was under constant surveillance by the Special Irish Branch and other British Intelligence departments, because it was thought to harbour not only radical would-be revolutionaries, but Anarchists and Fenians as well. In November 1890, just two years after the Whitechapel Murders, posters were put up across the East

End, proclaiming a mass meeting by the International Workingmen's Educational Club at the Great Assembly Hall, Mile End Road. A protest would be held there to highlight 'the inhuman treatment and persecution of Jews in Russia'. Among the printed names on that poster of the people attending the meeting, you will find William Morris, the British craftsman, designer, writer, typographer, and Socialist, as well as Eleanor Marx – the daughter of Karl Marx, and also Michael Davitt – the Irish social campaigner, nationalist politician and founder of the Irish National Land League.

In 1865 Davitt drifted into the ranks of the Irish Republican Brotherhood, the Fenians' organisation in Ireland, and was later imprisoned for treason-felony for sending guns to Ireland. He was sentenced to 15 years and served seven of them in isolation before being released on a 'ticket of leave'. Davitt subsequently joined up with the Irish Republican Brotherhood again. He gained quite a reputation as a defender of the disadvantaged, and today he is recognised as one of the founder members of the British Labour Party.

Davitt was a revolutionary, a writer, a Labour activist, a republican, an internationalist who sympathised with the down-trodden of every country – and, of course, he was a Fenian. Davitt was also a fierce supporter of the women's suffrage movement at a time when women hardly had any rights. His political ideas travelled far beyond the shores of Great Britain, and Davitt himself visited Australia, Tasmania, New Zealand, the Holy Land, Russia, South America, and Europe. He wrote a book about the persecution of the Jews in Russia, which woke America up to the pogroms, and he bitterly opposed the Boer War. Davitt compared the Boers to the poor of Ireland – people who had also been victims of British duplicity and

Michael Davitt was a revolutionary, a writer, a Labour activist, a republican, an internationalist who sympathised with the down-trodden of every country.

oppression, and he resigned his seat in Parliament in protest against the war in 1899. Gandhi was inspired by Davitt's ideals, and when he went to South Africa to organise and mobilise the Indian population, he was mindful of the Mayo man's struggles with the British.

Davitt then, was, in the eyes of the British Establishment of 1888, a dangerous missing link between Fenianism and Socialism. He was a nexus that amalgamated the Jewish Socialists and Anarchists with the Fenians into a formidable ally against the British Government. His presence at the Berner Street International Workingman's Educational Club highlights the political movement that had been imminent at the time of the Ripper murders: Fenian Irishman and radical Jew were ready to join forces.

139

6

THE LUSK KIDNEY

By now, the reader should be aware of a Fenian element that is slowly emerging in the Jack the Ripper murders case. This element becomes strikingly evident in the aftermath of the Stride and Eddowes 'Double Event' murders. On Monday, 1 October 1888, *The Times* reported:

> *Messrs George Lusk and Joseph Aarons, writing from 1, 2 and 3 Alderney Road, Mile End, September 29, on behalf of the Whitechapel Vigilance Committee, who communicated without result with the Home Secretary with the view of obtaining, on behalf of the public at large, the offer of a Government reward for the apprehension and conviction of the assassin or assassins in the recent East-End atrocities, say: – "We shall be glad if you will allow us to state that the committee do not for one moment doubt the sincerity of the Home Secretary in refusing the said offer, as he apparently believes that it would not meet with a successful result. If he would, however, consider that in the case of the Phoenix Park murders the man Carey, who was surrounded by, we may say, a whole society steeped in crime, the money tempted him to betray his associates, in our opinion, if Mr Matthews could see his way clear to coincide with our views, the Government offer would be*

Timothy Kelly, one of the Phoenix Park murderers aged 20.

*successful. The reward should be ample for securing the
informer from revenge, which would be a very great
inducement in the matter, in addition to which such offer
would convince the poor and humble residents of our
East End that the Government authorities are as much
anxious to avenge the blood of these unfortunate victims
as they were the assassination of Lord F. Cavendish and
Mr Burke."*

This letter, written the day before the Double Event, is
quite curious. An intriguing reference is made to a
politically-motivated double murder in Ireland, committed
six years before. The Phoenix Park murders were carried
out by a Fenian splinter group called 'The Invincibles' in
May 1882. The victims were the Chief Secretary for Ireland,

Lord Frederick Cavendish, and the Under-Secretary, Thomas Burke, and the way in which these men were killed was horrific.

At 7.17pm on the Saturday evening of 6 May 1882, they were both walking across Phoenix Park in Dublin, towards the Viceregal Lodge, when they were attacked. Fenian Joseph Brady cried out, "Ah, you villain!" and struck Thomas Burke with a knife that passed between his ribs and penetrated the left ventricle of the heart. Burke slumped to the floor and as he did so, Brady stabbed at his chest and neck. Timothy Kelly, the other Fenian assailant, had managed to stab Lord Cavendish in the right shoulder, and the thrust had been so forcefully delivered, the blade tip had emerged over the second rib of the victim's chest. Despite this wound, Cavendish turned around and tried to make a dash for the roadway of the park, but the ensuing great loss of blood caused him to sink to his knees. He raised his left arm defensively and it was almost severed by the unusually sharp knife. It was in fact, a twelve-inch-long Weiss surgical knife, and was one of a dozen purchased from a surgical instrument manufacturer of 287 Oxford Street, London.

Brady finished off a groaning Thomas Burke by drawing the surgical knife across his throat. Lord Cavendish was left barely alive, and by the time a surgeon was summoned from nearby Steeven's Hospital, he had stopped breathing and was pronounced dead soon afterwards. It transpired that the fearsome Weiss surgical knives, which had slain the two men, had been purchased in London and left with a Bethnal Green cobbler named Maurice Collins. He arranged for an associate named Deasy to fit special sheaths to hold the knives and then had them taken to the Land League office at Westminster Palace Chambers.

Then came the problem of how to transport the knives to

Aftermath of the Phoenix Park double murder 1882.

Ireland. The Fenians knew their usual messengers and couriers had a habit of attracting the attention of the police, and they wondered if there was any possible way of using a courier who would automatically be regarded as above suspicion. The wife of Liverpool Irishman and Fenian Frank Byrne volunteered to be the courier. Mrs Mary Byrne was seven months' pregnant at the time, an ideal condition to avert any suspicions of her carrying anything but her unborn baby. She was successful in taking the knives, hidden in her skirt, to Ireland. Also upon her person were revolvers and ammunition, and these, along with the twelve Weiss knives, were deposited

Liverpool Irishman Frank Byrne and his wife Mary.

with the Dublin conspirators. The Fenian splinter group had learned a valuable lesson; that female couriers were more successful because they were far less likely to be searched, or to find themselves under surveillance.

A reward of £10,000 for information leading to the arrest of the Phoenix Park murderers was quickly raised, and Superintendent John Mallon of the Dublin Metropolitan Police soon apprehended the assassins. Of the twelve smuggled-in, double-edged, surgical knives, only three were ever found.

Back to the letter of George Lusk and Joseph Aarons, published in *The Times* after the Double Event. It is a strange comparison indeed, to compare the enormous reward offered for the capture of the Fenians in the Phoenix Park double murder in Dublin with the lack of a reward in the Whitechapel Murders case in London. George Lusk was

George Lusk.

the president of the Whitechapel Vigilance Committee, formed by concerned local businessmen, tradesmen and residents, with a view to supporting and supplementing the police force at the height of the Ripper scare. The Whitechapel Vigilance Committee was just one of several vigilance organisations in operation at that time. The Central Vigilance Agency, based at the Adelphi, was concerned with the ever-present problems of prostitution and alcoholism, and the St Jude's committee – named after the local Reverend Samuel Barnett's Church – was also tackling crime in Whitechapel and Spitalfields. Without a doubt, Lusk's vigilance organisation was the one that featured mostly in the newspapers.

George Lusk was a widower in his late forties, living with seven children at 1 Tollit Street, Alderney Road, Mile End. His wife Susannah had passed away from diabetes on

5 February 1888, after lying in a coma for 18 months. Upon Susannah's death, George inherited her property, which he used to finance a building and decorating business. George's speciality was renovating old music halls, but he was also a member of the Metropolitan Board of Works, as well as a vestryman of his parish. On Monday, 15 October 1888, a strange incident took place involving Lusk. The *Daily Telegraph* of 20 October describes this peculiar event:

A statement ... was made last night by Miss Emily Marsh, whose father carries on business in the leather trade at 218 Jubilee Street, Mile End Road. In Mr Marsh's absence Miss Marsh was in the front shop, shortly after one o'clock on Monday last, when a stranger dressed in clerical costume entered and, referring to the reward bill in the window, asked for the address of Mr Lusk, described therein as the president of the Vigilance Committee. Miss Marsh at once referred the man to Mr J. Aarons, the treasurer of the committee, who resides at the corner of Jubilee Street and Mile End Road, a distance of about thirty yards. The man, however, said he did not wish to go there, and Miss Marsh thereupon produced a newspaper in which Mr Lusk's address was given as Alderney Road, Globe Road, with no number being mentioned. She requested the stranger to read the address, but he declined, saying, "Read it out," and proceeded to write something in his pocket-book, keeping his head down meanwhile. He subsequently left the shop, after thanking the young lady for the information, but not before Miss Marsh, alarmed by the man's appearance, had sent the shop-boy, John Cormack, to see that all was right. This lad, as well as Miss Marsh, gives a full description of the man, while

*Mr Marsh, who happened to come along at the time, also
encountered him on the pavement outside. The stranger is
described as a man of some forty-five years of age, fully
six feet in height, and slimly built. He wore a soft felt
black hat, drawn over his forehead, a stand-up collar,
and a very long black single-breasted overcoat, with a
Prussian or clerical collar partly turned up. His face
was of a sallow type, and he had a dark beard and
moustache. The man spoke with what was taken to be an
Irish accent.*

When Lusk was told about the strange Irish visitor, he was
baffled, as he knew no one of that description. On the
following day at around 5pm, a small parcel was delivered to
Lusk's home. It contained half of a human kidney, cut
longitudinally, accompanied by a menacing letter which read:

From hell

Mr Lusk

*Sor
I send you half the
Kidne I took from one women
prasarved it for you tother piece I
fried and ate it was very nise I
may send you the bloody knif that
took it out if you only wate a whil
longer
Signed Catch me when
you can*

Mishter Lusk

147

Lusk was naturally shocked by the grisly contents of the parcel and the accompanying warped letter. He wondered if the kidney belonged to a sheep or a dog, and was in two minds as to whether it was genuine or simply a macabre prank. He recalled a letter he had received a few days before:

Say Boss-

You seem rare frightened. Guess I'd like to give you fits, but can't stop time enough to let you box of toys [Cockney rhyming slang for 'boys'] play copper games with me, but hope to see you when I don't hurry too much.

Bye-bye, Boss

That letter bore no resemblance to the 'From Hell' letter; its calligraphy, grammar and punctuation were a world apart from the sinister missive delivered with the half a kidney. Lusk looked at the parcel and saw two penny stamps stuck to its wrapping with a single postmark that was indistinct. A Post Office official who scrutinised the postmark opined that the parcel had been posted in either the Eastern or East Central district of London. The wording of the letter from that parcel had either been written by an Irishman or someone who wrote to denote an Irish accent. The use of the word 'Sor' for 'Sir', 'prasarved' for 'preserved' and 'Mishter' for 'Mister' effectively conveyed the impression that the writer of what would become known as the Lusk Letter was an Irishman. Months before, the satirical magazine *Punch* had featured comical sketches of the Fenians talking to blundering Scotland Yard detectives in such phonetic words as 'Sor' and 'Mishter'. There was also a satirical weekly column syndicated in many newspapers that year called 'Mick Malone's Letters' – supposedly written by a stereotypical Irishman to a 'Mishter' McCarthy – which featured words such as 'Sor' and 'prasarved'. Lusk must have worried about the identity of the mysterious tall Irishman in black who had visited Emily Marsh at the shop in Jubilee Street, inquiring about his address, just a day ago. Miss Marsh had given Lusk's address as Alderney Road, Globe Road, without specifying a house number, and sure enough, on the parcel containing the kidney portion, there was no house number included in the address.

It is possible that the postal kidney incident was a disgusting hoax, perpetrated by Lusk himself, or a member of his vigilance committee, staged as a publicity gimmick, but Lusk would be risking a lot if this were so. He'd have had to have hired someone to visit Emily Marsh at the shop and he would also have had to obtain half a human kidney. Had Lusk been discovered to have been a man who wasted precious police time at the height of an unprecedented series of murders, as well as being involved with the theft of a body part from a dissecting room, his reputation would have been destroyed overnight.

Lusk was an expert in self-publicity, so why didn't he rush to the police station with the piece of kidney and the letter 'From Hell'? Instead, Lusk did nothing for two days. This is out of character for a publicity-seeking man such as Lusk. As we have seen, he had written inflammatory letters to the newspapers, criticising the Government for not offering a reward for the capture of the Whitechapel Murderer, and he had even sent a petition to the Monarch herself on 27 September 1888. In this petition, Lusk stated that he was a representative of the 'the inhabitants of the

East End districts' of the metropolis, and advised the Queen to offer a reward for the apprehension of the Whitechapel Murderer.

Two days after receiving the kidney portion, the Whitechapel Vigilance Committee had a meeting at Lusk's home, and Lusk showed the members the kidney and the covering letter. Joseph Aarons, the treasurer had already seen the kidney on the previous evening after Lusk had visited him in a terrified state after receiving the partial organ. The committee members urged Lusk to take the kidney to a medical man to see if it really had come from a human. They were all too keenly aware of the press reports stating that Jack the Ripper had not only removed the womb of Catharine Eddowes – he had taken out her left kidney as well. "Throw it away; I hate the sight of it," Lusk said. Nevertheless, the committee members persuaded him to have it analysed, and they visited the local surgery of Dr Wills on Mile End Road, but he wasn't in, so they showed the bisected kidney to his assistant, Dr Reed, and after a cursory examination of the organ he stated that it was indeed from a human and had been preserved in spirits of wine. Dr Reed then advised the men to take the kidney to Dr Thomas Openshaw, the curator of the pathological museum at the London Hospital, for an expert analysis.

Openshaw made a detailed and microscopic analysis of the kidney. The newspapers claimed that Openshaw had deduced that the kidney was from a woman of about forty-five years of age who had been in the habit of drinking, as the organ exhibited symptoms of Bright's Disease and that the woman had died around the time of the Mitre Square murder. In reality, Openshaw made no such claims. He merely deduced that the half of kidney was from a human, but he couldn't say if it was a male or female kidney, nor could he tell how long ago the kidney had been removed from the body as it had been preserved in spirits. The letter that came with the package was sent to Scotland Yard and the portion of kidney was sent to Dr Frederick Gordon Brown, the man who had performed the autopsy on Catharine Eddowes. Brown could see that the kidney portion had not been charged with formalin preserving fluid, so the organ had not been destined for the dissecting room for an anatomy lesson; instead the organ had been preserved in spirit. Brown wouldn't stick his neck out to say that the kidney was part of a left one, but he did say that it couldn't have been immersed in spirit for more than a week. He told a journalist from *The Sunday Times*:

> *So far as I can form an opinion, I do not see any substantial reason why this portion of kidney should not be the one taken from the murdered woman. I cannot say that it is the left kidney. It must have been cut previously to its being immersed in the spirit which exercised a hardening process. It certainly had not been in spirit for more than a week. As has been stated, there is no portion of the renal artery adhering to it, it having been trimmed up, so, consequently, there could be no correspondence established between the portion of the body from which it was cut. As it exhibits no trace of decomposition, when we consider the length of time that has elapsed since the commission of the murder, we come to the conclusion that the probability is slight of it being a portion of the murdered woman of Mitre Square.*

The jury then, is still out on the authenticity of the kidney portion, although Brown himself did state in his inquest deposition that the intact right kidney of Catharine

Eddowes was pale, bloodless with slight congestion of the base of the pyramids, and these are indeed the symptoms of Bright's Disease – the very same disease that Dr Openshaw allegedly observed when he analysed the Lusk kidney portion. It's a problem that will probably never be solved now, and it's a pity the piece of kidney Lusk received was not preserved, along with the right kidney of Eddowes, for today, forensic experts would have had no trouble determining whether they were from the same body.

We still have the Lusk Letter, of course, so perhaps by analysing its grammar, graphology and phraseology we can learn a little about its author. Graphology – the study of handwriting as an indicator of the writer's mental disposition or health – is still regarded by some as a pseudoscience, and some confuse graphologists with document examiners. The document examiner is more scientific in his or her analysis, whereas the interpretations of the graphologist tend to vary from one 'expert' to the other. In June 1975, Thomas J Mann, a charter member of WADE – the World Association of Document Examiners, published his analysis of the Lusk Letter. Mann deduced that the letter written 87 years previously had been penned by a semi-literate author. I disagree, and believe that the person who wrote the Lusk Letter was an educated man writing in disguised handwriting. Let us look at the letter again:

From hell

Mishter Lusk

Sor
I send you half the Kidne I took from one women
prasarved it for you tother piece I fried and ate it was

very nise I may send you the bloody knif that
took it out if you only wate a whil longer
Signed Catch me when you can

Mishter Lusk

The writer has put a heading – 'From hell' – as if he is used to doing that when he corresponds in his normal handwriting, and he has correctly spelt the phonetic Irish pronunciation for 'Mister' – 'Mishter'; if he was semi-literate, 'Mr' would have sufficed. He indents 'Sor' correctly and begins his missive with 'I send you'. Such three words are to be found in many letters of that period. For example, if we look at the correspondence of Lord Kelvin, the mathematical physicist and engineer, we will see he begins several of his letters with 'I send you'. The writer of the Lusk Letter is not very good at disguising his intelligence, and perhaps thinks that by omitting a handful of letters from the words, he will have covered his usual traits, but it's glaringly obvious that this man knows about the silent h in 'while' and the silent k in 'knife' and so on. He spells 'signed' easily enough but expects us to believe he can't spell a small word such as 'nice'. The writer has laboured slowly with his nib in some parts – the hallmark of a person taking their time to disguise their handwriting.

Who was the author of the letter, and why did he target Lusk? Lusk considered throwing the kidney away, initially dismissing it as belonging to an animal, and if he had thrown it away, then nothing more would have been heard about either it or the letter From Hell. Whoever sent the package and letter would have been better sending the kidney portion and the note to the Central News Agency. That's what the writer of the Dear Boss letter did, and he was given worldwide publicity. Perhaps, though, the sender of the package and letter didn't care for newspaper publicity at all; perhaps he specifically wanted to scare Lusk.

What possible reason would he have for wanting to frighten Lusk of all people, when he could have scared the metropolis via the newspapers? Well, Lusk was a man with heavy Socialist leanings, and his popularity was growing daily. He was recruiting what amounted to his own private army, and although Joseph Aarons, the treasurer of Lusk's vigilance organisation, told the newspapers that the Whitechapel Vigilance Committee was in no way antagonistic towards the police, Sir Charles Warren the Chief Commissioner of the Metropolitan Police, knew only too well what the mob was capable of, even if they claimed their intentions were honourable. He only had to recall the 'Bloody Sunday' riots of the year before. Lusk was an ambitious self-publicising profiteer, with heavy Socialist leanings, and many in the upper echelons of society would have noted his controversial mention of the Phoenix Park murders in his letter to *The Times* bemoaning a lack of reward for the capture of Jack the Ripper. Was he trying to say that the Government cared more about bringing Fenians to justice than catching a monster who was ripping unfortunate women apart on the streets of the East End? Perhaps Lusk had inadvertently made a comment that was too close to the bone about someone in high authority, or perhaps Lusk was a perceptive man who had realised that Jack the Ripper was in fact someone working for Salisbury's Government. This would mean that the Irish man in black who visited Emily Marsh, asking for Lusk's address, and the kidney delivered to his home were a warning from someone in Whitehall who had been monitoring Lusk's ambitious programme to create a 'people power' movement in the slums of Whitechapel. Salisbury expected an uprising among the working classes any day, and if anyone was capable of motivating a revolt, it was Lusk. Given his growing popularity among the forgotten people of Whitechapel and Spitalfields he could certainly have caused an uprising of some three million destitute and desperate people in the slums of the East End.

When we look at Lusk in this light, we start to see some sense in the mysterious Irish visitor inquiring after his home address, and the letter couched in a style of handwriting that seemed to be the work of an Irishman. Lusk would have realised that Lord Salisbury's cabal was on to him, and perhaps that's why he agonised over what to do for 48 hours before he finally took the kidney to the police. Had the kidney arrived minus the 'From Hell' letter, Lusk might have dismissed it as some ghoulish prank, but after reading the mock-Irish message he would have known he was being watched. The title of the letter, 'From Hell' is a curious choice of words, because those two words appeared in *The Times* on the day before the murder of Annie Chapman – 7 September 1888 – in an advertisement which read:

LETTERS from HELL. 14th Thousand. From the Danish. With an Introduction by Dr GEORGE MACDONALD. In one vol., crown 8vo., 6s. "Should be read by every thinking mind." – Morning Advertiser.

This advertisement was for a book translated by the popular author Dr George MacDonald, from the Danish. The book, *Letters from Hell*, first appeared in Denmark in 1868, and is about a man named Philip, who dies and tours Hell, describing his new abode in a first-person narrative, and telling the reader what sins he has committed while on earth.

155

It's a very bleak and shocking tome, and it would seem that MacDonald, a man with an amazing imagination who wrote such children's classics as *At the Back of the North Wind*, actually fabricated portions of the book, but claimed he'd merely translated the work from the original manuscript by a Danish priest named Valdemar Adolph Thisted.

So, here we have a book with the words 'From Hell' in its title, advertised in a newspaper that covered the Whitechapel Murders and also featured Lusk's letters. There is another connection between Dr George MacDonald and the Whitechapel Murders case. MacDonald was a close friend of Charles Edward Troup, who hailed from the same village as himself – Huntley in Aberdeen. In 1897, Troup married Dr MacDonald's youngest daughter, Winifred Louise after the many years of courtship. In 1888, Troup was the permanent under-secretary at the Home Office, and worked closely with senior police and other Home Office officials engaged in the investigation of the Whitechapel Murders. He had an in-depth knowledge of Sir Robert Anderson's secret service work and was also involved in Fenian surveillance work himself, often compiling files on the work of the Special Irish Branch and James Monro. Troup was also one of the few people who knew about the Jubilee Plot – the Salisbury Government's black operation in which the Fenians were framed for the attempted murder of Queen Victoria during her Golden Jubilee of 1887. Secret documents released in 2001 revealed a controversial memo from Troup to the British Prime Minister Herbert Asquith, in which he strongly advises the PM not to publish the truth about the killing of innocent people during the Easter Rising rebellion in Ireland in 1916. Troup writes:

I am strongly of the opinion that it would be undesirable to publish the evidence taken by the Courts of Public Inquiry. There are many points that could be used for the purpose of propaganda. Nothing but harm could come of any public inquiry that would draw further attention to the matter.

Troup was talking about the cover-up of atrocities committed by 5,000 British soldiers equipped with armoured cars and artillery who had been ordered to launch a savage attack on a mere 200 civilian rebels. Soldiers of the South Staffordshire Regiment bayoneted and shot innocent civilians during the battle with the rebels, and MPs later put pressure on the Prime Minister to hold a public inquiry into the indiscriminate slayings. But there was a cover-up, so most people never got to hear about Thomas Hickey and his 16-year-old son Christopher being dragged from their home by British troops and shot in a neighbouring house – even though father and son had had no involvement in the battle with the soldiers. These were just two of the many murders committed by the British soldiers during the Easter Rising of 1916.

After Lusk receives the kidney portion and the warning letter, he keeps a lower profile than before, and eventually vanishes into obscurity. By 1891 he is bankrupt, and by 1900 he is placing desperate-looking adverts in a local newspaper that read:

GEORGE LUSK
Builder & Decorator
Bricklayer, Plasterer, Carpenter, Plumber, Painter, Gasfitter
And Contractor for General Repairs
ROOFS AND DRAINS PROMPTLY ATTENDED TO

SANITARY WORK A SPECIALITY
*

THE CHEAPEST HOUSE IN THE TRADE.
HOUSE, ESTATE AND GENERAL INSURANCE
AGENT
RENTS COLLECTED AND ESTATES MANAGED
Please note the address:
ALDERNEY ROAD, GLOBE ROAD
MILE END EAST

We have seen how an Irish thread runs through the Whitechapel Murders, and later in this book we will see how this thread leads us to the killing of Jack the Ripper's final victim, an Irish girl named Marie Jeanette Kelly.

7

THE UNKNOWN VICTIM

At around 1.34am on the morning of the Eddowes murder, three Jewish men left the Imperial Club at 16-17 Duke Street – literally a stone's throw from Mitre Square – and headed in the direction of Aldgate. The three men were commercial traveller Joseph Lawende, butcher Joseph Hyam Levy and furniture dealer Harry Harris. At the inquest into the death of Catharine Eddowes, 41-year-old Lawende was sworn in and gave his address as 79 Fenchurch Street, Aldgate. The Aldgate High Street, you may recall, was the place where a highly intoxicated Catharine Eddowes mysteriously appeared out of nowhere after vanishing off the face of the earth for six-and-a-half hours.

It appears, however, that the address the witness Lawende gave was not his home, but a business address, which seems rather peculiar, for he lived in Norfolk Road, Dalston, in the borough of Hackney, with his wife and eight children. That morning then, it would appear that Lawende was not going home to his family, but to his business premises. His companion, 47-year-old Joseph Hyam Levy, gave his address as 1 Hutchison Street, which is also in Aldgate. Harry Harris, of Castle Street, Whitechapel, walked a little way behind Lawende and Levy when they left the Imperial Club shortly after 1.30am on that rainy morning when Eddowes was killed. The three men turned left when they left the club and walked down Duke Street,

159

passing the covered entry to Church Passage, which led directly to Mitre Square. This entry was just fifteen feet from the Imperial Club. Lawende, Levy and Harris said they noticed a man and a woman standing at the mouth of Church Passage. Here is what Lawende said at the inquest about this short sighting of what might have been Eddowes and her killer:

> *On the night of the 29th [September] I was at the Imperial Club. Mr Joseph Levy and Mr Harry Harris were with me. It was raining. We left there to go out at half-past-one, and we left the house about five minutes later. I walked a little further than the others. Standing in the corner of Church Passage in Duke Street, which leads into Mitre Square, I saw a woman. She was standing with her face towards a man. I only saw her back. She had her hand on his chest. The man was taller than she was. She had a black jacket and a black bonnet. I have seen the articles which it was stated belonged to her at the police station. My belief is that they were the same clothes which I had seen upon the Deceased. She appeared to me to be short. The man had a cloth cap on with a cloth peak. I have given a description of the man to the police. I doubt whether I should know him again.*

Unlike other witnesses in the sensational Whitechapel Murders case, the three Jewish tradesmen did not go to the police or the newspapers; instead the police became intrigued by the testimony of the men when they questioned them about their whereabouts during the house-to-house inquiries launched in the aftermath of the Mitre Square killing. One cannot help suspecting that Lawende, Levy and Harris knew more about the Eddowes murder than they would admit. A journalist writing for the *Evening News* on 9 October 1888 suspected as much, reporting that the police believed that the three Jews had seen the Ripper and Eddowes together, yet only Harry Harris was willing to talk to the Press. Joseph Hyam Levy, on the other hand, "is absolutely obstinate and refuses to give the slightest information. He leaves one to infer that he knows something, but he is afraid to be called on the inquest. Hence he assumes a knowing air."

When Joseph Hyam Levy saw the couple at the entrance to Church Passage that morning, he had supposedly remarked to Harris: "Look there, I don't like going home by myself when I see those characters about."

This remark does not ring true, and seems like invented fictitious dialogue. Levy seems to be overreacting to a couple who are not causing a disturbance, but quietly standing together in the street, and he later said he was unable to describe the couple, so he doesn't seem to have been too troubled by them. Even if he supposed that the man was with a prostitute, it was a very common sight on the streets of the East End, so why did he express fear by his curious remark?

Before the murder, Levy had remarked to Lawende that Mitre Square ought to be watched, because it was such a dark and secluded place, so he had probably walked through it during the day, and perhaps in the evenings. Was the couple that Levy and his two friends passed at Church Passage Jack the Ripper and Kate Eddowes? Well, according to Lawende, it was 1.35am when he, Levy and Harris passed the couple. Lawende not only checked the clock at the Imperial Club as he left, he also owned a watch. At 1.44am, just eight minutes after the three Jews had walked on to the Aldgate High Street, the extensively mutilated body of Eddowes was discovered by PC Edward Watkins. When we allow the couple a minute or two to move away down Church Passage into Mitre Square, this window of time becomes even shorter. Now, if we take the deposition of PC James Harvey into consideration, we shall see that something here is seriously amiss.

PC Harvey says he looked in on Mitre Square whilst on his beat between 1.41 and 1.42am, as timed by the post office clock, and stood at the end of Church Passage – yet he saw nobody and nothing suspicious at that time. We have to make allowances for the Ripper's escape, presumably into Mitre Street or the passageway into St James's Place, or he would have run straight into the arms of PC Harvey. This escape could be afforded within 30 seconds perhaps, which further shaves down the time Jack the Ripper had to inveigle Eddowes into the darkest corner of Mitre Square, strangle her and/or paralyse her by applying pressure to nerve-points in her neck and clavicle, cut her throat, search her pockets, write on her face, slice off her nose, rip her abdomen open, arrange her intestines, extract her kidney and womb, and cut off a piece of her apron. Jack had about two minutes to do what he did to Catharine Eddowes. Dr George William Sequeira believed the killer could have carried out his grisly work in three minutes, but the more experienced and senior City Police Surgeon Dr Frederick Gordon Brown said the Ripper would have needed at least five minutes, and, what's more, the kidney of the victim had been carefully extracted – a procedure that requires an inordinate amount of time – especially so if the surgeon finds himself working in the type of darkness found in that corner of Mitre Square.

The idea of the Ripper working at speed to entice, kill and mutilate Eddowes within two minutes has been deemed a knotty problem by most researchers and authors who have concerned themselves with the Whitechapel Murders. The clock rules all, and unless Jack could stop it, it stands to reason that he must have been almost superhumanly swift in Mitre Square – but what if the three Jews were lying?

The other victim that night was Elizabeth Stride, a woman who spoke fluent Yiddish, and like Eddowes, worked for the Jews regularly. Stride had asked Charles Preston, a resident at a Flower and Dean Street lodging house, if he had a clothes brush. Preston noticed that Stride was dressed up to go out, and at the time of her death she had acquired a rose in her lapel. She never told Preston where she was going, nor did she tell him when she would return. She had not paid for a bed for that night, although some lodgers didn't always book a bed that far in advance. It was as if Stride was going to meet someone; someone who didn't know her by sight, because she had a red rose in her lapel as an identifying mark. She was, perhaps, slain before she could keep the rendezvous, by the Ripper, but if he hadn't killed her, who was she going to see and how would she get there? Stride was found dead in the yard of a largely Jewish Socialist Club by Louis Diemschutz, the steward of the club. Diemschutz remarked that he didn't know Stride, and also that she was much better dressed than the previous victim, Annie Chapman. The question I posed in an earlier chapter was: how did Diemschutz know how Annie Chapman had been dressed in order to be able to make a comparison with Stride's attire? Chapman had been wearing three cheap brass rings shortly before her death, and the Ripper had wrenched them from her finger after killing her. It is my belief that Diemschutz gave Chapman those rings because she acted as a courier for the immigrant Anarchist

163

Jews who used the International Workingmen's Educational Club as their base. As I revealed in the chapter on Annie Chapman, she had been carrying an envelope that bore the crest of the Sussex Regiment, and although one lodger, a man named William Stevens came forward and claimed Annie had found the envelope on the floor of the lodging house's kitchen, not one person could be traced who had written that letter. Annie was undoubtedly a courier, and before she could deliver the envelope to someone, Jack the Ripper intercepted her and killed her.

Was Catharine Eddowes making her way to some prearranged meeting in Mitre Square when she was released from Bishopsgate Police Station at 1am that morning? Had this meeting involved the Jews from the Imperial Club? This possibility throws more light on the behaviour of Lawende, Levy and Harris. What if the couple at the entrance to Church Passage never existed in the first place? The Jews may have sent Eddowes into Mitre Square to meet someone who would either take a message from her or give a message to her. The Ripper then intercepted her as swiftly and silently as he did when he killed Stride. When Eddowes did not return to the Jews at the Imperial Club, one of them, or all three, either went down Church Passage and saw her dead in the corner, or assumed she had gone because it was too dark to see her body lying in the far corner. To deflect suspicion from themselves, Lawende, Levy and Harris would invent the mysterious man in the cloth cap standing with Eddowes at the entrance to Mitre Square. Eddowes would thus meet her death shortly after PC Watkins left the square. PC Harvey came down Church Passage at around 1.41am, but did not enter the square, and may not have seen the body of Eddowes lying on the ground in the dark far corner. Harvey would turn around and walk back up the passage to

Duke Street. This would give the Ripper around eight minutes to carry out his work. It is curious that the murderer then incriminated Jews in the Wentworth Model Dwellings by chalking a message in the doorway of one of their tenements, underlining his cryptic message with a portion of Eddowes' apron placed beneath it.

So, on the night of the Double Event, the first victim is found by a Jew, in the yard of a Jewish Socialist Club, and the second victim is within the vicinity of three Jews when she dies, and a piece of her clothing is left in the doorway of a tenement inhabited principally by trouble-making Socialist Jews, and the message scrawled in the doorway even makes a reference to 'Juwes'. As I pointed out in the chapter on Eddowes, the Jewish Anarchists and socialists were joining up with the Fenian dynamiters, and as a consequence they were under surveillance by officers of the newly-formed Special Irish Branch, as well as members of James Monro's Secret Department. Upon being appointed the Assistant Commissioner at Scotland Yard in 1884, James Monro took over from 'Spy-Master General' Edward Jenkinson, a dishonest and twisted shadowy man who had built up a vast network of secret illegal agents who spied on the Fenians and set up questionable plots to snare them which amounted to nothing short of entrapment. Harrow-educated Jenkinson, who was also private secretary to Earl Spencer, was running what would today be known as black operations out of Paris, Dublin, London, New York, and many other cities throughout the world, and his agents were answerable to no one but him. This network of illegal agents caused a rift between Jenkinson and the Metropolitan Police, and James Monro. Jenkinson was subsequently sacked for his illegal intelligence gathering and black operations against the Fenians in December 1886. Ironically, anti-Fenian Jenkinson had been converted to the idea of Home Rule for Ireland, and so he leaked sensitive information to Michael Davitt, the Irish Republican and Fenian mentioned in the chapter on Eddowes. Davitt, as you may recall, was a guest speaker at the International Workingman's Educational Club on Berner Street. In the yard of that club, Elizabeth Stride was found with her throat cut. In his memoirs, Inspector John Sweeney, of the Special Irish Branch, says of the period 1887 onwards, 'the Anarchists began to grow restless, they held frequent meetings, there was quite a small boom in the circulation of their revolutionary publications [such as the radical periodical *The Worker's Friend* which was printed in the yard belonging to the International Workingman's Educational Club on Berner Street, where Stride was murdered].'

Inspector Sweeney further reminisces about the Anarchists: 'One could never be sure of what those fellows would be up to at any moment, so that Scotland Yard had an anxious time keeping every movement of theirs under surveillance.'

Because the Anarchists, socialists and Fenians knew they were under such surveillance, they often used unremarkable-looking women from the lower classes to act as couriers to carry messages between the radical clubs and cells. In theory, women would be less likely to fall under the suspicious eyes of Whitehall's agents, and on a few occasions, the Fenians had asked women of the streets to go as far as planting bombs, as this report reveals, from the *Leeds Mercury* on 7 March 1885:

THE DYNAMITARDS ALLEGED ATTEMPT TO BLOW UP A POLICE STATION

*Shortly before ten o'clock on Thursday night, as the night
men were going on duty, a respectably dressed woman
entered the Commercial Road Police Station, London,
and made the following extraordinary statement to the
inspector on duty. She said that a few minutes previously
a man had stopped her in one of the main back streets
which run at the rear of the police station, and asked if
she would like to earn a good sum for doing a slight
service for him. He then showed her two sovereigns,
which he said he would give her on condition she placed
the parcel, which he was carrying in his hand at the time,
in the doorway of the police station. The man further
told her she could easily do it without fear of detection,
as, being a woman, no one would take any notice of her;
and that, as soon as she had deposited the parcel in the
place directed by him, she was to get away from the spot
as quickly as she could, or the consequences would be far
worse to her than she could imagine.*

*This statement somewhat alarmed her, and as she
suspected the man, who had the appearance and brogue
of an Irishman, and who was wearing a slouched hat, of
some evil intent, she refused to undertake the task offered
her, or to have anything to do with it. The man then
said, "Oh, if you don't want to earn two sovereigns
easily, I can soon get someone who will be glad to do it."
With that, the man then walked quickly away, holding
the parcel, which appeared to be a tin box wrapped in
brown paper, carefully in one hand. At that moment, she
saw a policeman, who appeared to be on duty, and
immediately told him what had occurred, and also
pointed out the man, who was then fast disappearing in
the distance. The constable, for some unexplained reason,
refused to credit her statement or to follow the man, and*

only laughed at her. As she was determined that the
proper authorities should know of the strange occurrence,
she came to the police station to tell what had occurred.
The woman's name and address were then taken, and
after being questioned, the police were satisfied her
statement was correct. A number of plain-clothed
constables were immediately told off to watch the precincts
and all approaches to the police station and barracks,
which cover a large area of ground. A number of
constables were also sent to try and find the man in
question, but of course by that time he had managed to get
clear away. The woman, who was a stranger to the
locality, was unable to point out the exact spot where the
man stopped her, and the statement was credited, as it was
afterwards ascertained she had to inquire her way to the
police station, and was naturally, as can be imagined, in
a condition of great excitement and nervousness.
It is also stated that Inspector Abberline, of the Criminal
Investigation Department, who has been largely
instrumental in bringing the now almost complete and
detailed evidence against Burton and Cunningham [the
Fenian bombers of Mitre Square], has received letters,
on more than one occasion of late, threatening him with
death for the part he has taken in bringing the two men
referred to justice. The letters have been signed on behalf
of a society of men who have pledged themselves to
avenge the arrest of the two men in question.

In the chapter on the Lusk kidney, I related how Weiss
surgical knives and other weapons were smuggled into
Ireland by female couriers for the assassination of Lord
Frederick Cavendish and his Under-Secretary Thomas
Burke in Phoenix Park, Dublin. The couriers were working-

class women, employed by the Invincibles, an extremist splinter group of the Irish Republican Brotherhood. I propose, from the information we have on the Whitechapel Murders, that, because of the concentration of surveillance (by Whitehall agents) going on in the East End, the Fenians, Socialists and Anarchists were forced to use women to carry their messages, but Jack the Ripper, whom I believe to have been an exceptional British Intelligence agent, resorted to killing these female messengers, not solely to prevent them from passing on messages, but to also create an unprecedented atmosphere of terror. There was a stark statement in those mutilated bodies which told the radicals attempting to incite a British Revolution that the Establishment meant business, even if it meant slaughtering traitorous women on the streets of London. In the eyes of the people behind the Whitechapel Murders, the victims of Jack the Ripper were immoral traitors to their country anyway, and punishment for treason had always been death in English Law. Under the Crime and Disorder Act of 1998, the penalty for treason was changed from death by hanging to life imprisonment.

The last person to be hanged for treason in Britain was William Joyce, the fascist politician and Nazi propaganda broadcaster nicknamed 'Lord Haw Haw' who attempted to scare the people of Britain into submission with his menacing radio speeches transmitted from stations at Berlin, Hamburg and Luxembourg. Joyce was hanged on 3 January 1946 at Wandsworth Prison. As Joyce had been born in the United States, many believed he could not be tried for treason against a country that was not his own, but on a technicality argued by Sir Hartley Shawcross, the Attorney-General of England and Wales, Joyce was convicted and sentenced to hang. Anne Boleyn, Catherine

169

Howard, Guy Fawkes and Sir Walter Raleigh were all executed for treason, and even in recent years the most serious crime in British Law has resurfaced on a few occasions, including the alleged treason committed by Princess Diana when she admitted to having an adulterous affair with Major James Hewitt in the 1980s. The editor of a tabloid newspaper at the time asked Scotland Yard detectives whether there were any plans to investigate Mr Hewitt under the 1351 Act of Treason for committing adultery with the wife of a future monarch. No action was taken by Scotland Yard.

In the 1880s, any such threats to the Monarchy would have been taken much more seriously, and any attempts to overthrow the Government, or to offer services to a hostile or foreign power, would constitute High Treason, an offence punishable by death, and before 1814, the death penalty was not at all swift. The traitor was dragged by a horse to the place of execution, where a noose was placed around his neck. However, there was no sudden neck-breaking drop, as with the gallows; instead the traitor was hanged until he was at the point of choking. Then he would be cut down. He was stripped of his clothes and his genitals were sliced off. Then the executioner would slit open the conspirator's abdomen and pull out the intestines. They would then be hurled on to a fire and burnt before the traitor's eyes if he was still conscious. The heart was removed and burnt, as well as the kidneys. Sometimes the internal organs would be gibbeted and left on display to the public as a warning.

In 1814 it was deemed that the traitor should be 'humanely hanged' first, but disembowelment would still take place after death. This was finally abolished as late as 1870. In four out of the five canonical Ripper murders, the abdomen was opened and the intestines were drawn out, and the doctors who surveyed the aftermath of the killer's work noted the eerie ritualistic element of the crimes. When Annie Chapman's body was discovered in the backyard of 29 Hanbury Street, her intestines had been placed over her right shoulder, and the disembowelled corpse was so extensively mutilated, the first three men to come upon it were too afraid to even venture into the yard. One of them was so shaken he ran off and gulped down brandy. In this respect, the Ripper arranged the bodies of his victims to cause maximum terror, and he was in essence, a terrorist. If men had been butchered by his hand, that would have been shocking enough, but these mutilated victims were members of the 'fairer sex' – and that trebled the shock value of the crimes. Jack the Ripper could have easily slit the throats of these women and left it at that, but instead he carried out a ritual of disembowelment and organ removal, just as the executioner did to traitors in bygone days. If this was the reason behind the murderer's acts of mutilation and disembowelment, then it suggests he was an educated man who knew his history.

In the month that followed the killing of Stride and Eddowes, October, the public and the police waited for the Ripper to strike again, and to make matters worse, a thick fog pervaded London to heighten the already nerve-wracking tension that was building up among the population of the metropolis. Businesses in the East End suffered, as people shunned Whitechapel and Spitalfields because of the sinister murders. Fewer prostitutes walked the streets of the East End, and people took to arming themselves against the mysterious phantom-like killer. Into this cauldron of fear and mounting panic, another element was added: scare letters, sent to the newspapers by hoaxers who signed their communications as 'Jack the Ripper'.

On Tuesday 2 October, a woman's body was found in a cellar of the foundations of the New Scotland Yard buildings being erected on the Victoria Embankment. The corpse was headless and limbless, and this torso, wrapped in broché satin cloth of Bradford manufacture, with pages from the Echo and Chronicle newspapers attached, was discovered by workmen. How the killer left the torso there was a baffling mystery, as there was a hoarding around the building site, and the unlit interior of the cellars was described by one workman as "dark as the darkest night". Whoever deposited the torso must have been fit enough to scale the 8-foot tall hoarding around the building site without being seen by anyone, whilst, of course, carrying the parcelled-up remains. The same person must have had inside knowledge of the cellars, and he also possessed enough anatomical know-how to enable him to expertly cut up a body, for he had severed the head and limbs perfectly with an exceedingly sharp knife.

Dr Thomas Bond, the Police Surgeon to A Division (Westminster), the very same surgeon who would later examine the body of the Ripper's final victim, Marie Jeanette Kelly, examined the torso, and when a leg and foot were also found, by a dog named Smoker, under the debris of the cellar where the trunk was discovered, along with an arm that had been recovered from the Thames the month before (11 September), Bond attempted to put together the grotesque jigsaw of the unknown female murder victim. At the inquest into the Whitehall Torso, Bond stated:

The trunk was that of a woman of considerable stature and well nourished. The head had been separated from the trunk by means of a saw. The lower limbs and the pelvis had been removed in the same way. The length of

172

the trunk was 17 inches, and the circumference of the chest 35 inches and the waist 28 inches. The parts were decomposed, and we could not discover any wounds. The breasts were large and prominent. The arms had been removed at the shoulder joints by several incisions, the cuts having apparently been made obliquely from above downwards, and then around the arm. Over the body were clearly-defined marks, where string had been tied. It appeared to have been wrapped up in a very skilful manner. We did not find marks indicating that the woman had borne any children. On opening the chest we found that the rib cartilages were not ossified, that one lung was healthy, but that the left lung showed signs of severe pleurisy. The substance of the heart was healthy, and there were indications that the woman had not died either of suffocation or of drowning. The liver and stomach, kidneys and spleen were normal. The uterus was absent. There were indications that the woman was of mature age – twenty-four or twenty-five years. She would have been large and well nourished, with fair skin and dark hair. The date of death would have been from six weeks to two months, and the decomposition occurred in the air, not the water. I subsequently examined the arm brought to the mortuary. It was the arm of a woman, and accurately fitted to the trunk; and the general contour of the arm corresponded to that of the body. The fingers were long and tapered, and the nails well shaped; and the hand was quite that of a person not used to manual labour.

The pleurisy that bond had mentioned at the inquest was not recent; the victim had suffered from the condition in the past.

The coroner, John Troutbeck, posed several questions

relating to the way the unidentified female had died and he also tried to discover what social class she had belonged to:

> *Coroner: Was there anything to indicate the cause of death?*
> *Dr Bond: Nothing whatever.*
> *Coroner: Could you tell whether death was sudden or lingering?*
> *Dr Bond: All I can say is that death was not by suffocation or drowning. Most likely it was from haemorrhage or fainting.*
> *Coroner: Can you give any indication of the probable height of the woman?*
> *Dr Bond: From our measurements we believed the height to have been 5ft 8in. That opinion depends more upon the measurements of the arm than those of the trunk itself.*
> *Coroner: Was the woman stout?*
> *Dr Bond: Not very stout, but thoroughly plump; fully developed, but not abnormally fat. The inference is that she was a tall, big woman. The hand was long, and was the hand of a woman not accustomed to manual labour.*
> *Coroner: Did the hand show any sign of refinement?*
> *Dr Bond: I do not know that a hand of that kind is always associated with any refinement of mind or body, but certainly it was a refined hand.*

So, we have gathered that the unknown victim had been around 24 to 25 years of age, about 5 feet 8 inches in height, and plump. She had not been accustomed to manual labour. It was also revealed that she had been dark-haired and fair-skinned. The victim seems to have been a lady of the middle, or possibly the upper classes, yet no one seems to have missed her, for no one came forward to report the disappearance of a fair-skinned dark-haired refined lady in her mid-twenties.

One of the newspaper pages attached to the torso was from an edition of the *London Echo*, dated 24 August 1888, implying that the murder and dismemberment might have taken place on or after that date. If so, it would put the killing close to the date when Mary Ann Nichols, the first of the accepted five canonical Jack the Ripper victims, was murdered. Marie Jeanette Kelly, the woman who would be the Ripper's final victim, was, like the Whitehall Torso woman, fair-skinned and dark-haired, and although never described as plump, most who knew Marie Jeanette said she was a bit stout. Like the Torso victim, not one relative comes forward when Marie Jeanette Kelly is slain.

Some believed that the Whitehall Torso victim had been murdered close to the Victoria Embankment. What person in his right mind would go to all the trouble of disposing of a torso (and leg) on the very site where New Scotland Yard was being built, when he could simply toss the trunk and other remains into the Thames? The arm belonging to the torso was thrown into the Thames, so why didn't the killer hurl the torso in as well? Why did the murderer make a hazardous climb over an 8-foot-tall hoarding, carrying the torso, and then make his way down to pitch-black cellars, where workmen would undoubtedly find the remains sooner or later? Was the murderer making a statement by placing the torso in the cellars of the future home of the Metropolitan Police?

Less than half a mile from the place where the torso was planted stood the offices of the Palestine Exploration Fund (PEF), in Adam Street. The PEF was a society founded in 1865 by a distinguished group of clergymen and academics to further research into the Holy Lands of the Bible. The PEF in the 1880s supposedly only concerned itself with the archaeology, topography, customs, culture, geology and natural science of the Levant, but this was not in fact so. Although the PEF had been established under the patronage of Queen Victoria, the War Office also used the society as a front to carry out covert surveillance in Palestine, which was then part of the Ottoman Empire. The Turkish government was trying to settle its unwanted Arab Christians East of the Jordan, and the Germans were making overtures to challenge British supremacy in Egypt by exploring plans to aid the Turks in building a railway. This railway – the Hejaz Railway – was later started in 1900 upon the orders of the Ottoman Sultan Abdul Hamid II, but became a success through German technical advice and support. The Hejaz Railway still exists in two sections. One line connects Amman in Jordan to Damascus in Syria, and the other line runs between phosphate mines near the city of Ma'an to the Gulf of Aqaba, east of the Sinai Peninsula.

In 1872 the Executive Committee of the PEF met a subcommittee of army men to discuss the names of various soldiers who could lead a survey party to map the Holy Land. Such a leader would not only be a supreme surveyor, he would require great courage, stamina and resilience in a climate of temperature extremes and bellicose tribesmen. A Captain Stewart of the Royal Engineers was a popular choice amongst the army men, and he was chosen to lead the expedition, but unfortunately, he succumbed to fever upon reaching Jaffa in Western Palestine, and became so ill he was forced to return to England.

A successor to Captain Stewart was needed urgently, and in desperation the PEF approached the War Office in search of the right man for the mission. The War Office supplied the

PEF with one of its toughest and most intelligent men – Claude Reignier Conder. Conder accepted the job as the principal surveyor for the Survey of Western Palestine, from 1872 to 1877, accompanied by his great friend Lieutenant (later Lord) Horatio Kitchener, along with a formidable team of NCOs and Royal Engineers.

The intelligence-gathering survey was a success. Maps were compiled in great detail – 3,000 square miles, mapped on a scale of six inches to the mile. Sir Charles Warren, who was then a captain in the Royal Engineers, became a great admirer of young Conder, who was then in his mid-twenties. As mentioned in a previous chapter, Conder went on to write the best-selling book *Jerusalem* with Warren, and the young explorer also wrote many other popular books alone, such as *Tent Work in Palestine*. In this book, Conder narrates the exploits of the grand survey, and along the way in this colourful record of adventure, danger and discovery, he fills us in on the ancient and legendary names of Biblical places and personages. He describes, for example, the blue hills of Moab, and among the 733 pages of his book he also happens to touch on 'the hosts of Midian'. Midian was a son of Abraham and Keturah.

Now, here is a curious thing. After the Whitehall Torso was found less than half a mile from the Adam Street offices of the PEF, a letter signed 'Jack the Ripper' was sent to the Central News Agency. It stated:

Dear Friend

In the name of God hear me I swear I did not kill the female whose body was found at Whitehall. If she was an honest woman I will hunt down and destroy her murderer. If she was a whore God will bless the hand

177

that slew her, for the women of of [sic] Moab and
Midian shall die and their blood shall mingle with the
dust. I never harm any others or the Divine power that
protects and helps me in my grand work would quit for
ever. Do as I do and the light of glory shall shine upon
you. I must get to work tomorrow treble event this time
yes yes [sic] three must be ripped. Will send you a bit of
face by post I promise this dear old Boss. The police now
reckon my work a practical joke well well [sic] Jacky's a
very practical joker ha ha keep this back till three are
wiped out and you can show the cold meat.

Yours truly
Jack the Ripper

This links Claude Reignier Conder once more with the
Ripper murders. You may recall how I revealed in the
chapter on Eddowes how Conder wrote extensively of the
Manchu language, as it belonged to the Altaic languages, of
which he was an eminent expert. After the Whitechapel
Murders, Conder had given a talk about the origin of the
Chinese peoples, presided over by his close friend
Sir Charles Warren, the man who had been the Metropolitan
Police Commissioner during the Ripper's Autumn of terror.
On the chalkboard at that talk, Conder had written the first
five numerals of the Manchu number system: 1.Emu 2.
Juwe 3. Ilan 4. Duin 5. Sunja.

Conder discussed the Manchu numeral juwe, and told
his audience that such English words such as dual, duo,
duplicate, duel, and duet – as well as the French for two –
deux – were connected with the Manchu language.
Sir Charles Warren looked on with interest, and few people
present would have recalled how he had washed away the

cryptic clue that Jack the Ripper had chalked on the wall on the night of the double murder:

The Juwes are
The men that
Will not
be Blamed
for nothing

Claude Reignier Conder wrote a popular book called *Heth and Moab*, about his explorations in Syria in 1881 and 1882. He had also written about Midian, and in his books he had also documented the story of the 'women of Moab and Midian' mentioned in the Jack the Ripper letter which was sent to the Central News Agency after the Whitehall Torso discovery. Without a doubt, there are some deranged killers who believe they are doing the work of God, but the writer of the 'Moab and Midian' letter seems to have in-depth knowledge of the Old Testament. Conder had written about women of Moab, and how the Moabites regarded prostitution as an act of worship to their god Baal. Conder wrote about the Israelites having sex with the Moabite women, and Moses ordering the Moabite chiefs to be 'hanged in the sun', as well as having the sex-crazed Hebrew men killed for their lustful behaviour.

If the author of the Moab and Midian letter is making a genuine claim, then he did not kill the Whitehall Torso victim, yet the wording seems to indicate that the writer has a changeable personality, for the first half of the letter is religious and the second half is deliberately sensational. I believe that the writer did indeed kill the Whitehall Torso victim, and that his sole motive for writing the letter was an attempt to throw the police off his trail, which led from the

179

East End to the Victoria Embankment, in the West End. I also believe that the murder victim – described as being 'refined' when she was alive – was perhaps a female Fenian or Anarchist spy, who had either tracked the Ripper down to his base in Westminster, or had been lured to this residence by him before being killed and dismembered. Her head was never found, and so no identification of the body took place. All of the Ripper's victims were identified, but only in the case of the last one, Marie Jeanette Kelly, did no relatives come forward, despite her death being one of the most publicised events across the world in the late nineteenth century. I believe that was because Kelly was a Fenian spy, and her relatives and comrades did not dare to show up at her funeral because the Special Irish Branch and other secret Government agents were keeping watch, and they would have promptly been arrested.

So, then, if we accept that the Whitehall Torso murderer, with his references to Moab and Midian, is Jack the Ripper, it puts paid to the hoary old notion of the killer being a local of Whitechapel.

8

MARIE JEANETTE KELLY

Chief Inspector Walter Dew of Scotland Yard, who had been a young detective constable in H Division (Whitechapel) in 1888, remarked in his memoirs (published in 1938) that 'there was no woman in the whole of Whitechapel more frightened of Jack the Ripper than Marie Kelly.'

Marie Jeanette Kelly was to be the final known victim of the Ripper, but of all the victims she stands out starkly as an enigma. With the exception of the Whitehall Torso victim, I have described the biographical backgrounds of Mary Ann Nichols, Annie Chapman, Elizabeth Stride and Catharine Eddowes, but Marie Jeanette Kelly seems to be a woman without a past. All of the Ripper's victims before her were killed on the street, but Kelly was killed indoors. The first four victims were all in their forties, but Kelly was only 25. Kelly also bore the full savagery of Jack's knife, and he took amazing risks when he killed her and extensively mutilated her body in the victim's small rented room. After her murder, the series of mysterious killings stopped for good. What's more, in the final weeks of her life, Kelly had apparently been living in fear of the Whitechapel Murderer, even though October had come and gone without a Ripper murder being committed, and by then, most of the prostitutes of the East End had felt safe enough to resume plying their trade.

181

I believe Marie Jeanette was expecting her Nemesis because she had seen how Jack had systematically killed women who had been acting as messengers and couriers for the Anarchists and the Fenians, and she had undoubtedly suspected that she was under surveillance, not just by Special Irish Branch agents and the men of Dr (later Sir) Robert Anderson's Secret Department, but by Jack the Ripper himself, and in my opinion, Kelly had finally realised that the Whitechapel Murderer was a military intelligence man. At the inquest into her death, Kelly's last boyfriend, Irish Cockney Joe Barnett stated: 'She had on several occasions asked me to read about the murders [in the newspapers]; she seemed afraid of someone.' Of course, most people living in Whitechapel and Spitalfields during the Ripper's Reign of Terror were naturally afraid of the faceless killer, but there are hints that Marie Jeanette Kelly actually believed she knew who the murderer was. She certainly told Barnett and a few close friends that she feared for her safety and in her final days she made it clear that she wished to leave the East End.

The history of Marie Jeanette comes down to us primarily from her boyfriend Joe Barnett, a 30-year-old unemployed Billingsgate Market fish porter (and occasional fruit hawker). According to Barnett, he met Marie Jeanette in Commercial Street on Good Friday, 8 April 1887, and on the following day they met again and decided to become a cohabiting couple, living together from then on. According to Kelly, she was born (around 1863) in Limerick – although she never made it clear whether she meant Limerick Town or the County Limerick. Kelly said her family had moved to Wales when she was a young girl, and that her father John had subsequently secured the post of foreman at an ironworks in either Caernarvonshire or Carmathernshire.

182

Joe Barnett, lover of Marie Jeanette Kelly.

The young Marie Jeanette in those days was known by her birth name Mary Jane Kelly. She maintained that she had a sister, six or seven brothers, one of whom was Henry (nicknamed 'Johnto') in the Scots Guards, and Kelly also told a young neighbour named Lizzie Albrook that she had a relative on the London stage.

The records show that the 2nd Battalion of the Scots Guards were stationed at Chelsea until 6 September 1888, when they sailed to Dublin (from Woolwich) to relieve the Coldstream Guards. Joe Barnett, Marie Jeanette's boyfriend, made a curious comment regarding this regiment within his statement to detectives on 9 November 1888. He says Marie Jeanette told him she had a brother named Henry serving in the Second Battalion of the Scots Guards – and then Barnett adds: 'I believe that regiment is now in

Ireland.' This was perfectly true, as I mentioned previously, but how did Joe Barnett know the whereabouts of the Second Battalion of the Scots Guards? The regiment had only been in Dublin for a matter of weeks, and Barnett knew this. The average Londoner in those days (and these days for that matter) would not know where the Scots Guards was stationed – but Barnett knew. Were Barnett and other men of Irish blood (ie Fenians) observing the movements of British Regiments?

If we cast our minds back to the murder of Annie Chapman, we may recall how an envelope bearing the crest of the Sussex Regiment was found close to the head of the victim. When she met her death at the hands of the Ripper, Chapman had been in possession of the envelope, which, Inspector Joseph Chandler discovered, had been posted near to the army barracks at Farnborough on Thursday, 23 August 1888. The origins of the baffling envelope were never determined, but it had been sent from a place close to a military barracks to a location in Spitalfields, and the person who sent the letter never came forward to throw light on the matter.

Marie Jeanette Kelly also maintained that she had married a collier named Davies or Davis at the age of 16 (in 1879), but there is no record of such a marriage in Wales for that period. Kelly said her husband died in a mine explosion. There was a mine explosion at Abercarn, Newport on 11 September 1878, in which 265 people died. This was the worst colliery disaster in Gwent, and 16 of the dead were surnamed Davis or Davies, with ages ranging from 16 to 47, but the mine explosion took place before the accepted year of Kelly's marriage, which was 1879. Furthermore, Kelly told Barnett she had lived with her husband for two or three years before he was killed, which puts the colliery disaster in the 1880s. There was a Thomas Davies killed in a Welsh mine explosion at Penygraig, Tonypandy, in January 1884. In November of that year, there was also a John Davies killed in an explosion at the mine in Tredegar, Blaenau Gwent, but each of these disasters is a little too late to be the one Marie Jeanette is referring to, and by 1884, she was in London. Here is what Joseph Barnett had to say about the potted history of his murdered girlfriend at the inquest into her death:

I reside at 24 and 25 New Street, Bishopsgate, which is a common lodging house. I am a labourer and have been a fish porter. I now live at my sisters at 21 Portpool Lane, Gray's Inn Road. I have lived with the deceased one year and eight months, her name was Marie Jeanette Kelly. Kelly was her maiden name and the name she always went by. I have seen the body. I identify her by the ears and eyes. I am positive that it is the same woman. I have lived with her at 13 room, Miller's Court, eight months or longer. I separated from her on the 30th of October. I left her because she had a person who was a prostitute whom she took in and I objected to her doing so, that was the only reason, not because I was out of work. I left her on the 30th October between 5 and 6pm. I last saw her alive between 7.30 and 7.45pm, the night of Thursday, before she was found [on Friday morning]. I was with her about one hour, we were on friendly terms. I told her when I left her I had no work and had nothing to give her, of which I was very sorry; we did not drink together, she was quite sober…
There was a female with us on Thursday evening when we were together; she left first and I left shortly afterwards. The deceased often told me … she was born

in Limerick – that she was 25 years of age – and from Limerick she went to Wales when very young. She told me she came to London about four years ago. Her father's name was John Kelly; he was a Gauger at some iron works in Caernarvonshire. She told me she had one sister who was a traveller with materials from market place to market place. She also said she had six brothers at home and one in the army; one was Henry Kelly. I never spoke to any of them. She told me she had been married to a collier; she told me the name was Davis or Davies; I think it was Davies. She told me she was lawfully married to him until he died in an explosion. She said she lived with him two or three years up to his death. She told me she was married at the age of sixteen years. She came to London about four years ago, after her husband's death. She said she first went to Cardiff, and was in an infirmary there for eight or nine months, and followed a bad life with a cousin whilst in Cardiff. When she left Cardiff she said she came to London. In London she was first in a gay house in the West End. A gentleman there asked her to go to France … she told me she did not like the part; she did not stay there long; she lived there about a fortnight. She did not like it and returned. She came back and lived in the Ratcliff Highway for some time. She was then living near Stepney Gas Works. Morganstone was the man she lived with there. She did not tell me how long she lived there. She told me that in Pennington Street she lived at one time with a Morganstone, and with Joseph Fleming; she was very fond of him. He was a mason's plasterer. He lived in Bethnal Green Road. She told me all this, but I do not know which she lived with the last; Fleming used to visit her.

The story Kelly told Barnett about the West End brothel is apparently backed up by a Mrs Mary Carthy, a landlady who gave Kelly lodgings at Breezer's Hill, Pennington Street, in the notorious Ratcliff Highway district from 1885 to around 1887. Mrs Carthy claimed that Kelly had come to her from another landlady with the (Polish) surname Buki, and this landlady had accompanied Kelly to a French lady's residence in the Knightsbridge area to fetch a box and several expensive dresses belonging to Kelly. The house Buki and Kelly visited was a 'gay house' – the Victorian term for a brothel. The location of this brothel has never been discovered. In the 1880s there was a French brothel at Portman Square, Westminster, but that is hardly in Knightsbridge. It was around the time of the jaunt to France when Mary Jane began to call herself Marie Jeanette, a French affectation of her name, and the name that would ultimately end up inscribed on her coffin plate. Kelly eventually left Mrs Carthy's lodgings in late 1886 to live with a man who worked in the building trade. After Kelly was murdered, Mrs Carthy told the *Star* newspaper that the man Kelly had left her lodgings with had obviously loved her so much, she believed he would have married her. This was probably the Bethnal Green plasterer Joseph Fleming. It might have even been the 'Morganstone' Marie Jeanette mentioned to Barnett.

Mrs Carthy presents us with a further intriguing mystery. She told the newspapers that Kelly and an unknown man called at her lodging house a "short time" before Kelly's murder, at two o'clock in the morning. Kelly had asked for a bed for the night. Mrs Carthy had asked her if she was still with the affectionate man who had taken her from the lodging house, and Kelly had said she wasn't. Mrs

187

Carthy's former tenant was never seen in the area again after that late-night call. Who was this man with Kelly? Yet another mystery in the life of the most unfathomable victim of Jack the Ripper.

Piecing together the last known movement of Kelly from the testimony of witnesses who saw her in the final hours of her life is highly problematic. I will shortly attempt to document her whereabouts in a chronological order to determine just when she was killed by Jack the Ripper, but firstly let me describe the background to this most shocking of all the Whitechapel Murders.

In a police interview in the aftermath of the Marie Jeanette Kelly murder, Joseph Barnett told Frederick Abberline – the Metropolitan Police Inspector who was in charge of all the detectives on the ground in the Ripper investigation – that he had lost his job at Billingsgate Market around late August, or early September. Barnett does not explain why he suddenly lost his job, but it's improbable that he simply couldn't afford to renew his market porter licence. It had to be renewed on 1 July each year, and this would have cost him just a few shillings. Barnett had been a market porter for around ten years, and a worker of his skill and experience could have been earning as much as £3 per week. In 1888 this was a small fortune, so surely he'd be able to spare a couple of shillings towards the renewal of his licence when he was bringing home around 60 shillings per week? To this day, no researcher has ever discovered just why Joseph Barnett was sacked from his job.

Barnett lived with Marie Jeanette Kelly at 13 Miller's Court, a 12-foot square room that was in fact the partitioned-off space of a shed at the rear of a house owned by a landlord and shopkeeper named John McCarthy. The grimy-wallpapered room Barnett and Kelly lived in was

13 Millers Court, off Dorset Street.

sparsely furnished, containing a small wooden-framed bed, two tables, a chair, a washstand and pail, and a small worn and faded woollen rug. Located off Dorset Street, one of the most notoriously rough streets in the East End, access to Miller's Court was via an arched passageway that ran between numbers 26 and 27, just two of the many properties owned by Mr McCarthy in that area. A villain named Arthur Harding, who was born in 1886, grew up in the East End and knew Charlie Kray, the father of the organised crime leaders Ronnie and Reggie Kray. Harding also knew John McCarthy (whom he recalled as 'McCarty'), and in his colourful and eye-opening memoirs, *East End Underworld: Chapters in the Life of Arthur Harding*, there is a very interesting description of Barnett and Kelly's landlord:

John McCarthy, landlord of Marie Jeanette Kelly.

Dorset Street had an even worse reputation than Flowery Dean Street. That's where Jack the Ripper done some of his murders. We just used to call it 'the street'. There was such a large number of doss-houses there that they called it 'Dossers Street' and they abbreviated it again to just 'the street' which is what we called it. There were doss-houses on one side, furnished rooms on the other. McCarty [sic] owned all the furnished rooms down there. He was an Irishman, a bully, a tough guy. Marie Lloyd used to see him, because there was a pub round the corner she used to go to. All his daughters were in show business on account of Marie Lloyd. They had plenty of money. McCarty lived down there and Danny Macarthur, and a chap I had some trouble with, Billy Macguire.

Not much is known about John McCarthy's background, beyond him being Marie Jeanette Kelly's landlord. He was born in Dieppe, France (as a Foreign Subject), in 1851, had a Spitalfields-born wife, Elizabeth, whom he married in 1877 at the Protestant church of St Mary's at Spital Square, Spitalfields. They had four children by 1891, and after 37 years of marriage, Mrs McCarthy died of bronchitis in 1914. Curiously, there is a census record of a John McCarthy who was born in France circa 1850, with a French mother and an Irish father. In 1880 this McCarthy lived in Franklin Greene County, Pennsylvania – a state that was a hotbed of Fenianism that dated back to the famous 1870s Irish secret organisation, known as the 'Molly Maguires'. This is surely just an extraordinary coincidence, though, as it is commonly accepted that McCarthy's Irish parents, Daniel and Margaret, hailed from Cork. Six years before the Whitechapel Murders, in 1882, McCarthy seems to have been involved in an illegal fist fight, according to this intriguing article from *The Times*, dated 29 March:

AN ALLEGED PRIZE FIGHT

Yesterday, at the Bow-street Police-court, before Mr. Vaughan, a man named Henry Goodson, a carman, living in Brick-lane, Spitalfields, was charged with committing a breach of the peace, and being one of the principals in a prize fight at St. Andrew's-hall, Tavistock-place. Aaron Moss, aged 48, of Corbet's-court, Andrew-street, Spitalfields, fishmonger; William Scoll, aged 22, 17, Lisbon-street, Cambridge-heath-road, fishmonger; John Satchell, Brick-lane, Spitalfields, beerhouse keeper; John McCarthy, 27, Dorset-street, Spitalfields, shopkeeper;

191

Thomas Moss, 2, New-street, Union-street, Lambeth,
bricklayer; Joseph Lilly, 76, Moneyer-street, Hoxton,
general dealer; Thomas Davis, Luke-street, Mile-end, gas
stoker; George Lewis, Vanston-place, Coalham-green,
carpenter; and R. Smith, Flower and Dean-street,
Spitalfields, general dealer, were charged with aiding and
abetting and taking part in the fight. Smith was further
charged with assaulting the police; and George Stevens, of
John's-place, Whitechapel, a blacksmith, was also charged
with assaulting a police constable.
Mr. Superintendent Thomson, on behalf of the police,
stated that it was only proposed at present to offer
sufficient evidence to justify a remand.
The first witness called was the constable who charged
Stevens with assaulting him by striking him on the mouth
while he was endeavouring to disperse the crowd
assembled outside the hall. The defendant declared his
innocence, and was remanded, to give him an
opportunity of calling witnesses on his behalf.
Inspector Arscott, of the Hunter-street Police-station,
then deposed that at about 3 o'clock on Monday
afternoon he received an intimation that a prize fight
was about to take place at the hall, which was formerly
used by Archdeacon Dunbar as a church. Witness secured
the assistance of two plain-clothes officers – Sergeant
Rowan and Detective Scandrell, and proceeded to the
place in question. He encountered at the door a man who
gave the name of John George Elliott, of 14, Finsbury-
square, and stated that he had "hired the hall for a few
amateur gentlemen to have a sparring match." This man
was admitting persons through a turnstile. Witness and
his companion, passing through, saw a large number of
persons assembled in the hall. Two men entered a ring

192

formed in the centre of the hall by means of ropes and stakes. A carpet was lying on the ground. The two men who entered the ring first were not arrested with the others. They sparred in the ring for some little time, and then gave place to two other men. The latter, who were also stripped, sparred with boxing-gloves on. After they had finished, the prisoner Goodson and another man (not in custody) entered the ring. They fought with gloves of a lighter kind than those used by the other men. Goodson knocked down his antagonist, who was unable to get up again for a second or more. He, however, rose and fought again. He was again knocked down, Goodson still striking him as he fell across the rope.

Mr. Vaughan: What, while he was down?

Witness said that the man was struck while across the rope and also kicked by Goodson. The bystanders struck both men with sticks. Witness entered the ring and said, "This must not be allowed; stop the fight." Immediately there was a general rush for the door. The defendants, however, were secured, and all, with the exception of Lewis, were identified as having been present when the fight was proceeding. They encouraged Goodson with cries of, "Go for it, 'Sugar'!" – a name by which he was known. Moss was acting as his second, and in the ring there was a small basket containing ice, some spirits in a bottle, jars containing water, zinc pails, and several sponges. There were some slight traces of blood on Goodson's face.

In cross-examination by Mr. Armstrong, on behalf of Goodson, witness said he saw one pair of gloves on the hands of the parties, but the gloves produced were not those worn by Goodson. He had a thin pair which was not padded. Witness heard nothing about the

193

*Queensberry Rules. Goodson kicked the other man in a
most brutal way.*

*In cross-examination by Mr. Clark, on behalf of
McCarthy and Satchell, it was stated that there were
about two hundred persons in the room, and the witness
expressed his belief that all the persons present were
mixed up in the affair. He thought that the first couples
had sparred fairly, but that Goodson and his opponent
did not use fair gloves.*

*Detective-sergeant Rowan deposed to having
accompanied the last witness to the scene of the fight. He
saw McCarthy and Lewis standing first outside the
turnstile. He asked what was going on. He was told that
it was a sparring match, and that the admission was one
guinea. McCarthy asked whether he had a guinea, and
upon receiving a reply in the negative, he made use of an
oath and told him to get outside. After some difficulty, he
was admitted by Elliott. The ring was formed in the
body of the hall, towards the chancel. Many persons were
in the body of the hall, and in the place where the
Communion table once stood were a number of raised
seats. Witness walked to a room adjoining the chancel,
where he found Goodson, Moss, Scott, and other men.
On a table were sponges, towels, ice, bottles of spirits,
and some India-rubber shoes. After examining these
articles, witness returned to the chancel. By that time
Goodson and his opponent had entered the ring. Each
had two seconds. Bets were made by the spectators on the
raised seats, the sums ranging from £2 to £20. The
defendants could hear the bets made. Witness then
described the way in which the other man was knocked
down and treated by Goodson. He further stated that
both men kicked each other. They put down their hands*

*when the officers entered the ring and called upon them
to stop. McCarthy said, "Never mind the police, fight it
out." The mob made a rush to the door, and all of them,
with the exception of the prisoners, succeeded in getting
out. Witness described the gloves worn by Goodson as
being thinner than ordinary boxing gloves. He added
that a person who acted as referee read some rules before
the fight commenced and held up a cup, which he said
was to be fought for in addition to so much per side.
Witness did not hear what the amount was. One of the
rules was that when either of the combatants was down
the seconds should not assist him, under pain of
disqualification, and he was allowed ten seconds to rise.
In cross-examination, witness said he remembered only the
above rule. He did not hear one providing that if a man
were knocked on the ropes in a helpless state with his feet
off the ground he should be deemed down. The gloves worn
by Goodson and his opponent were taken away in the
rush. The cup to be fought for was left at a public house in
the Euston-road, and handed to the police.*
*Mr Vaughan here granted a remand, agreeing to accept
two sureties in £40 each for the appearance of the
defendants, notice of bail to be given to the police.*
*Mr. Thomas, on behalf of Lewis, submitted that this
client was quite innocent of taking any part in the
proceedings, as he had merely brought up the turnstile
from Walham-green for his employer, Mr. Starke, who
had received the order for it from Elliott by telegram
now produced.*
Mr. Vaughan declined to discharge Lewis at present.

From this article we can see how McCarthy was not only
involved in an illegal activity – the clandestine sport of

prohibited prize fighting, his audacious disregard for the law is also evident when he shouts to the boxers, as the venue was being stormed by policemen: "Never mind the police, fight it out." McCarthy is obviously a man who would resort to illicit means to make a quick buck. Some researchers into the life of Marie Jeanette's landlord have assumed McCarthy to be a Cockney, but he is known to have spoken with an Irish accent. In the January 1894 edition of *Harper's New Monthly Magazine*, McCarthy's quoted reply, when asked what he thinks about police inspectors calling at his lodging houses in the middle of the night, is: "It droives away trade".

The Irish landlord of Kelly has a history which suggests he is not averse to making money underhandedly, and I believe he was being paid by someone to look after Kelly, and I will explore that theory later, but first let me detail the last known movements of Kelly before she was murdered in Miller's Court, as well as the background to the time-line of her final days.

On Wednesday, 7 November 1888, Marie Jeanette Kelly entered John McCarthy's shop at 27 Dorset Street to buy a halfpenny candle. McCarthy would later tell the police on the day of Kelly's murder that her rent was 29 shillings in arrears, so why didn't he press her for this owed rent when she came into his shop to buy a candle? Even if these rent arrears were for consecutive non-payments, it is still a sizeable sum to owe a landlord in 1888. It was standard practice at that time for the landlords in Whitechapel to confront irregular payers early in the morning and demand a day's rent in advance from them.

There is also a mystery surrounding the reasons why Kelly rented the room at Miller's Court in her own name rather than the name of her boyfriend Joseph Barnett. He had lived with her for eight months at that address until leaving her on 30 October, supposedly after a quarrel because he had objected to Kelly allowing a German prostitute named Julia to live in her room. In those days, it was the usual practice for the bread-winning male to rent accommodation in his name, and such male chauvinism went unquestioned, yet Kelly had rented the room under her own name. Why? Why would a tough, streetwise, money-oriented man like John McCarthy even allow Kelly to stay in one of his rented rooms when she wasn't far off being two months in rent arrears?

Some have conjectured that Kelly was paying McCarthy off with sexual favours, but he was living with his wife and children just a few feet away from her door. Admittedly, Kelly and McCarthy could have met elsewhere if this was the case, but the astute people of the overcrowded East End would have noticed these meetings and rumours of the affair would have circulated. There is a possibility that Kelly and McCarthy were related in some way, perhaps as cousins or as niece and uncle. If that were the case, it would explain McCarthy's lenience towards her rent arrears.

It is interesting to note that, after Kelly's horrific murder, a showman offered John McCarthy £25 (about £3,000 today) for the use of Kelly's room for a month, but this offer was declined by McCarthy. Another showman offered to buy Kelly's blood-soaked bed, and the landlord turned down this offer as well. Why did McCarthy want to keep the bed Kelly had slept on? Today, Kelly and McCarthy rest in their graves close to one another at St Patrick's Roman Catholic Cemetery, Leytonstone. Furthermore, it is recorded that both Barnett and McCarthy wished Kelly to be interred at that church with the full ritual of the Catholic Church.

197

On the Thursday morning of 8 November 1888, Marie Jeanette Kelly was seen having breakfast in her room with a woman, according to Julia Venturney, a charwoman who lived at Number 1 Room Millers Court. Incidentally, Julia Venturney was not the German prostitute named Julia who had been lodging with Kelly. The identity of that prostitute, who was the cause of the split between Barnett and Kelly, has never been established. That same Thursday morning, Kelly told Elizabeth Prater, the woman who lived in the room almost above 13 Miller's Court, how she hoped the weather would be clement on Friday. "I hope it will be a fine day tomorrow, as I want to go to the Lord Mayor's Show," were her exact words, according to Mrs Prater. The previous year's Lord Mayor's Show had been a complete wash-out due to an unrelenting downpour of November rain which left the people on the procession floats soaked to the skin. The Lord Mayor's procession of 1888 was to be closely watched by policemen, plain-clothed detectives and the intelligence agents of Whitehall, as the city-wide event would be an excellent opportunity for Socialists, Fenians and Anarchists to create disturbances, with the regular police force already stretched to deal with the hundreds of thousands of Londoners lining the route of the pageant. On 5 November, Sir Charles Warren had publicised a warning to any radical troublemakers in *The Times* newspaper:

> *Sir Charles Warren has issued a notice prohibiting*
> *processions or speechmaking in or near any thoroughfare*
> *through which the Lord Mayor's procession will pass or*
> *in Trafalgar-square. This has been called for by a*
> *suggestion, on the part of persons who have before*
> *organised disturbances, that a red-flag procession shall*
> *pass through the route of the Lord Mayor's procession on*

November 9. Sir Charles Warren also states that the
order of November 18, 1887, shall not apply to the Lord
Mayor's procession, but otherwise remains in force in
respect to the prohibition of public processions through
the metropolis.

Warren was only too aware of a possible hijacking of the
Lord Mayor's Parade by Anarchists, Socialists and Fenians.
It had been reported in the press that 'Bloody Sunday' – the
name given to the Trafalgar Square demonstration against
coercion in Ireland which Warren had severely dealt with 12
months previously – would be commemorated on Tuesday
13 November with a torchlight assembly on Clerkenwell-
Green, where the radicals would demand the right to hold
meetings in Trafalgar Square and call for the dismissal of Sir
Charles Warren. One of the firebrand speakers addressing
this gathering would be none other than Michael Davitt, the
Fenian, and one of the founder members of the British
Labour Party, who had given incendiary speeches at the
International Workingmen's Educational Club at 40 Berner
Street – the scene of the Elizabeth Stride murder.

After Marie Jeanette Kelly told Elizabeth Prater she
hoped the weather would be fine on Friday for the Lord
Mayor's Show, we next hear of her in the Ten Bells public
house, situated just around the corner from Kelly's home, on
the corner of Commercial Street and Church Street. Kelly
spent some time there in the company of her friend
Elizabeth Foster until 7.05pm, when she left the pub.
Foster had known Kelly for 18 months and stated that her
friend had told her she was from Limerick. Foster had no
idea where Marie Jeanette went to when she left the Ten
Bells, but it was probably Dorset Street, because Joseph
Barnett, Kelly's estranged boyfriend, visited 13 Miller's

Court that evening between 7.30 and 7.45pm (as he had been doing on an almost daily basis) and he found his former girlfriend in her room, with a friend named Lizzie Albrook. Albrook left shortly after the arrival of Barnett, but she would later tell a newspaper reporter a curious thing. On 12 November, three days after Kelly's murder, the St James Gazette reported:

> *Lizzie Allbrook, a young woman of twenty, who resides in Miller's Court, and works at a lodging-house in Dorset Street, says: "I knew Mary Jane Kelly very well, as we were near neighbours. The last time I saw her was on Thursday night, about eight o'clock, when I left her in her room with Joe Barnett, the man who had been living with her. About the last thing she said to me was, 'Whatever you do, don't you do wrong and turn out as I have.' She had often spoken to me in this way, and warned me against going on the streets, as she had done. She told me, too, she was heartily sick of the life she was leading, and wished she had money enough to go back to Ireland, where her people lived. I don't believe she would have gone out as she did if she had not been obliged to do so in order to keep herself from starvation. She had talked to me about her friends several times, and on one occasion told me she had a female relation in London who was on the stage.'*

Kelly had told Joseph Barnett and other people she knew that she had come to live in South Wales with her parents when she was a child, yet now she was saying "her people" lived in Ireland, but how could this be so? Landlord John McCarthy stated that Kelly regularly received letters from Ireland, and he had assumed they were from her mother.

Joseph Barnett also asserted that Kelly had received letters from Ireland. We shall look at the significance of these letters later in the book.

Barnett talked with Kelly at 13 Miller's Court for about a quarter of an hour, then left, and the whereabouts of Kelly after this period is a mystery. There were unconfirmed reports that she was in the Britannia, one of the pubs at the end of Dorset Street, at around 11pm that night, drinking with a well-dressed respectable-looking man with a black moustache. If Kelly was in the Britannia, we must assume she had no money to buy drinks, as the unemployed Barnett had not given her any money when he called. We can only assume that the well-dressed stranger with Kelly in the Britannia was buying her drinks.

At a quarter to twelve that night, 31-year-old Mary Ann Cox of 5 Miller's Court, returned home from Commercial Street, where she had been soliciting. Cox felt a severe chill in the autumn air that night, so started to walk home where she could warm herself for a while before going out again to look for clients. As she walked down Dorset Street from Commercial Street, she saw a familiar person walking ahead of her – Marie Jeanette Kelly – and she had a stout man, about 5 feet 5 inches in height at her side. He was around 36 years of age, wore a billycock hat, was dressed rather shabbily in a long overcoat, and carried a pail of beer. It's possible that Kelly and the man had just left the Britannia pub. Kelly wore a maroon knitted 'crossover' shawl and a linsey frock. As usual, she was bare-headed; Kelly never wore a hat, and sported a fine head of long hair. The couple turned into the arched passage that led from Dorset Street into Miller's Court, and Cox followed close behind. She had noticed – probably from the swaying gait and slurred speech – that Kelly was quite drunk, and by the light of the lamp facing the door of 13 Miller's Court, Cox had a look at the face of the stout stranger accompanying her neighbour. It was blotchy and he had a full carroty moustache, small side-whiskers and a clean-shaven chin. A moment later the man with the quart can of ale entered Kelly's small room as Mrs Cox bid her neighbour goodnight. Kelly replied, "Goodnight, I am going to sing."

Mary Ann Cox walked on down the court to the last door on the left, where she lived, and not long afterwards, perhaps a minute or two, Marie Jeanette Kelly started to sing 'A Violet from Mother's Grave', a song written by Will Fox in 1881. The first verse of this Victorian 'bereavement broadside' runs thus:

> *Scenes of my childhood arise before my gaze,*
> *Bringing recollections of bygone happy days,*
> *When down in the meadow in childhood I would roam,*
> *No one's left to cheer me now within that good old home,*
> *Father and Mother, they have passed away;*
> *Sister and brother, now lay beneath the clay,*
> *But while life does remain to cheer me, I'll retain*
> *This small violet I plucked from mother's grave.*

Some Ripperologists have assumed that 'A Violet from Mother's Grave' is an Irish song, but the song is, in fact, American in origin. In October of 1884 – the year Marie Jeanette is said to have come to London – the song was played with great emotion on a harp by a Mrs Ives (wife of the singer, dancer and instrumentalist Joe) at the Royal Foresters' Music Hall, Cambridge Road, Bethnal Green. Her performance evoked thunderous applause, but in the minds of the public, the song was always associated with the Mohawk Minstrels, an immensely popular troupe of English

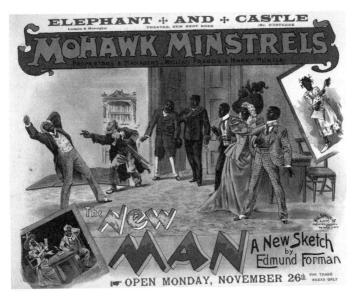

Mohawk Minstrels at the Elephant and Castle, 1888.

singers who blacked-up their faces with theatrical make-up to affect the countenance of the American Southern Negro – white people acting out black stereotypes. Such minstrel shows were incredibly popular because of their mixture of pathos, glamour, humour, and catchy songs. The Mohawk Minstrels were formed in 1873 by brothers James and William Francis – two Londoners who worked for a music publisher. The Mohawks were inspired by the Manhattan Minstrels from the United States, and the Francis brothers became so well-received with their act, they attracted new members and moved from the small-scale Berners Hall in Islington to the nearby Agricultural Hall, which was capable of seating fifty-thousand people. The Mohawk Minstrels also played regularly at the Elephant and Castle Theatre in the 1880s, and this leads us to a quaint possibility regarding Marie Jeanette Kelly.

Kelly often visited a woman in the Elephant and Castle district, but very little is known about this individual. Kelly said the woman was very much like herself, but why she journeyed two-and-a-half miles across the Thames to see her remains a mystery. The Elephant and Castle district was not only largely inhabited by Irish people at that time; it was also an area where many Fenians had safe-houses. In August 1887, for example, two American Fenians were followed by the agents of James Monro – head of the Secret Department – from the House of Commons to the Red Lion public house in Westminster. From there one of these two Fenians headed towards the Elephant and Castle district, and was seen to go into a Southwark lodging house at 7 Gladstone Street. Monro's men kept the Fenian under surveillance, and he subsequently left the lodging house and went to Paris, a city swarming with Fenian spies, Anarchists and British Intelligence agents.

Now, we return to Miller's Court on that fateful November night. Around 15 minutes after midnight, prostitute Mary Ann Cox left her room and walked down the court towards the arched passage that led to Dorset Street. She walked the streets of Whitechapel in search of a paying customer, but could find none. Mrs Cox persisted in her search for clients for as long as she could. She had to find money for her rent somehow, and her landlord was not as lenient towards her as he was towards Marie Jeanette.

At half-past midnight, 30-year-old flower seller Catharine Picket was awakened from her precious slumbers by Marie Jeanette's singing. Picket lived in the court, quite close to Kelly, and she complained about the noise to her husband David, and then she told him she was going to have words with her noisy neighbour. "You leave that woman alone," her husband told her grumpily, and rather

204

reluctantly, Mrs Picket turned over and went back to sleep.

Around 1am, Mrs Cox returned to her little room in Miller's Court to warm herself at the embers of her fire, and as she passed Number 13, she saw a light through the windows and heard Marie Jeanette still singing. Around this time, as rain began to fall, Elizabeth Prater, the woman who lived in Room 20, almost directly above Kelly's room, was standing in a drunken state beneath the shelter of the arched passage that formed the entrance to the court. She was waiting for a man she lived with to turn up, but he never arrived, and during the 20-minute wait, Prater went into McCarthy's shop and chatted with him for a while. McCarthy remembered hearing Kelly singing during this period, yet at the inquest into his tenant's death days later, Prater stated that she did not hear her late neighbour singing that Friday morning. Shortly after one o'clock on what was to be the morning of the Ripper's last murder, Mrs Cox decided to go in search of a client again, and must have passed McCarthy's shop before Prater arrived, or perhaps when the latter was talking to McCarthy on the premises. At 1.20am, Prater went up to her room and put two tables up against the door as a primitive security measure, no doubt mindful of the mysterious killer at large. She lay on the bed, fully dressed, and fell into a deep (and most probably, gin-induced) sleep.

At 2.30am, Sarah Lewis, a laundress of Great Pearl Street, came down Dorset Street from the Commercial Street end. She was heading for Miller's Court to stay with the Keylers, who were friends of hers (or possibly even her parents) after having an argument with her husband. Just before Sarah turned right into the archway leading to Miller's Court, she noticed two things. Firstly, there was a lone stranger on the other side of the street, standing outside Crossingham's Lodging House, and he was staring at the arched entrance to Miller's Court across the road. Secondly, Sarah could see a man and a drunken woman further down Dorset Street, coming towards her from the direction of Little Paternoster Row and Crispin Street. Sarah recalled that the solitary man standing opposite Miller's Court was stout-looking, and not very tall. He wore a black 'wide-awake' hat, and Sarah had the impression that the loiterer in Dorset Street was looking up the arched passage of Miller's Court as if he was waiting for someone to come out. Sarah walked down the passage and knocked on the door of 2 Miller's Court, the home of the Keylers. We are not yet done with Sarah Lewis, for she will claim to hear a woman – possibly Marie Jeanette Kelly – crying out later that morning. We shall look a little further into the testimony of Sarah in a while, but now for an extraordinary version of an incident which initially seems to throw light on the ghastly fate of Marie Jeanette Kelly.

A 'witness' named George Hutchinson was to come forward after the short inquest into Kelly's murder had ended, on 12 November. Hutchinson, an unemployed labourer lodging at the Victoria Workingmen's Home on the corner of Wentworth and Commercial Streets, went to his nearest police station and made a startling statement. He had seen the murdered woman Kelly on the morning she was killed with a man who could have been Jack the Ripper. This is the very wording of this astonishing statement:

> *About 2.00am, 9th, I was coming by Thrawl Street,*
> *Commercial Street, and just before I got to Flower and*
> *Dean Street I met the murdered woman Kelly, and she*
> *said to me, "Hutchinson, will you lend me sixpence?" I*
> *said, "I can't , I've spent all my money going down to*

Romford." She said, "Good morning, I must go and
find some money."

She went away towards Thrawl Street, a man coming in
the opposite direction to Kelly tapped her on the shoulder
and said something to her. They both burst out laughing.
I heard her say, "Alright" to him, and the man said,
"You will be alright, for what I have told you."
He then placed his right hand around her shoulders. He
also had a kind of a small parcel in his left hand, with a
kind of strap round it.

I stood against the lamp of the [Hutchinson said Ten
Bells first but it is crossed out in the statement] Queens
Head public house and watched him. They both then
came past me and the man hung down his head with his
hat over his eyes. I stooped down and looked him in the
face. He looked at me stern.

They both went into Dorset Street. I followed them. They
both stood at the corner of the court for about 3 minutes.
He said something to her. She said, "Alright, my dear,
come along, you will be comfortable." He then placed his
arm on her shoulder and gave her a kiss. She said she
had lost her handkerchief. He then pulled his
handkerchief – a red one – out and gave it to her. They
both then went up the court together. I then went to the
court to see if I could see them but could not. I stood
there for about three quarters of an hour, to see if they
came out. They did not so I went away.
Description: age about 34 or 35. Height: 5ft6.
Complexion: pale, dark eyes and eye lashes, slight
moustache, curled up each end, and hair dark. Very surley
[sic] looking. Dress: long dark coat, collar and cuffs,
trimmed astrakhan, and a dark jacket under. Light
waistcoat, dark trousers, dark felt hat pulled down in the

middle. Button boots and gaiters with white buttons. Wore
a very thick gold chain. White linen collar. Black tie with
horseshoe pin. Respectable appearance. Walked very
sharp. Jewish appearance. Can be identified.

[signed]
George Hutchinson
E. Badham Sergt
E. Ellisdon Insp
Submitted FG Abberline Inspr T Arnold Supdt

Before we continue to look at the incidental occurrences
taking place around Miller's Court on the morning of the
Kelly murder, let us scrutinise the claims of George
Hutchinson. Almost nothing is known about him. He was an
unemployed labourer, and some who have tried to research
his background have said he had been a night watchman
and also a groom. His age is not recorded, but he was
described by a reporter from *The Times* as looking like a man
'of the labouring class, with a military appearance'.

The first unanswered question concerning Hutchinson
is his whereabouts on the morning of the Kelly murder. He
says he was walking up Commercial Street, passing Thrawl
Street, heading towards Flower and Dean Street. This
means he was walking away from his lodgings – the Victoria
Workingmen's Home at 39-41 Commercial Street and
heading north. Where was he going? Hutchinson does not
say. He told Kelly he couldn't give her sixpence because
he'd spent what money he had going down to Romford.
Perhaps Hutchinson had been walking the streets, hoping
to borrow money from any friends who came his way so he
could pay for a bed for the night at his lodgings. Romford is
about 13 miles east of the City of London and is part of the

London borough of Havering. Hutchinson's business there in November 1888 is not known. He may have been visiting relatives or friends in the town, or looking for work. Romford at the time was still recovering from a serious flood, caused by unusually heavy August rains that burst the banks of the River Rom, so perhaps Hutchinson had hoped to find a job repairing flood-damaged properties.

The morning of 9 November was one of the coldest on record, with temperatures in London falling as low as 32 degrees Fahrenheit – zero degrees centigrade, and before and during this icy cold spell, which lasted from 2am to 4am, rain and sleet fell heavily on the East End and the rest of London, driven by a glacial knife-edged wind. During this freezing period, George Hutchinson, who had just walked over 13 miles from Romford in around three hours or more, would have been soaked, and yet he states that he stood in Dorset Street for three quarters of an hour, gazing down the arch of Miller's Court. Hutchinson said he was curious as to why Marie Jeanette Kelly – a girl he'd known for about three years – was with such a respectably dressed stranger. This selfless concern for Kelly, regardless of the 45-minute wait that ice-cold morning in Dorset Street, seems a little too altruistic to be true. Perhaps Hutchinson was naturally concerned at the presence of such an eccentric stranger with Jack the Ripper still being at large in the area. If Hutchinson had known Kelly since 1885, then wouldn't Kelly's ex-boyfriend Joe Barnett have known Hutchinson, if only by sight? Barnett makes no references at all to Hutchinson either on or after the Kelly murder inquest, yet Marie Jeanette knew his surname, and asked him for money. Was Hutchinson trying to say he was an occasional client of Kelly's, or just a friend of hers who sometimes gave her money? He told both Inspector Abberline and a journalist that he had generously given Kelly a shilling now and then.

Hutchinson describes the well-to-do stranger in the astrakhan coat with amazing detail, considering the fleeting glimpse he had of him as he passed under the lantern of a pub. Hutchinson is so ultra-observant, he is even able to note the colour of the affluent outsider's eyelashes, but does not mention in what type of accent the stranger spoke. Was it upper-class? He doesn't say. He also fails to mention the dapper stranger's build; was he stout, thin or of medium build? Dorset Street was just 25 feet wide, and Hutchinson stated that he had watched Kelly and the foreign-looking man as they stood on the pavement in front of the entrance to Miller's Court. Surely Kelly and the stranger would notice that they were being observed by Hutchinson, who, if he was standing in front of Crossingham's, would be directly under the lodging house light that even threw its rays into Elizabeth Prater's room.

Would the Ripper (if that was who the ostentatious man with Kelly actually was) be foolish enough to go and kill and mutilate a victim in a room in Miller's Court when he knows a witness has seen him enter the building? That witness could still have been waiting outside, or might have gone to Commercial Street police station to alert the law. And what are we to make of Hutchinson's description of the thick gold (watch) chain, supposedly worn by the mysterious dandy? To put such gold on show in a street renowned to have been the roughest in a notorious district of the East End would be asking for trouble. Organised mobs of cut-throat criminals such as the Friar's-mount Gang, The Green Gate Gang and other bands of murderous thieves (similar to the mythical Old Nichol Gang) prowled the dark warren of streets in Bethnal Green, Spitalfields and Whitechapel, so the "toff in the astrakhan coat" – if he ever existed – would have put his life in grave danger by showing off his thick gold chain in Dorset Street in broad daylight, never mind two o'clock in the morning.

After Hutchinson had finished his 45 minutes of surveillance on Miller's Court, he claimed to have wandered the streets all night. Around the time Sarah Lewis passed Kelly's room – at 2.30am – she heard nothing and saw no light from any candle or fire, yet according to Hutchinson, Kelly is entertaining her rich-looking client in there at that time. Which leads me to ask, was Hutchinson actually there in Dorset Street that morning? Well, Sarah Lewis did see a man standing outside the lodging house opposite Miller's Court at 2.30am, but does her description of that man tally with the scant description of Hutchinson? The man Lewis saw was described by her as short and stout, whereas Hutchinson is described as having the appearance of a military man – upright, smart, fit-looking (and he probably was fit, considering the walk of over 13 miles from Romford through rain and bitterly cold weather). If Hutchinson was the short stout man Lewis saw, then why didn't he mention seeing Lewis in his statement? Such a mention of Lewis would have given his statement more credibility. Or, did he not see Sarah Lewis because he was never in Dorset Street to begin with?

Lewis saw a drunken woman, accompanied by a man on Dorset Street that morning. Unlike the outlandishly dressed man Hutchinson saw with Kelly, the man Lewis saw with the woman was dressed rather mundanely, and this couple were coming from the western end of Dorset Street. Hutchinson's couple – Kelly and the swell – were said to have walked from the eastern end of the street. Is it possible that George Hutchinson was a publicity seeker? Or was he

211

simply out to make easy money from the newspaper hounds who were desperate for any copy on the Ripper crimes? We only have to cast our mind back to Matthew Packer, the lying fruiterer who claimed he had sold grapes to Jack the Ripper in Berner Street the night Elizabeth Stride was killed, to realise that this is a possibility. If Hutchinson had read the *Star* newspaper on the evening of Saturday 10 November, he would have seen that one 'Mrs Kennedy' – a journalist's misidentification of Sarah Lewis – had given a story about seeing a respectably dressed man with a woman in Dorset Street. This was the *Star's* garbled version of Sarah Lewis's sighting of the couple walking up Dorset Street. Could Hutchison have read the Lewis story and decided to insert himself into it? Did he expand on the description of the respectable stranger mentioned in the *Star* and create the ostentatious stranger who accosted Marie Jeanette Kelly?

I believe that was the case with George Hutchinson. I think he was just a fantasist who didn't come forward until three days after the Kelly murder. After all, Abberline stated in 1903 that the only possible witnesses who might have seen Jack the Ripper had only had rear views of him. Abberline was referring to witnesses like Mrs Elizabeth Long, who said she saw Annie Chapman talking to a man on Hanbury Street around 5.30am on the morning she was murdered. Unfortunately though, the man had his back to Mrs Long. Surely, by 1903, Abberline would have mentioned Hutchinson's sighting of Kelly with the man in the Astrakhan coat if he had given the report any serious thought?

Let us return again to that morning in Miller's Court, and look at the testimony of more credible witnesses than George Hutchinson.

At 3am, Mrs Cox returned to the court. She had had

enough of a blustery cold rainy night devoid of clients. She passed Kelly's room and heard nothing from within and noticed no light through the window. Mary Ann Cox, described by an insensitive journalist from the *Star* as 'a wretched-looking specimen of East End womanhood', went into her humble abode, warmed herself at the dying vestiges of her fire, and listened to the bitterly cold rain, which was now heavy, falling on the flags of Miller's Court. She was unable to sleep, and throughout that rainy night she occasionally heard the distinctive faint footfalls of men entering and leaving the court, and in particular, Cox recalled hearing someone going out of the cul-de-sac at 5.45am, but was unable to establish which room this person had left, as she heard no door shut.

Mrs Cox certainly heard no screams that morning, but Elizabeth Prater claimed she did. She was awakened by her kitten Diddles walking gently over her neck between 3.30am and 4am. The window next to Prater's bed looked into Dorset Street, and she established the time because the lodging house light, a lantern hanging on the wall of Crossingham's lodging house across the road, was out. As Diddles woke her up, she allegedly heard a cry of, "Oh! Murder!" It seemed to come from somewhere close by, but Mrs Prater admitted such cries of murder during domestic squabbles had been heard quite a few times before in the neighbourhood, so she took little notice. She heard no further sounds and went back to sleep. She later rose from her bed at 5am and went out to the Ten Bells pub for a glass of rum. At 5.45am she recalled seeing several men harnessing horses in Dorset Street. After drinking her rum on that cold rainy November morning, Mrs Prater went back to her room in Miller's Court and slept till 11am.

Sarah Lewis, who had been staying at the Keylers home

at 2 Miller's Court after the argument with her husband, had been dozing in a chair until 3.30 that morning, when she heard the Spitalfields church clock striking the half hour. She was unable to get back to sleep until almost 5am, but before then, at around a minute before 4am, she heard a young woman's voice scream out "Murder!" The scream seemed to have come from the direction of Kelly's room. Sarah Lewis attached hardly any significance to the cry for the same reason given by Elizabeth Prater – cries of murder were fairly common in that rough neighbourhood.

Catharine Picket, the flower seller in Miller's Court who had been awakened by Kelly's singing at half-past midnight, woke up around 7.30am, and by 8.am had ventured out into the court, ready to go to the market to buy flowers, but, seeing how rainy and chilly it was that Friday morning, went to knock on the door of Kelly's room, as she wanted to borrow her shawl, or 'pelerine' as Mrs Picket called it. The flower seller told a newspaper reporter that her own shawl was "as thin as a cobweb", but after knocking at Kelly's door for a short while, and believing the young woman to be fast asleep, she left Miller's Court and headed for the market.

Around this time, a Dorset Street tailor, Maurice Lewis, said he actually saw Marie Jeanette Kelly briefly leave her room at Miller's Court and return moments afterwards. Lewis also maintained that he had known Kelly for five years, which was unlikely, as she hadn't arrived in London until 1884, and had only been living in Miller's Court since the beginning of the year. Before that she had lived briefly on Little Paternoster Row, off Dorset Street. The tailor even described his friend of five years as being 5 foot 3 inches in height, when she was, in fact, 5-foot 7.

Lewis also claimed he had seen Kelly in the Britannia pub at around 10am on the morning of her murder, but this claim was not taken seriously by the police, as doctors attending the crime scene had calculated that Kelly had been dead several hours by then. Maurice Lewis did not make an appearance at the Kelly murder inquest.

Another person who was either lying or genuinely mistaken about the whereabouts of Kelly that Friday morning was Mrs Caroline Maxwell, the wife of Henry Maxwell, a lodging house deputy, who lived at 14 Dorset Street. Maxwell testified to seeing Marie Jeanette Kelly standing on the corner of Miller's Court at around 8.30 that morning. This would be around the time Catharine Picket was knocking on the door of 13 Miller's Court and getting no answer. "What brings you up so early?" Mrs Maxwell asked Kelly from across the street.

"I have the horrors of drink upon me, as I have been drinking for some days past," replied Kelly.

"Why don't you go to Mrs Ringers [the landlady of the Britannia pub] and have half a pint of beer?" Mrs Maxwell suggested.

"I have just had a drink of ale and brought it all up," Kelly told her, nodding to either the vomit in the roadway or the Britannia pub up the street; Mrs Maxwell wasn't sure what the motioning head gesture meant.

However, when Mrs Maxwell testified at the inquest into Kelly's death, she added first names into her version of the aforementioned dialogue, suggesting that she and Kelly were not just people who knew one another by sight. In her second version of events, Mrs Maxwell states that she said, "Why Mary, what brings you up so early?"

And, according to Mrs Maxwell, Kelly replied thus: "Oh, Carry, I feel so bad."

During the inquest, Mrs Maxwell admitted that she had only known Marie Jeanette for four months. The coroner asked Mrs Maxwell if she was sure of the time of the encounter with Kelly, as the woman had been dead for several hours when the alleged meeting took place, and Maxwell said she was adamant that she had met Kelly, as she had been returning china that her husband had borrowed to the house opposite. "I am positive the time was between eight to half-past eight," Maxwell insisted, and continued her recollections of that morning: "I left her saying I pitied her feelings. I then went to Bishopsgate. [to get her husband's breakfast]. As I returned, I saw her outside the Britannia talking to a man; the time was then about ... a quarter to nine. I could not describe the man. I did not pass them. I went into my house. I saw them in the distance. I am certain it was the deceased. The man was not a tall man. He had on dark clothes and a sort of plaid coat. I could not say what [type of] hat he had on. Mary Jane had [on] a dark skirt; velvet body, and maroon shawl, and no hat."

Despite the coroner warning her that her testimony ran against all the known facts, 'Carry' Maxwell stuck to her story about Kelly. Police made inquiries with the landladies and landlords at the Britannia pub, Blue Coat Boy, Horn of Plenty, Ten Bells and other pubs in the area, and not a single person recalled serving Kelly that morning. Caroline Maxwell was either a blatant publicity-seeking liar (and we have seen how she added first names to the second version of her story) or, she had simply got the days mixed up. The Maxwell story is an enduring puzzle within the larger enigma of the Whitechapel Murders, and it has stubbornly refused to be explained away for well over a century.

The accounts of the discovery of Marie Jeanette's body that Friday morning in November 1888 seem to throw up even more perplexing questions. At 10.45am, John McCarthy told his assistant, Tom Bowyer, of 37 Dorset Street, to go to

Marie Jeanette Kelly's room to collect the rent she owed. Bowyer knocked on Kelly's door, but there was no answer, so he turned the doorknob, and decided the door was locked. Bowyer therefore knocked again, and getting no answer, peeped through the keyhole, but saw no one and heard no sounds within the room. Number 13 had two windows, and Bowyer turned the corner and went to the first one. Kelly or Barnett had broken a pane in this window during an altercation some time before, and, because the couple had lost the key to their room some weeks previously, either of them could reach in through the hole in the windowpane to unfasten the door-latch of the spring-lock. Tom Bowyer reached in through this hole in the windowpane and lifted up the curtain. His eyes adjusted to the dim interior of the room, and he suddenly saw what looked like two lumps of something unfamiliar on a table straight ahead. That table was quite close to the bed on which Marie Jeanette slept. Bowyer brought his eyes nearer to the aperture in the pane, looked again and squinted to behold a scene that would stay with him for the rest of his life. There was a body on the bed, and blood on the floor. The body was hardly recognisable because it had been butchered.

Dropping the curtain, Tom Bowyer walked in shock back to his employer, and told him what he had just seen through the window of 13 Miller's Court. McCarthy immediately went back to Kelly's window with Bowyer and reached in through the hole in the window pane to see the same ghastly sight that his assistant had described. McCarthy seemed mute for a while, as if he was too deeply shocked to utter a word. He later claimed that he and Bowyer had then dashed about 416 yards (380 metres) to Commercial Street police station to notify the law of the barbaric murder which had taken place within 20 feet of his shop.

Marie Jeanette Kelly's body on her bed.

When we analyse the statements McCarthy and Bowyer made to the police with their inquest testimony, odd gaps appear where the information seems rather fuzzy. At the inquest into Kelly's death, McCarthy stated that he had sent his hired assistant Tom Bowyer to Kelly's room (just 20 feet away) and he had returned five minutes later. Also, in his police statement, McCarthy said he had sent Bowyer to the police station after seeing the body through the window, and that he had then followed him to the station on Commercial Street. In the inquest, however, McCarthy stated that he accompanied Bowyer to the station. Bowyer made the same amendment to his story at the inquest. He said McCarthy followed him to the station in his statement to the police but at the inquest he said he and his employer went to Commercial Street police station together. Five minutes is a long time to walk 20 feet, knock twice on a door, look through a window to see evidence of a gruesome murder and return 20 feet to report it – but that's how long Bowyer took to report a murder that would have sent most people running for a policeman within seconds. McCarthy then waits around as Bowyer goes to report the stomach-churning murder of unprecedented savagery, and then follows his assistant to the police station. Why? Perhaps McCarthy went to lock up his shop first, but surely that would take a minute at the most; merely the turn of a key? Perhaps McCarthy went to inform his wife Elizabeth about the murder, if she was there in the shop or at home (both at number 27 Dorset Street). In his inquest testimony and police statements, McCarthy did not mention Mrs McCarthy nor her whereabouts, nor did he refer to the whereabouts of his children at the inquest. It's possible that the Lord Mayor's Show Day, being a public holiday, would have meant that McCarthy's children, who were of schooling age, would have been off school that day? Perhaps Mrs McCarthy had taken her girls to see the Lord Mayor's pageant, but if she was at 27 Dorset Street when her husband saw the grotesque aftermath of Jack the Ripper's most violent crime, then surely John McCarthy would have either taken his wife and children to the police station with him, or at least to a neighbour's, purely out of concern for their safety? For all McCarthy knew, the Ripper – assumed

219

by most to be a homicidal maniac – could have still been in Kelly's locked room. The four previous canonical victims had all been found within minutes of their deaths, so many who learned about Kelly's body being found in Miller's Court at 10.45am would possibly have surmised that she had only recently been murdered.

Twenty minutes after the discovery of Kelly's body, Bowyer, and then McCarthy, arrived at Commercial Street police station, shortly after 11am. According to the memoirs of Detective Walter Dew, who was in the police station that morning, Tom Bowyer burst into the building with his eyes bulging out and was unable to utter a word for a while, until he gasped out, "Another one ... Jack the Ripper ... awful! Jack McCarthy sent me."

McCarthy duly arrived some time later to give his version of the discovery of Kelly's body to Inspector Walter Beck. Beck and Sergeant Edward Badham went at once to Miller's Court. After taking a look at the carcass of Marie Jeanette Kelly through the hole in the window pane, Inspector Beck sent for divisional surgeon Dr George Bagster Phillips and police assistance. He then closed off the court, which effectively barred people from entering the cul-de-sac. Those who were already in Miller's Court were not allowed to leave, and Sarah Lewis, the laundress staying with the Keylers, was one of the people confined to the court by the police. She was not allowed to leave until 5.30pm.

Dr Phillips arrived at the scene of the crime at 11.15am. The door to Kelly's room was apparently locked, so the surgeon viewed the body through the window. It was evident that the mutilated corpse on the bed was in no need of immediate medical attention from Dr Phillips, and he could see that there was no one else in the small room to which he could render professional assistance. Dr Phillips would later

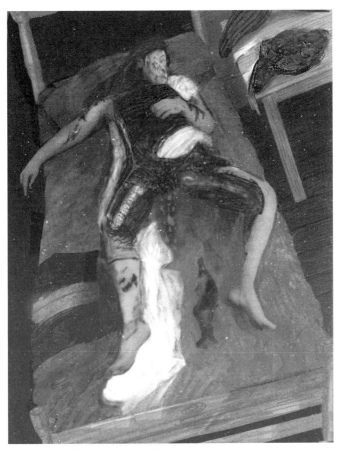

Marie Jeanette Kelly on her deathbed.

tell the coroner at the inquest that: "Having ascertained that … it was advisable that no entrance should be made into the room at that time, I remained until about 1.30pm, when the door was broken open, I think, by Mr McCarthy."

The idea was to leave the body of Marie Jeanette in the room and wait until the bloodhounds, promised by Sir Charles Warren, arrived. Warren had personally tested

221

out two bloodhounds, named Barnaby and Burgho just the month before in Hyde Park, using himself as the 'fox'. The trial was a success, and Warren was traced and 'caught' by the dogs. It was thought that the bloodhounds would be able to pick up the scent of the Ripper if the dogs were brought to the victim immediately after the murder. In Kelly's case, the body was in a room, so the weather would not have affected the strength of the killer's scent. There were claims that the police believed that Barnaby and Burgho would not be able to pick up the murderer's scent through the crowded streets of Whitechapel, yet bloodhounds were subsequently used in other urban murder investigations. In August 1908, a bloodhound named Czar was used to track the murderer of 7-year-old Madge Kirby through the crowded streets of Liverpool to a train station where the killer managed to flee to Birmingham. One of the most successful canine 'sleuths' of all time was a bloodhound named Nick Carter (after the fictional American detective) which was responsible for the conviction of over 600 criminals in the 1930s. On one occasion this bloodhound successfully scent-trailed a murder suspect to the door of his home after four days.

Fifteen minutes after the arrival of Dr Phillips at Miller's Court, half a dozen hansom cabs trundled into Dorset Street carrying Inspectors Abberline and Reid and other detectives – directly from the Criminal Investigation Department in Whitehall, according to most newspapers. If Inspector Beck had despatched a telegram to Abberline just after 11am, then this was an incredibly rapid response time. Not only had Abberline and the other policemen travelled from Scotland Yard in Whitehall to Spitalfields within 25 to 30 minutes, they had travelled through roads and thoroughfares in London that had been closed to wheeled traffic from 10am because of the Lord Mayor's Show. Gresham Street West, St Martin's-le-Grand, Cheapside, Mansion House Street, Leadenhall Street, Fenchurch Street, Mincing Lane, Great Tower Street, Cannon Street, St Paul's Churchyard, Fleet Street, Ludgate Hill, the Victoria Embankment and numerous other streets were closed to wheeled vehicles, and yet half a dozen cabs from Scotland Yard, Whitehall Place (also closed because of the Mayoral procession), reached Dorset Street within 25 minutes. This is almost 40 days after the last Ripper murder, and Abberline's plain-clothed detectives arrive in Dorset Street in unmarked hansom cabs which have travelled through roads choked with Londoners out to see the Lord Mayor's Procession and thoroughfares congested with vehicles taking alternative routes because of the major disruptions caused by the closed roads. The most direct route from Scotland Yard to Dorset Street would involve traversing the very streets closed to wheeled traffic. Even if Abberline had possessed the Victorian equivalent of a red flashing police light on the roof of his hansom cab, he would have been hard pushed to arrive so quickly in Dorset Street on one of the busiest mornings in the capital. If the newspaper reports were wrong, and Abberline and his detectives were already in Whitechapel, then that would be quite a coincidence, because there had not been a Ripper murder for 40 days. Of course if Abberline and his men were in Whitechapel on the morning of the Kelly murder, then why would they take 25 to 30 minutes to get to Dorset Street?

Abberline took a look at Kelly's body via the smashed window, and agreed with Dr Phillips that a forced entry should not be made into the room until the bloodhounds had arrived. A photographer in his late thirties, Joseph Martin, was summoned to Miller's Court. This photographer would be responsible for taking several photographs of Marie

Jeanette Kelly's ripped and slashed corpse, including the haunting picture of the body lying on the bed with its face turned towards the windows of the room. How this photograph was taken remains something of a mystery. The angle it was taken from suggests the camera lens was pointing through the larger window of 13 Miller's Court. A pane of glass would surely have been removed to facilitate this famous shot. Some have suggested that the police simply lifted the window open and stepped inside Kelly's room, but that seems unlikely, as Abberline later asked John McCarthy to make a forced entry into the locked room. One account given by a Ripperologist in 1970 maintains that the police broke into Kelly's room and took several photographs of the body. This Ripperologist does not explain why McCarthy then still broke into the room after this supposed event took place. Other crime historians have maintained that a whole window frame was removed to enable the photographer to record the horrendous murder scene. The truth is probably more straightforward; Joseph Martin may have simply set up his camera in the room after the forced entry by McCarthy. Before McCarthy forced the door open, there was something of a fiasco unfolding in Dorset Street.

A soft drizzling rain began to drift down from a darkening sky on to Miller's Court, and Abberline and the detectives were left in a bureaucratic limbo for two hours until 1.30pm when Superintendent Thomas Arnold arrived on the scene. Arnold, the man who had sent an inspector with a wet sponge to wipe out the chalked 'Juwes' message on the night of the Stride and Eddowes murders, had some startling news that proved to be an utter embarrassment to Abberline. Sir Charles Warren had countermanded the order to use the bloodhounds, so now the dogs were not coming to Miller's Court.

The day before – 8 November – Sir Charles Warren had tendered his resignation, supposedly because of tensions that had built up between himself and the Home Secretary. In the spring of that year Warren had offered to resign but his offer was turned down. The refusal was no surprise, as Anarchy, Socialism and Fenianism were undoubtedly ready to explode on the streets of the capital, and an unpopular reclusive sovereign did little to help the political situation. Only Warren could tackle the rioters and keep mob rule at bay. Warren was certainly no quitter and yet he resigned on the eve of the last and most violent murder committed by Jack the Ripper. He did remain in office for a short while after his resignation, until he was succeeded by the enigmatic James Monro, head of the so-called Secret Department, a special unit created specifically to spy on Anarchists, Fenians, Socialists, and any other subversive faction out to overturn the Establishment.

Sir Charles Warren left Scotland Yard in November 1888 and returned to the War Office on Pall Mall. Warren was a steely-nerved time-served soldier who was renowned for seeing things through to the end, whether on the battlefield or in his personal life. Even in the face of the gravest adversity, the history books tell us that Warren would see a task through to completion, and yet we are asked to believe that Sir Charles would simply give up on the world-famous Jack the Ripper murders at the height of the atrocities, because he was thin-skinned enough to be offended by the Home Secretary's opinions. This explanation simply does not ring true. Queen Victoria had been following the news of the Ripper murders and had even been aware of the rape, robbery and murder of one Emma Elizabeth Smith, who had been set upon by three youths in Whitechapel in April 1888 – five months before Mary Ann Nichols was slain. A blunt instrument was rammed into Smith's vagina after the sexual assault and robbery, and she later died of peritonitis. The perpetrators of this shocking crime were never brought to justice.

On the night of the Double Event, when Stride and Eddowes were killed by the Ripper, the Monarch was at Abergeldie in Scotland with Prince Albert Victor, and when the news of two killings reached her, she used one of the new-fangled telephones to call the Home Office to express her shock at the murders. The Monarch also sent a cipher telegram from Balmoral to the Prime Minister, the Marquis of Salisbury, on the day after the murder of Marie Jeanette Kelly which read: 'This new most ghastly murder shows the absolute necessity for some very decided action. All the courts must be lit, and our detectives improved. They are not what they should be. You promised, when the first murders took place to consult with your colleagues about it.'

The Queen was outraged at the brutal slaughter of such women in the East End, and she had entrusted her loyal subject Sir Charles Warren to defend the people of the Metropolis and to keep the growing mobs of radicals in the capital at bay. On 26 December 1887, the Sovereign had been so impressed with Warren's handling of the Bloody Sunday Riots, she had decided to knight him. On that date, the Prime Minister, Lord Salisbury wrote to the Chief Commissioner:

December 26th, 1887

Dear Sir Charles,

> *I am very glad to be the channel informing you that in special recognition of the services you have performed in maintaining order in the Metropolis during the past*

difficult year, the Queen has been pleased to confer upon you a Knight Commandership of the Bath.

Believe me,

Yours faithfully

Salisbury

Warren's wax replica was being exhibited at Madame Tussauds by January 1888, such was his heroic status to those of the upper classes of the West End in the aftermath of the Bloody Sunday Riots. Why on earth would a Royalist as strong-minded as Warren throw in his hand, and in effect, desert a royally-appointed duty? On 13 November that year, the Queen dictated a letter to her Private Secretary Sir Henry Ponsonby, who in turn forwarded the missive to Home Secretary Henry Matthews. The letter expressed her 'sincere regret' about Warren's resignation. She also believed that Warren's untimely resignation would encourage the lawbreakers of London to defy the Police. Could it be that Warren was trying to impede the Whitechapel Murders investigations? It certainly seemed as if that were the case. First of all, Warren had washed away a major clue in the case – the cryptic message chalked on a wall, and then he had countermanded the decision to use bloodhounds to detect the Ripper's scent, and now he had resigned on the eve of the Ripper's most shocking murder. In that cold, wet bleak yard in Miller's Court, many of the detectives must have suspected that someone in high places was out to hamper their attempts to solve this unprecedented series of crimes.

After the fruitless two-hour wait outside Kelly's room,

Superintendent Arnold declared that the door to number 13 would have to be forced to gain entry. John McCarthy, a landlord who surely should have possessed a spare key to Kelly's room, prised open the door with a pickaxe. Who had locked the door in the first place? The key had been missing since around the end of October, so we are left to ponder a few possibilities. If Kelly had found the key days before, then perhaps she had locked herself in her room that night, but the key was never found in her room. If the door was not locked at all, but able to be opened by inserting a hand through the broken window to undo its catch, then why didn't Abberline or McCarthy simply reach through the hole in the windowpane and do just that? If the Ripper had locked the door, then how had he come to have the key in his possession? Had he found it in Kelly's room? Or was he some Raffles-like character who could open or lock a door with a skeleton key?

Abberline later states that, after interviewing Marie Jeanette's boyfriend Joseph Barnett, he was convinced that the Ripper had not come into possession of the key because it had already been lost, weeks before the murder. Abberline also added that, "It is quite simple" to open the door of 13 Miller's Court by putting one's hand through the broken window to move back the latch. If it was as simple as Abberline claims, then why was McCarthy ordered to use a pickaxe to open the door?

The scene that greeted Abberline in Kelly's room was horrific, and many of the seasoned detectives who saw the extremely mutilated corpse lying on the bed were undoubtedly traumatised by the sight. Marie Jeanette Kelly, described by many in life as an attractive and likeable woman, was now barely recognisable. A wooden partition wall, to the right of her bed, was splashed with arterial blood

228

where the Ripper had slit her throat, perhaps as she slept on that side of the mattress. The degree of mutilation inflicted upon the corpse was unprecedented. The killer had removed Marie Jeanette's breasts and placed one under her head and the other by her right foot. Her excised liver had been placed between her legs, and her face was a gashed mess of tattered flesh. The nose had been sliced off, and the only way Joseph Barnett would later succeed in identifying Marie Jeanette would be by recognising her eyes and ears, even though the ears had been removed. The head might have lolled left so the disfigured face was presented to the window – or perhaps the Ripper deliberately posed the head that way so the first people to peep into the room would see the corpse looking at them and be thoroughly terrorised. The killer had cut off flaps of flesh from the abdomen and thighs and piled them on the bedside table, and beneath the bed there was a large pool of blood.

Some crime historians have hypothesised that Kelly had been killed that morning much later than the doctor's estimated time of death (around 2am). One researcher into the fifth (canonical) Jack the Ripper murder has seriously conjectured a time of death as late as 10am, but surely it would take more than 45 minutes for Kelly's blood to percolate through her mattress and create a pool two feet square on the floor? And what's more, this pool of blood was clotted.

Dr Phillips gave an exceedingly sparse account of the position and state of Kelly's body at the inquest:

> *The mutilated remains of a female were lying two thirds*
> *over towards the edge of the bedstead, nearest to the door*
> *of entry. She had only her under linen garment on her,*
> *and from my subsequent examination I am sure the body*
> *had been removed subsequent to the injury which caused*

*her death from that side of the bedstead which was
nearest to the wooden partition, the large quantity of
blood under the bedstead, the saturated condition of the
paliasse, pillow, sheet, at the top corner nearest the
partition leads me to the conclusion that the severance of
the right carotid artery which was the immediate cause of
her death was inflicted while the deceased was lying at
the right side of the bedstead and her head and neck in
the top right-hand corner.*

At 1.50pm, a hansom cab rolled into Dorset Street and came
to a halt at the archway that gave access to Miller's Court.
Robert Anderson, the Assistant Commissioner of the
Metropolitan Police alighted from it and was ushered to the
Kelly murder scene by constables guarding the archway to
Number 13. According to the *Daily Telegraph* for 10
November 1888, Anderson stayed at Miller's Court for some
time. Apart from his police and secret service duties,
Anderson was a religious man, a theologian and a
millenniarist (one who was looking forward to the Second
Coming of Christ) and he also wrote many theological
volumes, covering a plethora of religious subjects, including
the long-awaited arrival of the Anti-Christ, the Whore of
Babylon, and various Biblical prophecies marking the so-
called 'End Times'. In one of Anderson's religious books,
The Gospel and its Ministry, there is a surprising reference to
Marie Jeanette Kelly in a chapter entitled 'Atonement'.
Amongst references of blood sacrifices, meat-offerings, the
Paschal Lamb (Lamb of God), and quotes from the Book of
Leviticus within this chapter, Anderson writes:

*The sight of a room thus stained will not easily fade
from my memory. It was the scene of the last and most*

fiendish of the crimes known as the "Whitechapel
murders" in London. Blood was on the furniture, blood
was on the floor, blood was on the walls, blood was
everywhere. Did this speak to me of life? Yes, but of life
gone, of life destroyed, and, therefore, of that which is the
very antithesis of life. Every bloodstain in that horrid
room spoke of death.

At 2pm, police surgeon Dr Thomas Bond arrived at Miller's Court, directly from his home at the Sanctuary, Westminster Abbey. Bond was the surgeon who had dealt with the Whitehall Torso case (previously mentioned in the 'Unknown Victim' chapter of this book). Bond had been brought in to look at the Whitechapel Murders case by Robert Anderson as late as 25 October 1888. Why? Weren't the medical opinions of doctors such as George Bagster Phillips and Frederick Gordon Brown, Rees Ralph Llewellyn and George William Sequeira enough to go on? What was Anderson's motive for bringing in a doctor from Westminster who had conducted a post-mortem on a torso found at Whitehall? Well, there is a possibility that Anderson knew, or suspected, that there was a connection between the murderer of the torso woman and the killer of Marie Jeanette Kelly, all because of a curious clue overlooked by most Ripperologists for over a century. This clue can be clearly seen in two gruesome photographs of Kelly's corpse. The Whitehall Torso and the leg, foot and arm that belonged to it, had all been tied with a miscellaneous collection of strings and sash cord of varying thicknesses. Now, on the right calf of Marie Jeanette Kelly's leg, there is a strange circumferential 'band' which, upon first glance, appears to be a very thin garter, or perhaps a cut that was carved out by the Ripper, but if we take a closer

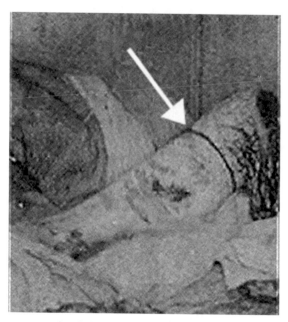

Cord tied around Kelly's right calf.

look at this dark line encircling Kelly's leg, we will see that
it has none of the smears or drips of blood which are evident
in the other cuts on her body. The circumferential mark on
closer inspection looks like string – a shoelace even. In hi-
resolution scans of the photograph you can actually see how
this string has a small bow protruding slightly from Kelly's
leg, and you can also see how it pinches in the skin of the
calf with its tightness. If this unusual mark was a cut, then
surely it would have been mentioned by the two doctors
who examined the body – Thomas Bond and George
Bagster Phillips – but no reference at all is made to the
'binding' around Kelly's leg. Even the small, superficial
marks and cuts on the body are mentioned, such as the 1-
inch-long incision in Kelly's right thumb, noted by Bond,

but in his report and post-mortem examination he makes no mention of the dark line encircling the victim's right calf. Here is Bond's initial report:

Notes of examination of the body of a woman found murdered & mutilated in Dorset Street.

Position of the body,
The body was lying naked in the middle of the bed, the shoulders flat, but the axis of the body inclined to the left side of the bed. The head was turned on the left cheek. The left arm was close to the body with the forearm flexed at a right angle & lying across the abdomen. The right arm was slightly abducted from the body & rested on the mattress, the elbow bent & the forearm supine with the fingers clenched. The legs were wide apart, the left thigh at right angles to the trunk & the right forming an obtuse angle with the pubes.
The whole of the surface of the abdomen & thighs was removed & the abdominal cavity emptied of its viscera. The breasts were cut off, the arms mutilated by several jagged wounds & the face hacked beyond recognition of the features. The tissues of the neck were severed all round down to the bone.
The viscera were found in various parts viz; the uterus & kidneys with one breast under the head, the other breast by the right foot, the liver between the feet, the intestines by the right side & the spleen by the left side of the body.
The flaps removed from the abdomen & thighs were on a table.
The bed clothing at the right corner was saturated with blood, & on the floor beneath was a pool of blood

*covering about 2 feet square. The wall by the right side of
the bed & in a line with the neck was marked by blood
which had struck it in a number of separate splashes.*

Postmortem Examination.
*The face was gashed in all directions. The nose, cheeks,
eyebrows & ears being partly removed. The lips were
blanched & cut by several oblique incisions running
obliquely down to the chin. There were also numerous
cuts extending irregularly across all the features.
The neck was cut through the skin & other tissues right
down to the vertebrae – the 5th and 6th being deeply
notched. The skin cuts in the front of the neck showed
distinct ecchymosis [bruising].
The air passage was cut through at the lower part of the
larynx through the cricoid cartilage.
Both breasts were removed by more or less circular
incisions, the muscles down to the ribs being attached to
the breasts. The intercostals [breathing muscles] between
the 4, 5 & 6 ribs were cut through & the contents of the
thorax visible through the openings.
The skin & tissues of the abdomen from the costal arch to
the pubes were removed in three large flaps. The right
thigh was denuded [stripped of fat] in front of the bone,
the flap of skin, including the external organs of
generation & part of the right buttock. The left thigh was
stripped of skin, fascia & muscles as far as the knee.
The left calf showed a long gash through the skin &
tissues to the deep muscles & reaching past the knee to 5
inches above the ankle.
[The reference to the circumferential mark/object on
Kelly's right calf would have been here in Dr Bond's
Post-mortem Examination report, but was omitted.]*

234

Both arms & forearms had extensive and jagged wounds. The right thumb showed a small superficial incision about 1 inch long, with extravasation [leakage] of blood in the skin & there were several abrasions on the back of the hand moreover, showing the same condition.

On opening the thorax it was found that the right lung was minimally adherent by old firm adhesions. The lower part of the lung was broken & torn away.

The left lung was intact; it was adherent at the apex & there were a few adhesions over the side. In the substances of the lung were several nodules of consolidation.

The Pericardium was open below & the Heart absent.

In the abdominal cavity was some partly digested food of fish & potatoes & similar food was found in the remains of the stomach attached to the intestines.

The allusion in this post-mortem report to the 'absent' heart has been interpreted ambiguously by criminologists and Ripperologists since 1987, when Dr Bond's long-lost report on Marie Jeanette Kelly was mailed anonymously back to Scotland Yard. Some believe that when Dr Bond stated that 'the pericardium was open … and the heart absent' he was merely saying that the heart was absent from the place where it would normally be situated – within the double-walled sac of the pericardium in Kelly's chest. Other Ripperologist have interpreted the statement in Bond's post-mortem as a reference to an organ theft by the Ripper, because Bond didn't say where the heart was in the room, yet he had mentioned the locations of all the other excised organs and body-parts. Surely Bond would not forget to mention where a major organ such as a heart was in Kelly's room?

On the day after the Miller's Court murder, shortly after the inquest, the coroner, Roderick Macdonald and

Dr George Bagster Phillips made an afternoon visit to 13 Miller's Court and sifted through the ashes of the fire grate. When Abberline and the other detectives had searched Kelly's room for clues, they had noticed the large amount of ash in the fire grate, and seeing a kettle hanging over the remains of the previous night's fire with its spout and handle melted off, they naturally assumed that Jack the Ripper had burnt several items of fabric to generate some light by which he could work. Amongst the ashes and carbonised vestiges of the fire, the remnants of women's clothing as well as a felt hat (possibly a woman's) were discovered. Macdonald and Phillips sifted through the residue of Kelly's fire with a sieve, apparently to see if they could detect any human remains. The newspaper reports of the day never stated if any parts of Kelly's body were ever found in the ashes of her grate, and neither did doctors Phillips and Macdonald ever comment on the outcome of their search. If the doctors really were looking for partial remains from Kelly's corpse, then we have to concede that something was missing from the victim's body.

Caroline Maxwell – who maintained she had seen and talked to Marie Jeanette Kelly as early as 8.30 on the morning of the murder, said the latter had vomited in the roadway on Dorset Street, but during the post-mortem on Kelly's body, doctors had noted the partly-digested remains of fish and potatoes in the stomach, which led Dr Bond to believe that the meal had been eaten at around 11pm, with death taking place between 1am and 2am in the morning.

The muscles of a person after death remain relaxed for about three hours before rigor mortis usually sets in. The muscles then remain stiff for a length of time that can vary between three and thirty-six hours, and after this stiffening they become relaxed again. However, determining the time of death of a person by rigor mortis is problematic, because the onset of the stiffening is dependent on the amount of work the muscles have done just prior to death. Most meals leave the stomach and enter the large intestine within three to four hours, and upon that salient fact, Bond based his belief that Kelly had met her death between 1am and 2am – long before Sarah Lewis and Elizabeth Prater heard the cry of 'Oh murder!' at around 4am, and around six hours before Caroline Maxwell's alleged meetings with Kelly in Dorset Street. The time of death does concur with the testimony of Mrs Cox, who said Kelly's room was in darkness when she passed it on her way home at 3am.

Roderick Macdonald, the coroner who conducted the unusually short (day-long) inquest into Kelly's death at Shoreditch Town Hall on 12 November, stated at the conclusion to the enquiry, "There is other evidence which I do not propose to call, for if we at once make public every fact brought forward in connection with this terrible murder, the end of justice might be retarded."

What was this 'other evidence' withheld from the inquest? Was something being suppressed? By the Statute de Coronatore, a coroner is legally bound to inquire the nature, character and size of every wound on a dead body, and to enter the same on his roll. It is the duty of the coroner to explain the effect of wounds and markings on a corpse. At the very beginning of the Kelly inquest, before the jury of twelve 'respectable gentlemen' was even sworn in, there was a jurisdictional dispute between the coroner, Macdonald and a juryman, who argued (quite rightly) that, as the body of Kelly had been found within Whitechapel, Wynne E Baxter – the coroner who had presided over the inquests of Ripper victims Nichols, Chapman and Stride – should have been directing the inquest. Macdonald was at fault when he argued in reply that, as Kelly's body had been brought to the mortuary within his district, he was fully entitled to preside over the inquest. Macdonald must have known full well that it was illegal to transport a corpse from one district to another, and yet he chided the dissenting juryman: "Do you think that we do not know what we are doing here, and that we do not know our own district? The jury are summoned in the ordinary way, and they have no business to object. If they persist in their objection I shall know how to deal with them. Does any juror persist in objecting?"

The rebuked juror replied, "We are summoned for the Shoreditch district. This affair happened in Spitalfields."

"It happened within my district!" Macdonald loudly insisted.

Another juror voiced his concern at the apparently illegal proceedings: "This is not my district. I come from Whitechapel, and Mr Baxter is my coroner."

His patience wearing thin at the protestations from the jury, Macdonald adamantly pushed on with proceedings, stating, "I am not going to discuss the subject with jurymen at all. If any juryman says he distinctly objects, let him say so. I may tell the jurymen that jurisdiction lies where the body lies, not where it was found, if there was doubt as to the district where the body was found."

The inquest was held with indecent haste, and at one point, when the jury expressed their wish to adjourn for a while, Macdonald waspishly told them they could rest until he resumed proceedings in 15 minutes. Inspector Abberline took the jury to the mortuary where Marie Jeanette lay in a coffin with a dirty grey sheet covering a body whose organs had been pieced together like some grotesque jigsaw puzzle and stitched up. Only Kelly's face was visible through the ash-grey shroud, and, according to the *Pall Mall Gazette*,

'The eyes were the only vestiges of humanity.' The rest of the victim's face was so scored and slashed, it was difficult to determine where the flesh began and the cuts ended. The jury was then taken to Miller's Court, to the little room where Marie Jeanette had died after having her right carotid artery severed by the Ripper's blade. Within a few hours the inquest was over. The verdict: wilful murder against some person or persons unknown.

As I mentioned earlier, shortly after the inquest had been held, the coroner and Dr George Bagster Phillips made their way to Kelly's room to sift through the ashes of the fire grate, but far more sinister visitors were also making their way to Miller's Court that day. Three MPs, two members of the Royal Irish Constabulary and a prominent high-ranking Post Office official visited the murder scene under a cloud of secrecy. What was the purpose of their visits to Miller's Court?

Later that day at 6pm, George Hutchinson visited Commercial Street Police Station in Spitalfields and told them the tall tale we analysed further back in this chapter. Hutchinson's yarn only added to the confusion surrounding the whereabouts of Kelly in the hours leading up to her baffling murder.

A week later, on 19 November 1888, the remains of Marie Jeanette were interred at the Roman Catholic Leytonstone Cemetery. Not a single family member or relative of the murdered woman attended the funeral, despite every attempt being made by The Royal Irish Constabulary to trace them in Ireland, and in Limerick in particular, but they failed to find anyone. The Ripper murders were hot news across the world with press coverage in every country, including Ireland, so Kelly's parents must have known their daughter had been murdered, but they never came forward. Marie Jeanette had told Joseph Barnett and others that she had six or seven brothers, (one of whom was a soldier serving in the Scots Guards, Henry 'Johnto' Kelly), and a relative on the London stage, but not a single person came forward to say they were the sister, brother, cousin, father or mother of Marie Jeanette, and yet she had been receiving letters from Ireland regularly at Miller's Court; John McCarthy and Joseph Barnett both attested to this fact.

What happened to the letters Kelly received? Perhaps the prominent Post Office official who visited Miller's Court with the two Royal Irish Constabulary officers had been summoned to Kelly's room to view a franking mark on one of these letters. The fact that the letter was not taken to the Post Office to be analysed suggests that it couldn't be moved from Miller's Court for some reason. Perhaps the envelope had been partly burned in some attempt by Kelly – or someone else – to destroy it. Modern forensic experts can use various chemicals, ultraviolet and infrared light as well as digital photography to reveal printed information and handwriting on burned or charred paper, but back in 1888, such science was in its infancy and simple magnifying glasses, lamps, basic photographic techniques and plain old human eyesight would have been used in an effort to decipher writing and postal franking marks on burnt envelopes and their contents.

Marie Jeanette was known to wear a maroon shawl most of the time, along with a spotless white apron over her skirt, but surely she would have made an effort to dress up a little for the day of the Lord Mayor's Show? According to upstairs neighbour Elizabeth Prater, Kelly had told her she wanted to go and see the show and hoped the weather would be fine. In the nightmarish photograph of Kelly's body, lying on her bed, we can plainly see a bundle of clothes folded on the mattress, to the right of her right calf. Maria Harvey, one of Kelly's few close friends, was a laundress who had been occasionally staying at 13 Miller's Court. At the inquest she stated that she had slept two nights with Kelly – the Monday and Tuesday nights before the murder. Harvey said that she had spent all of the afternoon of Thursday 8 November in her home at 3 New Court (off Dorset Street) with Kelly, and further stated that she had been in the room on the evening Joseph Barnett called, yet it is clear that Mrs Harvey is either mistaken or lying about this latter point, because Lizzie Albrook was undoubtedly the woman with Kelly when Barnett called at Miller's Court. Nevertheless, at the inquest, Mrs Harvey said she had left some clothes with Kelly. They were two men's shirts, a boy's shirt, a man's black overcoat, a black crepe bonnet with black strings, a child's white petticoat, and a pawn ticket for a shawl valued at two shillings. Only the coat was returned to Harvey after the murder, and it was mooted that this outer garment might have been the very same pilot coat that had been hanging over the broken window, serving as the ad hoc curtain which Thomas Bowyer first pushed aside to view the carnage. While this is a possibility, Harvey's coat might in reality have been the one folded up to the right of Marie Jeanette in the crime scene photograph of her lying on her deathbed. Why did Harvey leave her bonnet and clothes with Kelly anyway? Why couldn't she have taken them home to New Court, which was just 50 yards from Miller's Court?

We can conjecture that Mrs Harvey might have left the bonnet for Marie Jeanette to wear at the Lord Mayor's Show – even though it is known that Kelly had never been known to wear a hat. Unanswered questions galore are to be found in the life and death of Marie Jeanette. Here are just a few more of the many question marks hanging over the last Ripper murder victim. If Kelly was so afraid of the Ripper, why didn't she have the broken window in her room replaced? If the Ripper was not a client who had slept with Kelly and then killed her as she slept, then he must have been an intruder who had simply put his hand through the hole in the window pane to unlatch the door-lock. If this scenario is correct, then why didn't Kelly put a table against her door? Elizabeth Prater, Kelly's upstairs neighbour, pushed two tables against her door in order to feel safer, but Kelly did not do likewise. Why was this? Did Kelly believe the Ripper would never venture into the enclosed yard of Miller's Court? The Whitechapel Murderer had, after all, never killed indoors before.

How much did John McCarthy know about his murdered tenant and the mysterious individuals in Ireland that Marie Jeanette mentioned to Lizzie Albrook? Marie had told Lizzie she wished she had enough money to go back to "her people" in Ireland. Who were these elusive people? Were they Kelly's family? McCarthy gave the impression that he knew nothing about them; he merely admitted that letters addressed to Marie Jeanette came from "somewhere in Ireland" to Miller's Court, but McCarthy's wife Elizabeth later told journalists that Kelly's family were well-to-do and that Marie Jeanette was a scholar and an "artist of no mean degree". How did Mrs McCarthy know all of this?

After the murder of Marie Jeanette Kelly, the public began to lose faith in the police, and who could blame them? It seemed as if some invisible ghoul with a knife was prowling the East End at leisure, and the forces of law and order were powerless to stop him. Why wasn't the Government offering a reward to catch the Ripper? That was the question on everyone's lips. On Saturday 10 November, the Government had declared that any accomplice of Jack the Ripper would receive a pardon from Her Majesty if he gave himself up. This was seen by many East-Enders as a feeble ploy to make it look as if the Government was actually doing something to catch a killer who had largely confined his grisly work to the slum areas of the capital.

The funeral of Marie Jeanette Kelly took place on Monday 19 November. Kelly was not laid in a pauper's grave, thanks to a very charitable gesture by Henry Wilton, the verger of St Leonard's Church, who paid for the entire funeral service, as well as the impressive coffin of oak and elm with gleaming metal fittings. A simple inscription on the coffin plate read, 'Marie Jeanette Kelly, died 9 November 1888, aged 25 years.' Upon this coffin were two crowns made from artificial flowers and a cross made of violets. These floral tributes had been bought by the poor lodgers of Dorset Street who had known Marie Jeanette. Joseph Barnett and John McCarthy made sure the girl from Limerick was buried according to the Rites of the Roman Catholic Church. Barnett, Maria Harvey, a representative from McCarthy's Rents, and several of the women who testified at the inquest rode in the two mourning coaches behind the hearse that slowly drew towards Marie Jeanette's final resting place. The funeral procession had been lined by solemn men, women and children. Men removed their hats, and women wept openly as the hearse went by with its coffin fully displayed for all to see. At St Patrick's Roman Catholic Cemetery, Leytonstone, the burial service was conducted by the Reverend Father Columbant. He blessed the grave and coffin, raising the swinging censer of sweet-smelling incense to his eye level. As the coffin was lowered into the cold damp earth, Father Columbant sprinkled it with holy water as Joseph Barnett, Maria Harvey and several women from Dorset Street knelt at the graveside.

In the aftermath of the Kelly murder, a widespread panic erupted in the East End and spread to the rest of the capital. Now the fiend was striking indoors. Who would be the Ripper's next victim? Where would he strike next? The streets of Whitechapel and Spitalfields were deserted after nightfall because of the terror hanging in the air; a fear spread by sensational radical newspapers such as the *Star*, which had a record circulation of 298,000 copies for 9 November 1888 – the day Kelly's body was discovered. The *Star* headlines announced that day:

ANOTHER CRIME BY THE MURDER-MANIAC
MORE REVOLTING THAN EVER
THIS DEMONIACAL DEED DONE IN A HOUSE

A Woman is found in a house in Dorset-street
Decapitated and with Her Body Mutilated in a Manner
that Passes Description.

At a quarter to eleven this morning a woman was found murdered, with her head nearly cut off, in a room in a house in McCarthy's-court [sic], a turning out of Dorset Street – the street in which the lodging-house is situated where the Hanbury-street victim slept occasionally. Whitechapel is seething with excitement. Cordons of police are drawn up at all the entrances to Dorset Street, and no one is allowed to enter it. A Star man went to Commercial-street Police station to learn some further particulars, but was politely – but firmly – referred to Scotland-yard.

Such sensationalist newspaper copy did little to ease the nervous tension of London's denizens, and the following incident caused a short-lived Ripper scare. At 7.30 on the Wednesday morning of 21 November 1888, 40-year-old Annie Farmer, a prostitute who had separated from her husband for some time, 'picked up' a man in a suit (who she described as "shabby genteel") and took him to Satchell's Lodging House in George Street, Spitalfields. The man paid eight pence for a double bed to share with Annie, but at 9.30am, her screams of "Murder!" pierced the air, and she was seen by startled witnesses clutching at her throat, which had sustained a number of minor grazes from a knife. Annie's client darted out of the lodging house while Annie, wearing only a short knitted petticoat, and her breasts exposed for everyone to see, shouted "Darkie! Darkie!" – the nickname of the black lodging house watchman. To William Sullivan, a lodger at the doss-house, she pointed at the doorway leading to the street and cried out: "A man has cut my throat! Follow him!" Sullivan went outside but could see nothing of the assailant, but he did ask a coke man in the street named Frank Ruffell if he had seen the knifeman. Ruffell said a man had rushed past him moments before, panting, with a distressed expression. The stranger had blood on his mouth and a scratch, and gesturing towards the injury to his mouth he had said, "Look at what she has done!" and "What a cow!" before hurrying off towards Thrawl Street.

A *Star* newspaper reporter interviewed Ruffell, who described the assailant as a respectably-dressed man in his thirties; about 5 feet 4 inches tall with a red fresh-looking face and a fair moustache He wore a hard felt hat and a black diagonal suit. The *Star* thought this description of

Annie Farmer's attacker tallied well with the description of the blotchy-faced man Mary Ann Cox had seen with Marie Jeanette Kelly in Miller's Court. The attack on Farmer was magnified into a Ripper attack by rumours which flew around Whitechapel and beyond. The police later came to the conclusion that Annie had inflicted the wounds upon her own neck with a blunt knife after her client had discovered that she was robbing him. She had then accused him of being Jack the Ripper whilst hiding the coins she had stolen from him in her mouth. It had all been a clever distraction from the real crime that had taken place that morning – robbery.

Twelve days after the funeral of Marie Jeanette Kelly, on 1 December 1888, Sir Charles Warren issued a personal message of gratitude to the Metropolitan Police Force:

> *Sir C. Warren having resigned the office of Commissioner of Police of the Metropolis, which he has held since April, 1886, desires to convey to the members of the force his hearty appreciation of their efforts to do their duty during a time of unexampled difficulty, and in bidding them farewell, Sir Charles Warren wishes to express his earnest thanks to all those members of the force who, in loyally serving their country, have given him so much support and assistance in carrying out the re-organization entrusted to him.*

Is it not strange how Warren thanked his detectives and police constables for 'loyally serving their country' when he himself resigned from his highly important duties at the height of the Ripper murders on the very eve of the most violent atrocity committed by the killer? On 4 April 1889, Warren left the country to take up his command in

Singapore, where he had been appointed General Officer Commanding in the Straits Settlements. He left his wife and four children behind at 44 St George's Road, SW London, and arrived at Singapore on Monday, 6 May 1889. There he remained for five years, in a far-flung corner of the British Empire, over six thousand miles away from London and the aftermath of the mysterious and unsolved Whitechapel Murders. Warren was a prominent Freemason, and from 1886 to 1888 he had been active masonically, but there is no evidence of Warren using his Masonic connections to instigate a cover-up to protect Jack the Ripper. In fact, Warren's professional life took precedence over his Masonic duties during the time he was Chief Commissioner. In November 1887, at a Masonic meeting of the Quatuor Coronati Lodge No 2076 EC, held at Freemasons' Hall, London, Warren announced: "I have had a good many difficulties to contend with in the last few days, and have been a good deal harassed on your behalf, in securing the safety of the Metropolis. In doing this I have not had the time to turn my attention to the subject of this lodge and am not, therefore, enabled to reply in a manner suitable for the occasion ... At the present moment, working at a critical time in your history, I am endeavouring to keep peace in the Metropolis, but my position, you must remember, is precarious, for as I have been twice turned out and recalled by a paternal government, so may I probably be turned out again. I assure you as a Mason that I will do my duty and ask no man's favours."

The post of Chief Commissioner of the Metropolitan Police vacated by Warren was taken up by James Monro, a position the latter would hold for only 18 months before suddenly resigning on 12 June 1890. This was the shortest term ever served by a Commissioner in the history of the

Met. Monro became a missionary in 1890 and founded the Abode of Mercy medical mission at Ranaghat, West Bengal. The newspapers gave the impression that Monro had resigned as Chief Commissioner because of clashes with the Home Secretary Henry Matthews, but in 1903, 13 years after his controversial resignation, Monro broke his silence, and stated, rather enigmatically, that he had not resigned because of squabbles with the Home Secretary, but because he had refused to do 'something' which he considered to be wrong. In his 18 months as Chief Commissioner of the Metropolitan Police, James Monro made no breakthroughs in the search for Jack the Ripper, nor did his successor, Sir Edward Bradford, Chief Commissioner from 1890 to 1903. Colonel Bradford had a military background, just like Warren, and during his years in India he had been the General Superintendent of the secret police organisation known as the Thuggee and Dacoit Department. In 1887, Bradford had also held a position as Secretary of the Political and Secret Department of the India Office.

The winter of 1889 soon arrived, and still the police were no nearer to catching the Ripper. Walter Dew tells us in his memoirs just how maddeningly intangible and mysterious the phantom-like killer was: 'Huge numbers of police, both from the uniformed and plain clothes branches, were on patrol from dusk till dawn. Yet he must have passed through the ring of watchers, not once but twice. Small wonder that the superstitious-minded began to whisper that such an escape was possible only to a supernatural being. With luck – and the killer must have had the devil's own luck – a man of his undoubted cunning always had slightly more than even money chance of getting away.'

The long hard winter that ushered in 1889 soon wore down the vigilance patrols, and forced them to disband. The number of plain-clothed policemen in Whitechapel and Spitalfields also dwindled because of two factors, a lack of outrages being committed in the East End, and the cost of the special plain clothes police patrols. Sir Richard Pennefather, Crown-appointed Receiver-General – the chief financial officer of the Metropolitan Police – was very concerned by the substantial expense of Monro's undercover police operation, but not long after the patrols were ended, there was another false alarm, and they were started up again.

This second Ripper scare took place in July 1889 when the body of a 40-year-old prostitute named Alice McKenzie was found at 12.50am by a policeman on the beat in Castle Alley, Whitechapel. When PC Walter Andrews discovered the body, blood was still running from a slashed throat into the gutter. The skirts of the woman had been rolled up, exposing a series of abdominal wounds, though none as severe as the deep wounds inflicted by the Ripper. Jack had a tendency to cut the throats of his victims with such ferocity, the vertebrae were notched by the blade, but the cut to Alice's throat had not even divided the air passages, and there were two jagged wounds on the left side of the neck, each no longer than four inches. The majority of the wounds to Alice's abdomen were superficial scratches compared with the trademark deep zig-zag cuts the Whitechapel Murderer made when he opened up the abdominal cavity. The knife was, in the opinion of Dr Bagster Phillips, smaller than the Ripper's weapon. No organs had been removed and death had resulted from severance of the left carotid artery.

Dr Phillips opined that the Alice McKenzie killing could not be attributed to the Ripper. Dr Thomas Bond disagreed with this opinion, but he did not inspect

McKenzie's body until the day after the post-mortem, when decomposition had altered the features of the wounds. Robert Anderson did not share Bond's views; he believed McKenzie had not been a victim of the Whitechapel Murderer. Chief Commissioner Monro, however, thought McKenzie's murder was the work of Jack, and lost no time requesting allowances for additional plain-clothed officers who were to be drafted in to Whitechapel. The killer of Alice McKenzie was never brought to justice, despite Monro's extra police presence, and the perpetrators of two other killings in the East End after the McKenzie murder also got away scot-free.

On Tuesday 10 September 1889, PC William Pennett was on his beat in the parish of St George's-in-the East, when he came across the torso of a woman, minus head and legs, under a railway arch in Pinchin Street, about 270 yards from the spot in Berner Street where Elizabeth Stride had been murdered almost a year before. Although the hands of the unknown woman showed no signs of manual labour, the police speculated that she had been a factory worker. There was no evidence of the murder being committed where the torso was found, or in the immediate locality, and, according to Dr Charles Hibbert, the murder had been committed 24 hours prior to the discovery of the body. Dr Bagster Phillips' assistant, Mr Clark, disagreed, and believed the unidentified woman had met her death 48 hours before her torso was found, which would mean that the murder had taken place on 8 September, the anniversary of Annie Chapman's death at the hands of the Ripper, which was something of a black coincidence. The mutilated abdomen of the torso was eerily reminiscent of the Ripper's handiwork, but the crime was ultimately deemed to be the work of some other murderer, and on this occasion, James

Monro agreed with the verdict.

Around the time of the Alice McKenzie murder, Inspector Henry Moore – described by the *Pall Mall Gazette* as a well-dressed gentleman of athletic build – took over from Inspector Abberline in the ongoing investigation into the Whitechapel Murders. There was to be one more Ripper-like murder committed in the East End, and this was the killing of 31-year-old prostitute Frances Coles, who was found barely alive at 2.15am on Friday, 13 February 1891, beneath a railway arch at Swallow Gardens, a short dimly-lit alleyway that led from Chambers Street to Rosemary Lane (today's Royal Mint Street). PC Ernest Thompson lit his bull's eye lantern, trained its beam on the woman lying on the ground, and immediately saw that her throat had been cut, with blood flowing copiously from the wound. As he took in this horrific sight, he saw that the victim's eyes were open, and she was alive, but only just. Thompson heard footsteps running off in the darkness towards Rosemary Lane, but instead of chasing the possible attacker, he decided to stay with the victim.

Young Constable Thompson, who had been in the force less than two months, blew hard on his whistle to summon help. Sadly, the victim, who was later identified as Frances Coles, died on the stretcher on the way to hospital. Dr Phillips examined the wounds on the back of her head and it was deduced that these had been caused by the murderer throwing Frances to the ground before cutting her throat with a blunt knife as she lay on the pavement. Unlike four of the Ripper victims, there were no abdominal mutilations, and, furthermore, the victim's clothes had not been disarranged. Dr Phillips believed that Jack the Ripper had not killed Coles.

For a while, an acquaintance of the deceased, merchant

251

seaman James Thomas Sadler, was believed to be the culprit, and he was charged with the murder of Frances Coles on 16 February 1891, at Thames Magistrates' Court. A few detectives believed Sadler was the Ripper, but all their hopes were ultimately dashed when Sadler was not only found not guilty of murdering Coles, but enquiries into his whereabouts during the Ripper's reign of terror established that he had been at sea from 17 August 1888 until 1 October of that year.

There is a sad footnote to the murder of Frances Coles. PC Ernest Thompson, the policeman who came to her aid, was racked with guilt for the remainder of his life because he had not gone after Coles's killer that morning. He often tormented himself, brooding on that missed opportunity. He believed that the grim incident was some type of sinister omen pertaining to his own fate, and his dark forebodings became a reality when Thompson was stabbed to death in 1900, as he interceded in a brawl at a coffee stall on Commercial Road.

As previously mentioned, in March 1889, Abberline left the Whitechapel Murders investigation, and charge of the case was taken on by Inspector Henry Moore. Abberline left to investigate the Cleveland Street Scandal, which I shall look at in the last chapter. In July 1889, the heavily bloodstained room in which Marie Jeanette Kelly had been murdered, was re-let to a new tenant by landlord Jack McCarthy. By 1892, the Whitechapel Murders Case was officially closed, and Abberline retired that same year.

Abberline, a man with a thorough knowledge of the East End and its underworld, believed that the Ripper was not to be found in the lower classes. His network of informers in Whitechapel and Spitalfields could tell him nothing about Jack; he didn't seem to be a local man at all. In May, 1892,

Abberline stated in *Cassells Saturday Journal* that, in his opinion, Marie Jeanette Kelly had been the final victim of the Ripper, and in 1903, he told the *Pall Mall Gazette*:

> *Scotland Yard is really no wiser on the subject [of Jack the Ripper] than it was fifteen years ago. It is simple nonsense to talk of the police having proof that the man is dead. I am, and always have been, in the closest touch with Scotland Yard, and it would have been next to impossible for me not to have known about it. Besides, the authorities would have been only too glad to make an end out of such a mystery, if only for their own credit.*

So, in 1892, the hunt for Jack the Ripper ended unsuccessfully, but the mysterious killer was never forgotten, and his name and heinous crimes became the stuff of legend. Today, the world still wants to know the identity of the mysterious fascinating Victorian killer, and theorists of every generation are obsessed with unmasking him, but up to now, they have all failed. The theory I will present in the final chapter will be one that has never been proposed before. I would be extremely arrogant and unrealistic if I were to claim that this theory was unquestionably the final solution to the Whitechapel Murders mystery, but all the same, I believe that the theory has a lot going for it, and may help to sweep away the Red Herring League of usual Ripper suspects that has led us away from the truth for over a hundred years.

9

NATION ON A KNIFE-EDGE

I believe that the key to the identity and motives of Jack the Ripper lies in the political backdrop to his crimes, and so it is necessary for the reader to assimilate the following outline of the turbulent historical events that led to the climate of extreme radicalism in 1888.

Across the globe, there have been revolutions and rebellions since the beginning of recorded history, from the Ionian Revolts of 499-493 BC, to the Bolshevik Revolution of 1917. Britain has not experienced a violent revolution since the Civil Wars of 1642-1651, but there have been close calls. The Bastille prison fell in July 1789, a pivotal event in European history, for it marked the beginning of the French Revolution – a violent overthrowing by the masses of an absolute monarchy, as well as the aristocracy and clergy, in a country just 21 miles from England's shores. The shockwaves of the French Revolution reverberated throughout most countries in Europe, including Britain. Some in the higher echelons of English society feared an English Revolution would soon be inspired by the new democratic French society. The French revolutionaries had adopted the Declaration of the Rights of Man, a document modelled on the American Declaration of Independence, which consisted of a preamble and 17 articles stating such things as, 'Men are born and remain free and equal in rights. Social distinctions can be founded only on the common utility,' and 'The principle of any sovereignty resides essentially in the Nation. No body, no individual can exert authority which does not emanate expressly from it.' The noble tripartite motto of the new Republic was 'Liberty, Equality, Brotherhood (Fraternity)' and many people of the working and middle classes in Britain admired their continental counterparts and regarded their ideals as a workable template for change in class-ridden Britain.

Some thought the French Revolution was reminiscent of England's Glorious Revolution of 1688. Of course, many of these fans of Robespierre were labelled 'radicals' by the authorities in Britain, and on 25 January 1792, a group of these advocates of outright democracy founded the London Correspondent Society, which was concerned with Parliamentary reform and giving working class people a greater platform to have their say. The members of the London Correspondent Society also opposed England's war with France, which lasted from 1793 to 1802, and this naturally worried the Establishment. The society was investigated by spies of the British Secret Service, who infiltrated their ranks with ease. Espionage activities had been stepped up since the French Revolution. To British minds, the French could simply not be trusted, especially as the French revolutionaries had vowed, in 1792, to help the people of other European countries to overthrow their own monarchies.

In 1767 Lord Chatham had coordinated the theft of the French military plans for an invasion of England via the south coast. Those plans had been drawn up with the assistance of one Colonel Grant, of Blairfindy, a Scotsman employed by the French as a spy. Jacobite Grant had provided the French with elaborate details for landing four thousand troops at vulnerable locations on the south coast of England. Fortunately, Grant was not a realistic man, and he told the French that just four thousand grenadiers could overcome the entire militia of England and march in two columns to take London!

In October 1793 two main representatives of the London Correspondent Society, Joseph Gerrald and Maurice Maragot, were arrested, found guilty of sedition, and promptly sentenced to 14 years' transportation. The remaining members of the radical society went underground for a while before joining other reformist groups to print seditious pamphlets and periodicals. British culture and the traditional way of life were being challenged on all sides, and for a while it looked as if anarchy was set to rear its ugly head.

Mary Wollstonecraft, the writer, feminist and philosopher, had published *A Vindication of the Rights of Men* in 1790, in which she advocated republicanism and attacked the aristocracy, and in 1792, Thomas Paine published *The Rights of Man*, a work so pro-revolutionary, the author was forced to flee to France from England and was tried *in absentia* as a traitor. The widespread emergence of radicalism in Britain led to the Government resorting to all kinds of Draconian measures to prevent Republican ideas from taking hold of the minds of the masses, and so, in May 1794, William Pitt's Government declared war on the radicals, accusing them all of treason.

The 1794 Treason Trials took place solely to cripple British radicalism, and although the punishment for High Treason was to have the culprit hanged (in such a way so that death was not immediate) and to have his bowels drawn out before his eyes and burnt, followed by castration, this barbaric penalty was never enacted, but many freethinkers who were found guilty during the trials were instead transported.

In October of the following year, King George III was on his way to open Parliament when his coach was attacked by

256

crowds of people who threw stones, refuse and other missiles at it as they cried out, "Peace!", demanding a cessation of the war with France. There were also chants of "Bread!" in protest at the high price of bread due to a series of bad harvests. In response to this, Parliament, believing a revolution was imminent, rushed through two controversial 'gagging acts': the Seditious Meetings Act and the Treasonable Practices Act, which effectively prohibited public meetings. Freedom of Speech had once again been stifled in a so-called democratic country, but the British Crown and the land-owning classes remained alarmed by the power of popular agitation and the prospect of a revolution.

On 21 February 1803, Edward Marcus Despard, an Irish-born British colonel, was found guilty, along with six co-conspirators, of High Treason. Government informers had accused Despard of plotting to assassinate King George III and also conspiring to seize the Tower of London and the Bank of England. The evidence against Despard was very slight, and Lord Nelson himself appeared at the trial as a character witness for Despard, but to no avail. The colonel and his six fellow conspirators were sentenced to be hanged, drawn and quartered. Fears of a public outrage at the barbaric sentence resulted in the 'commutation' of punishment to a hanging and beheading instead.

In November and December of 1816, a number of incendiary mass-meetings of pro-radicals took place at Spa Fields, Islington, Greater London. Revolutionary Arthur Thistlewood, referred to by police spies as "a very dangerous character" was a member of the Society of Spencean Philanthropists, which was formed by the admirers of the radical democrat Thomas Spence, an advocate of the common ownership of land. Although the meetings at Spa Fields were peaceful, Thistlewood and several other Spenceans eventually encouraged rioting, and at the second meeting, a small body of protesters went to the Tower of London, intending to storm the fortress. A gun shop was looted at one point during the march, and when protesters reached the Tower, they were met by guards and forced to disperse. John Castle, a former member of the Spenceans who had been coerced into becoming a spy for the Home Office because of his criminal record, reported on the clandestine activities of the pro-revolutionary society, but ironically, his testimony was deemed to be unreliable because of his criminal record. All the same, it was known that the Spenceans intended to overthrow the Government by seizing the Army arsenal at the Tower of London, before taking control of the Bank of England's vaults. Thistlewood and other conspirators were charged with High Treason but subsequently acquitted. However, as we shall soon see, the Establishment had not seen the last of Thistlewood.

Open-air meetings during this politically unstable period were viewed as potential revolution-starters, and on 16 August 1819 there was a peaceful rally for Parliamentary reform and a repeal of the Corn Laws at St Peter's Field, Manchester. Some 63,000 pro-democracy reformers, mostly impoverished workers and their families, were charged by armed cavalry after the authorities feared the mass meeting would end in a riot. Eleven people were killed, and 600 (including women and children) were severely injured. During the massacre, the Manchester and Salford Yeomanry also injured a mother and killed her two-year-old child, William Fildes, as they made their way to St Peter's Field. This brutal dispersal of the crowds of peaceful demonstrators was known for evermore as the Peterloo Massacre – a sarcastic comparison to Waterloo.

The Government passed legislation to prevent any

future 'disturbances' of the type that had taken place at St Peter's Fields. The Six Acts prohibited any meetings for radical reform, and anyone who defied the acts would be guilty of 'an overt act of treasonable conspiracy'. Five months after the horrendous attack on the peaceful protesters at Manchester, King George III died, aged 82, on 29 January 1820. A band of 27 radical extremist conspirators, many of them angered by the Peterloo Massacre and the passing of the Six Acts, saw the monarch's death as an opportunity to cause a massive uprising against the Government. One of the dominant members of this group of revolutionaries was none other than Arthur Thistlewood of the Spa Field Riots. The plan was to invade a Cabinet dinner at the home of Lord Harrowby with pistols and grenades. One of the conspirators, former butcher turned coffee-house keeper, James Ings, had grisly plans to decapitate each member of the Cabinet so he could exhibit their heads on spikes at Westminster Bridge.

The headquarters of the conspirators was a hayloft in a small house on Cato Street, near London's Edgware Road, where plans were drawn up in detail to remove the Cabinet and declare a People's Parliament, but unfortunately for the plotters, a Home Office spy named George Edwards, acting as an agent provocateur, reported back to the authorities, informing them that Thistlewood and his cohorts intended to carry out his plan for mass murder. The Home Office decided to pounce on the conspirators, and on 23 February 1820, a dozen Bow Street Runners, a magistrate, and a police spy, stormed the Cato Street loft and in the resulting fracas, Thistlewood killed a policeman with a sword, before escaping through a back window with three other conspirators, but they were all arrested a few days later. Arthur Thistlewood and four of the other conspirators were

259

hanged at Newgate for the crime of High Treason. Five others involved in the conspiracy were transported for life.

The Government used the Cato Street Conspiracy as an example to justify the necessity for the Six Acts, but in the House of Commons, Matthew Wood revealed that he had evidence which proved that Lord Liverpool's Government had in fact orchestrated the Cato Street Conspiracy by printing an advertisement in the *New Times* detailing the very time and place of the Cabinet dinner. Then the Government had used their spy, George Edwards, to incite the conspirators to carry out the plans to massacre the Cabinet. This surely was a case of entrapment? Furthermore, Matthew Wood told the House that the Government wanted to smear the campaign for Parliamentary reform.

From 1830 to 1832, England was undoubtedly close to a full-scale revolution. Political unions were being formed in towns and cities throughout the land, and Parliamentary reform was reaching unprecedented heights. The Tory Government, led by the Duke of Wellington, was forced to resign; he was victorious at Waterloo, but as a politician he was a man to repress reform and his popularity, whilst in office, sank as a result. In the autumn of 1830, Countess Dorothea Lieven, the wife of Prince Khristofor Andreyevich Lieven, Russian ambassador to London, wrote to her brother Alexander, about the threat of revolution hanging in the air throughout England:

> *We, too, in England, dear Alexander, are just on the brink of a revolution. For the last two days agitation reigns in London. It began to show itself on the day of the opening of Parliament. The Duke of Wellington's peremptory declaration against any sort of reform has*

dissatisfied the upper classes, aroused fear in the middle class, and exasperated the populace. Disturbances have taken place and troops have been brought up to London. In view, moreover, of the threatening attitude assumed by the Government, it was asserted that the occasion of the King and Queen's visit to the City tonight was to be taken to make a popular demonstration, of which the object was to assassinate the Duke of Wellington and to create confusion and provoke disorder. Ministers having been informed of these intentions, persuaded their Majesties to give up their visit to the City, thereby causing general consternation and nervous anxiety. All yesterday was passed in comings and goings, and the public of all classes never for an instant doubted that the Ministry would be dismissed forthwith, on the ground that the King could not submit to be made the victim of the Duke of Wellington's unpopularity. Matters have turned out quite otherwise. I dined last night with the King and all his ministers. He treated them with greater cordiality and attention than ever. The Duke, for most of his part, told me that he was quite right in his course, that as for the disorders of the mob he knew how to repress them, and that as for reform it was with it as it had been with the Catholic Question, that it could not be passed without him, and that he would have none of it, therefore it would not pass at all. I have never seen anyone take a firmer and more confident attitude than the Duke. Meanwhile it is generally believed that there will be riots; but precautions have been taken, and 10,000 troops, who can be relied on, are quartered in London. Moreover, the London parishes have spontaneously offered to provide their own special constables and to answer for the peace of their respective

divisions. Permission has been accorded to them, but no
arms are to be issued to them.
This is the exact state of things at the moment of my
writing to you.

The Reform Act of 1832 introduced wide-ranging changes
into the United Kingdom's electoral system. In 1831, just
214,000 men in England and Wales were entitled to vote.
The combined population of the two countries at that time
was eight million, so only three per cent of the people were
voting in Parliamentary elections. The large industrial cities
such as Birmingham, Leeds and Manchester did not possess
an MP between them, whereas the so-called 'Rotten
Boroughs' in the south of England were sending two MPs to
Westminster. The Reform Act of 1832 reapportioned
representation in Parliament for the under-represented
industrial cities of England, especially the northern ones.
Those on the lower rungs of the country's social and
economic ladder were at last given the power of the vote.
The Reform Act was nothing short of revolutionary, but it
still did little to settle the nerves of the Establishment, who
remained worried about the widespread unrest and the
possibility of a working-class uprising. In the words of Lord
Grey, Prime Minister from 1830 to 1834, the 1832 Reform
Act was passed to "prevent the necessity of revolution".

The transference of power to people who ordinarily had
been unable to vote was compared to the transference of
power that had been achieved by bloody means over in
France.

The Factory Act of 1833 was designed to protect the
working-class children of England against exploitation and
oppression. Orders in Council for November 1831 had made
it illegal – throughout the British Empire – to make a black

slave of any age work throughout the night, and for any black child slave to work more than nine hours – and yet Michael Sadler MP, the Derbyshire-born reformer, campaigned unsuccessfully to limit the hours of labour for children in Britain to ten hours a day. At that time, it was legal to allow a girl of six to crawl on all fours through the dirt and mud of a mine gallery as she dragged a truck full of coal. The law also permitted sleep-deprived nine-year-olds in factories to work for 39 hours at a stretch. Most of the child workforce for the factories was made up of orphans, marshalled from the poorhouses of England. The orphaned children were 'recruited' because they would have no parents raising objections to the dangerous and highly unhealthy conditions the youngsters would be working in. On Sunday, the owners of the factories and mills would go to church, and their machines were stopped. Even then, the pre-teen workers still had to clean the machines, and that took all day, before they started work in the early hours of Monday morning, with shifts that typically lasted between 13 and 16 hours. In the so-called 'Rush Seasons' the children worked for 24 hours with a half-hour break for dinner.

Most factories and mills that resorted to this disgraceful child-labour had a man known as the 'Overseer' in charge, and it was his duty to strike any child flagging in his work with a strap. Each morning, sleep-starved girls were dragged from their beds by their hair to the machines by the Overseer, and this brute sometimes broke the skull of a child with a wooden roller pin when he or she became drowsy. The young workers were treated like hard-labour convicts when they were 'escorted' from the factory or mill to their bothies (huts), which usually had barred windows. They were then locked in for the night. The Factory Act came into force on 29 August 1833. From then on, for children under the age of

13, the hours of labour were limited to 48 per week, and 9 hours per day. Youths under the age of 18 were not allowed to work for more than 12 hours a day, or 69 hours per week. In all mills except silk mills, the employment of children under the age of 9 was prohibited.

Two more Reform Acts followed in 1867 and 1884, but the menace of insurrection by the working classes did anything but go away. In 1848, one of the world's most influential political documents was published – *The Manifesto of the Communist Party* by Karl Marx and Friedrich Engels. The Manifesto called for the abolition of private property, and for the workers of the world to unite, revolt and overthrow the Bourgeoisie to bring about a classless, stateless society. In 1849, whilst in Cologne, writing for *The New Rhenish Newspaper*, Marx was charged with inciting an armed rebellion, and was therefore forced to flee to Paris, where he expected a Socialist revolution to occur at any time. However, within weeks, the French police forced Marx to leave the country, and he came to settle in London, where he lived until his death, aged 64, in 1883. The Father of Communism was dead, but Marx's ideas and ideals lived on with a vengeance throughout Europe and took on flesh.

By the 1880s, the decade in which the Whitechapel Murders took place, revolution was once again in the air. These were very troubled times for the British Government. Britain was the richest nation on earth, and her Empire, which stretched across the globe from Canada to Australia, was romantically described as the 'Empire on which the sun never set'. Colvin R de Silva, one of the founders of the first Marxist party in Sri Lanka, later quipped that the sun never sets on the British Empire, "because God does not trust the British in the dark." Despite the British Empire being the largest empire in the history of the world in the 1880s, in the capital of England, at the very heart of the Empire, Queen Victoria's poverty-stricken subjects were dropping dead of starvation. On 7 November 1888, the *Star* newspaper reported one such death in its letters column:

Dear Sir,

Last week a poorly-dressed but respectable old man, cleanly in appearance and with well-blacked shoes, staggered into the People's Palace dying of starvation. He was supplied with food, which his famished stomach was unable to retain, and on being removed to the London Hospital he died in about an hour. The coroner returned a verdict of 'Death from starvation'.

W. Knight Chaplin,
Pastor,
Poplar and Bromley Tabernacle,
Brunswick Road
East London.

Just a short carriage trot from Buckingham Palace, many homeless subjects of Her Majesty began their mornings being rudely awakened from their alfresco slumbers by a policeman in Hyde Park, or on the Thames Embankment, and over in nearby Trafalgar Square, it was as common for the police to move on the abject poor as they swilled their faces in their communal 'toilets' – the Square's fountain pools. In a so-called Christian society, hundreds of thousands of people, many of them children, went without food and dropped dead in the streets in Victorian times. Under the reign of Queen Victoria, the Empress of India (from 1877) it has been estimated that between 12 and 29 million Indians died from famine. Queen Victoria – who was, of course, the Queen of the United Kingdom and Ireland – once said, in 1867, that the Irish had never "become reconciled to English rule, which they hate – so different from the Scots, who are so loyal. We shall have to hang some, and it ought to have been done before."

Between 1845 and 1850, over a million Irish people starved to death, as massive cargoes of food and drink were shipped from Ireland at gunpoint to England. Half a million Irish people were evicted from their homes during this so-called 'potato-bight' and a million and a half more emigrated to America, Australia and Britain. In 1997, British Prime Minister Tony Blair attempted to heal this great wound in Anglo-Irish history by apologising for the actions of the Governments of Sir Robert Peel and Lord Russell, stating: "Those who governed in London at the time failed their people through standing by while a crop failure turned into a massive human tragedy. We must not forget such a dreadful event."

And what of the poor of England in the realm of Queen Victoria? In 1851, as the capital of England and the 'first city in the world' was being trumpeted by the Great Exhibition as the premiere world-leading metropolis of industrial triumphs, the English social researcher, journalist, playwright and advocate of reform, Henry Mayhew, drew attention to the underbelly of London in his three-volume collection of investigative research of the poor and labouring classes. His *London Labour* and *London Poor* make both entertaining and grim reading, and in the preface, Mayhew says of his landmark work:

My earnest hope is that the book may serve to give the rich a more intimate knowledge of the sufferings, and the

frequent heroism under those sufferings, of the poor –
that it may teach those who are beyond temptation to
look with charity on the frailties of their less fortunate
brethren – and cause those who are in 'high places' and
those of whom much is expected, to bestir themselves to
improve the condition of a class of people whose misery,
ignorance and vice, amidst all the immense wealth and
great knowledge of 'the first city in the world' is, to say
the very least, a national disgrace to us.

This national disgrace was brushed under the carpet by those in 'high places'. The Bastilles of the Poor – the dreaded Workhouses – continued to swallow up entire families of destitute souls, and many of those unlucky enough to enter these battlements of hard labour often emerged only to be lowered into a pauper's grave. The East End of London, was, as Individualist Anarchist John Henry Mackay (1864-1933), called it, "The Hell of poverty". The American Socialist novelist Jack London concurred in his classic, *The People of the Abyss*, a first-hand study of poverty in Edwardian London, written during his time among the 500,000 of the East End's poor. Jack London paints some very disturbing word-scenes in his book, especially those concerning children:

Fresh in my mind is the picture of a boy in the dock of
an East End police court. His head was barely visible
above the railing. He was being proved guilty of stealing
two shillings from a woman, which he had spent, not for
candy and cakes and a good time, but for food.
"Why didn't you ask the woman for food?" the
magistrate demanded, in a hurt sort of tone. "She would
surely have given you something to eat."

267

*"If I'd asked 'er I'd a got locked up for begging," was
the boy's reply.
The magistrate knitted his brows and accepted the
rebuke. Nobody knew the boy, nor his father or mother.
He was without beginning or antecedent, a waif, a stray,
a young cub seeking his food in the jungle of empire,
preying on the weak and being preyed upon by the strong.*

That was in 1902, but life was even tougher 14 years further
back in time, in 1888. The constituency of Whitechapel
then had a population of 71,314, yet the electorate was just
6,110. The population of St George's in the East was 49,382
but only 4,317 people were allowed to vote there.
Parliamentary representation was denied to many.

At a Salvation Army shelter in Burne Street,
Westminster, the homeless were forced to sleep in coffin-
beds, which, as their name implies, were simply oblong
wooden coffin-shaped boxes (minus the lid of course) with
a pillow and sheet inside. The same coffin-beds were used
in a Salvation Army shelter at 212 Hanbury Street – the very
same Whitechapel street where Annie Chapman met her
death at the hands of the Ripper. This shelter was opened
in 1884 as a refuge for young women who had been forced
to resort to prostitution because of poverty. A few were
'saved' from their life of depravity. This often entailed
falling prone on the floor, and rising, redeemed, as a
penitent 'Magdalene'. These conversions took place against
a strict regime at the Hanbury Street shelter. The women
had to be in their coffin-beds by 9pm, and after rising at
6am, everyone had to vacate the shelter by eight. In the
shelter's dormitory there was a rather morbid religious
slogan painted in huge letters across the walls which asked:
ARE YOU READY TO DIE?

Outside the shelter, in the warrens of filthy hovels in Whitechapel and Spitalfields, there were horrors that rarely reached such staid newspapers as *The Times*, for they would have upset the people of the West End and reminded them of the existence of the lost and forgotten souls of their East End. It was difficult to shake the self-righteousness church-going middle classes out of their pipe-dream views of a society, in which people were poor from choice.

On 13 June 1888, 24-year-old alcoholic Theresa Smith, of 68 Catherine Buildings, Cartwright Street, Whitechapel, branded the back of her illegitimate young child Henry (aged four years and ten months) with a glowing hot poker for three minutes. Before that barbaric, sadistic act, Smith had rammed filth from a pond into the boy's mouth and forced him to swallow it. That same day she knocked the child down with a punch, kicked him in the ribs repeatedly, and afterwards jumped on him with full force. Miss Smith then knocked Henry's head against the door so violently, the sickening sound of the loud thump alerted a neighbour, Mrs Sullivan, who came out to witness further violent acts of child cruelty. Another neighbouring witness, Annie Edwards, told the court how, six month's previously, Smith had smashed the child's head open with a quart pot. Mrs Edwards also saw Smith bite a lump out of her boy's arm on one occasion. David Macluish, a surgeon, examined the unfortunate child, and saw that as well as being extremely malnourished, he had sustained a great number of scars from burns and injuries with blunt objects. The boy's legs were also ulcerated. Smith was imprisoned and the child was put in an orphanage. This disturbing story was barely mentioned in the newspapers, and nor was that of the five human skeletons found in a Whitechapel cellar in 1892. The skeletons were of people who had starved to death, yet the story was only allotted 13 words by the Press Association.

In 1887, a writer for the *Whitehall Review* commented on the approaching 'ominous cloud' of revolution that was hanging on the horizon in the East End, and warned the upper-classes to open their eyes to the disgraceful miasma of poverty in Whitechapel and Spitalfields before it was too late:

> *Many, it is true, are insensible to the danger. Many, unless roused, would go on in their fool's paradise, eating and drinking, dancing and leaving cards, until the scaffolds were up in Grosvenor Square ... In the words of Cardinal Manning, "Upon the multitudes among us there is an unconsciousness like sleep. They have never known poverty or want. Their well-provided life is, they think, the lot of all, or might be, and therefore ought to be; so they will not even read or listen. They do not know the condition of our poor, but the fault is their own."*

A year before, in the summer of 1886, a journalist writing for *The Referee* newspaper had predicted a revolution in England. He not only noted the spirit of rebellion that existed across the land, but also stated that half the working families in the United Kingdom were without bread, and that more than half of the shop-keeping classes were on the verge of bankruptcy. The author of this inflammatory article, which was entitled 'Impending Revolution', wrote:

> *We do not think that the long-suffering of this terribly cruel town [London] do not intend to go on living much longer, if it can be called living, upon what the dogs in good families would disdain. Does anybody suppose that the French Revolution would ever have come into effect*

270

if the masses had not been driven mad by sheer
starvation – not starvation that came all at once, but
starvation that went on, as it has been going on here, for
years upon years until the people could endure it no
longer? A hundred years ago France had an absentee
monarchy, much the same as the one we have here now,
except it was not a tithe as bad as our own. The Court
was held at Versailles, which as everybody knows, is less
than a fiftieth part the distance from Paris that lies
between London and Balmoral.

For the labouring classes and the destitute poor, 1886 had
been a particularly appalling year with a reduction of wages,
but also because of the severe snowstorms that punctuated
the harsh winter of 1886-87. It was sheer hunger, as well as
socialistic and political ideals, that spurred the hard-pressed
workers and workless alike to assemble at Hyde Park and
Trafalgar Square to protest against unjust social conditions
in 1887. The year before, on 11 February, Queen Victoria
had dictated a letter for Prime Minister Gladstone at
Osborne House on the Isle of Wight, which stated:

The Queen cannot sufficiently express her indignation at the
monstrous riot which took place the other day in London,
and which risked people's lives and was a momentary
triumph of socialism and disgrace to the capital.

Many of the downtrodden, starving, penniless, unemployed
people of outcast England had yearned for some political
Messiah to deliver them from the unjust state of affairs that
existed throughout the country. Some dreamt of Britain
becoming a republic, with a non-hereditary Head of State
replacing Queen Victoria, while others wanted nothing

more than sufficient money to live a decent civilised life.

On Sunday 13 November, 1887, there was a huge demonstration by the unemployed, radicals, Anarchists, Irish Home Rulers and Socialists in Trafalgar Square. Weeks prior to the demonstration, marching files of the unemployed had been invading the West End under a black flag, and these processions were always broken up by the police when they got to Trafalgar Square. By October of that year the Socialists joined in the black flag demonstrations and the flag's colour was changed to red. The red flag of Socialism was repeatedly seized by police who also arrested many of the marchers. On that historic Sunday 13 November, the Radical Federation intended to hold a demonstration in Trafalgar Square against coercion in Ireland. The demonstrators also called for the immediate release from prison of MP William O'Brien, the Irish nationalist who had been jailed for charges of incitement when he helped organise a rent strike at the estate of Lady Kingston near Mitchelstown, County Cork.

Sir Charles Warren had expressly forbidden organised processions into Trafalgar Square, but the discontented masses flouted his proclamation, and were probably testing the ban. Ten thousand Anarchists, radicals, and Socialists gathered in various areas of the Capital that Sunday, intending to rendezvous at the Square. Among the demonstrators that day marched the Socialist playwright George Bernard Shaw. William Morris, the artist, writer and dedicated Socialist, along with women's' rights activist and Marxist Annie Besant, addressed 5,000 demonstrators at Clerkenwell Green, advising their comrades to proceed to Trafalgar Square like good citizens – in an orderly manner. A rousing band and banner-wavers led the way, and everyone was unaware of the strategic traps that 'Warren's

Wolves' (as the *Star* nicknamed the Police Commissioner's policemen) had laid around the centre of the metropolis, at a distance of about a quarter of a mile from Trafalgar Square. The Socialist League were marching down Shaftesbury Avenue on their way to the Seven Dials when the police charged, first to the front of the column, and then to the rear. In minutes, the column was dispersed with shocking, brutal police assaults. Morris, Shaw and many others who took part in the demonstration later realised that Socialism through marches and revolution was doomed to failure. Morris himself later admitted, "Sir Charles Warren has given us a lesson in street-fighting."

The attack on Morris and Besant's column was a carbon copy of the other police onslaughts that took place elsewhere during the demonstrations. Robert Cunninghame Graham, Member of Parliament for Lanark, and a man who was to become a key figure in the formation of the Labour Party, found himself caught up in the Bloody Sunday riots as he walked across a street in the centre of London with John Burns, a member of the Social Democratic Federation. Cunninghame Graham, writing a year after the Establishment's most brutal put-down of a demonstration in the history of London, recalled:

> *I ... found myself a prisoner in the Square with a broken head. Whilst in there though I had ample time to observe a good deal. I watched the crowd and the police pretty carefully; I saw repeated charges made at a perfectly unarmed and helpless crowd; I saw policemen not of their own accord, but under the express orders of their superiors, repeatedly strike women and children; I saw them invariably choose those for assault who seemed least able to retaliate. One incident struck me with considerable force*

and disgust. As I was being led out of the crowd, a poor woman asked a police inspector (I think), or a sergeant, if he had seen a child she had lost. His answer was to tell her she was a "damned whore" and to knock her down. I never till that time realised how utterly servile and cowardly an English crowd is. I venture to say that had it occurred in any other country of the world, the man would have been torn to pieces. But no! In England we are so completely accustomed to bow the knee before wealth and riches, to repeat to ourselves we are a free nation, that in the end we have got to believe it, and the grossest acts of injustice may be perpetrated under our very eyes, and we will slap our manly chests and congratulate ourselves that Britain is the home of liberty. I saw much too, to moralise on. The tops of the houses and hotels were crowded with well-dressed women who clapped their hands and cheered with delight when some miserable and half-starving working-man was knocked down and trodden underfoot. As I stood there I saw the gross over-fed faces at the club and hotel windows, as I heard the meretricious laughter of the Christian women on the housetops (it is a significant feature of the decadence of England, that not one woman of the upper classes raised her protest by pen or on platform to deprecate the treatment of her unarmed fellow-countrymen; no – all pity was with the police). I thought yet, still – I have heard that these poor working-men, these Irish and Radicals have votes, and perhaps even souls, and it seemed impossible but that some day these poor deceived, beaten, down-trodden slaves would turn upon their oppressors and demand why they had made their England so hideous, why they ate and drank to repletion, and left nothing but work, starvation, kicks, and curses for their Christian brethren?

Both Cunninghame Graham and Burns were sentenced at the Old Bailey to six weeks' imprisonment with hard labour for allegedly breaking through the police lines, assaulting police officers and causing a riot.

Incidentally, amongst the battling masses that day was one Albert Bachert, the man who would succeed George Lusk as the chairman of the Whitechapel Vigilance Committee in 1889. Bachert was called as a witness for Cunninghame Graham at the Old Bailey trial. Three demonstrators died of injuries sustained on Bloody Sunday, including Socialist, Alfred Linnell, who had been marching beside George Bernard Shaw. He was run down by a police horse and passed away later in hospital. One-hundred thousand mourners attended Linnell's funeral, the greatest attendance figure for a funeral procession since the Duke of Wellington's death in 1852. Over two hundred people were severely injured by police and soldiers during the riots, and many more seriously wounded people stayed away from hospitals, fearing the authorities would arrest them before they could be treated.

The soldiers Warren had drafted in, namely Grenadier Guards, had taken up defensive positions with fixed bayonets, though they did not fire at the crowd. Likewise, the Life Guards had carried their swords but had not drawn them during the confrontations. All the same, what little respect the public had had for the police was shattered by Warren's brutal military tactics. Warren had temporarily destroyed all hope of the widely anticipated revolution-around-the-corner at Trafalgar Square on Bloody Sunday, but ideas and concepts are indestructible, and the golden promise of Socialism remained in the air.

As 1888 began, it really did look as if it would be the year of the British Revolution. The radical publication *Freedom* summed up this optimism in January 1888:

275

Socialism is in the air. It is the talk of the workshop and club, ale-house and street corner, throughout the civilised world. It is whispered in drawing rooms and seriously discussed in professional lectures and scientific assemblies.

In December 1888, Monsignor Gilbert, the Vicar General of the Archdiocese of Westminster, gave seven-hundred destitute Whitechapel people a Christmas dinner, and used the poignant charitable occasion to show the Press of the awful, disgraceful poverty that was so widespread throughout the East End. The Monsignor told journalists how 100,000 men in Whitechapel and Spitalfields were unemployed and unable to find work even for starvation wages. Women were working from six in the morning until midnight, and some were even working from 6am till 3am the following morning for a few extra pennies. The Monsignor said, "With miserable wages like these, East End families were driven from their homes, because they could not pay their rent, and women were turned out of their humble lodgings in Spitalfields and Whitechapel after midnight, because they could not pay for a bed."

That year, in the Metropolitan District of London alone, 32 people had died from starvation.

This shocking poverty existed in the very heart of England, at the hub of the British Empire, yet it was never addressed or even acknowledged by the Conservatives in the House of Commons. Instead, the right-wing MPs spent more time discussing the issue of Home Rule for Ireland.

In December 1888, as Monsignor Gilbert was feeding 700 of the 100,000 destitute people of the East End, Lord Salisbury, in Edinburgh, said, "To give Ireland the management of her own affairs would lead to the disruption

Prime Minister Lord Salisbury.

of the Empire." The Liberal party were of the opposite opinion, for they believed that Home Rule for the Irish would make Ireland contented, prosperous and loyal. Salisbury, however, feared that Home Rule for Ireland would lower the prestige and influence of the monarch and the aristocracy.

In 1888 the Establishment was faced with the rising threat of revolutionary Socialism, and the incendiary issue of Irish Home Rule, which refused to go away. "The Irish people are a really shocking abominable people – not like any other nation," Queen Victoria had remarked in 1867, and 21 years later, her attitude towards the Irish had not changed.

In the chapter on Catharine Eddowes, I told you about the underhand tactics of Prime Minister Lord Salisbury and the British Government in the 1887 black operation known as the Jubilee Plot, which was devised to undermine Irish

MP Charles Stewart Parnell.

Home Rule, MP Charles Stewart Parnell and Irish Republicanism. The Jubilee Plot had been kept secret for 113 years before it was finally declassified and released for public inspection at the Public Records Office in south-west London. The declassified document stunned historical researchers, for it had long been assumed that the Fenians had been behind the plot to kill Queen Victoria during her Golden Jubilee at Westminster Abbey, when, in fact, a secret agent, 'General' Francis Millen, hired by Conservative Prime Minister Lord Salisbury, had led the Irish plotters to attempt regicide.

In 1882, Parnell had made a speech in which he condemned the Phoenix Park murders – the gruesome assassinations of Chief Secretary of Ireland Lord Frederick Cavendish and Permanent Under-Secretary Thomas Burke by the Fenian splinter group 'The Invincibles', and I have mentioned this double murder in some detail in the chapter about the 'Lusk kidney'. Parnell's condemnation of the political murders increased his already growing popularity. Gladstone called him "an intellectual phenomenon" and this was certainly true, for Parnell seemed to be the man who could obtain self-government for Ireland, better known as Home Rule.

In 1886, Parnell joined up with the Liberal Party and defeated Lord Salisbury's Conservative Government, proving he was a force to be reckoned with. William Gladstone became Prime Minister, and he attempted to pass a badly-drafted and deeply flawed Home Rule Bill through the House of Commons. Parnell saw that the Bill had major faults but voted for it anyway, as he had been campaigning for Home Rule since the 1870s. The Bill split the Liberal Party and never made it through the House of Commons. Gladstone's Government fell soon afterwards.

In March 1887, *The Times* newspaper published the first of a series of articles, entitled 'Parnellism and Crime' – which supposedly showed how the Parnell movement had a sinister agenda with intentions to overthrow British authority in Ireland. On 18 April, the newspaper published what was alleged to be a facsimile of a letter written by Parnell, condoning the Phoenix Park murders. The letter, dated 15 May 1882, stated:

Dear Sir,
I am not surprised at your friend's anger, but he and you should know that to denounce the murders was the only course open to us. To do that promptly was plainly our best policy. But you can tell him, and all others concerned, that, though I regret the accident of Lord Frederick Cavendish's death, I cannot refuse to admit

279

*that Burke got no more than his deserts. You are at
liberty to show him this, and others whom you can trust
also, but let not my address be known. He can write to
House of Commons.
Yours very truly,
Chas S. Parnell.*

The Times was regarded across the globe as the premier
newspaper of the civilised English world, a paragon of
factual journalism since the days when it was published as
The Daily Universal Register in 1785. Parnell read the
shocking facsimile of the letter he had purportedly penned
and replied:

*I cannot imagine how the managers of a responsible, and
what used to be a respectable, journal could have been so
hoodwinked, so bamboozled – and that is the most
charitable interpretation which I can place on it – as to
publish such a production as that as my signature, my
writing ... I unfortunately write in a very cramped
hand, my letters huddle into each other, and I write with
great difficulty and slowness.*

The publication of the forged letter caused a great stir in
Parliament as well as in the country at large. In the House
of Commons, Parnell stated that the letter was a forgery and
requested the appointment of a select committee to
determine if the letter was a fake. His request was turned
down by the Government, and a special committee,
composed of a trinity of judges was appointed instead, to
investigate the serious charges made against the Irish leader
by *The Times*. This so-called Parnell Commission, dragged
on for almost two years. Some 445 witnesses were

examined, 150,000 questions were asked, and the Commission sat no fewer than 128 times. In February 1890, the Commission published its report, and among the 35 volumes of papers it had amassed, it stated that the letter alleged to have been written by Parnell was a forgery, and that he was not in league with the Fenians:

> *We entirely acquit Mr Parnell and the other respondents*
> *of the charge of insincerity in their denunciation of the*
> *Phoenix Park Murders, and find that the 'facsimile'*
> *letter on which this charge against Mr Parnell is chiefly*
> *based is a forgery.*

A forgery by whom? Well, the forger was one Richard Pigott, a Dublin journalist and one-time proprietor of three Irish Nationalist newspapers, *The Irishman*, *The Flag of Ireland* and *The Shamrock*. His chronic alcoholism and heavy gambling landed him in deep debt, and so, by 1881 he had sold his interest in the papers to the Irish National Newspaper and Publishing Company – an agency of Charles Stewart Parnell and the Irish Land League. This disenchanted nationalist, who also eked out a living by selling pornographic photographs and books, began to betray and blackmail his former political allies. He was contacted by a shadowy intermediary who offered a guinea a day, travelling expenses and hotel accommodation if he could prove Parnell was in league with the Irish terrorists. Pigott forged a number of letters associating Parnell with the Fenians and Invincibles, and he was paid £2,500 – a huge sum in those days – by the editor of *The Times*, who published the clumsy forgeries. It is now known that the British Secret Service contributed to the funds which *The Times'* Editor George Earl Buckle paid to Pigott, and there is also a Ripper connection.

Several of the anonymous articles attacking Parnell in *The Times* in 1887 – entitled 'Behind the Scenes in America' – had in fact been written by none other than Robert Anderson, Assistant Commissioner of the Metropolitan Police and the officer in charge of the Whitechapel Murders investigation from 6 October 1888. This was not made public at the time. In his controversial articles, Anderson had claimed that Parnell and other Irish parliamentary leaders were colluding with Irish-American revolutionaries. In 1910, when Anderson revealed he had written some of the anti-Parnell articles, he almost lost his pension, and the confession caused a scandal.

Not only did Anderson try his utmost to smear Parnell, the Metropolitan CID Chief also put his greatest spy – Thomas Billis Beach (also known as Henri Le Caron) in the witness box to testify on behalf of *The Times*. Beach's cover was now blown, and his life was certainly in jeopardy. He was given an annuity by *The Times* and a house, as well as a Special Branch Bodyguard to protect him and his family (who had been brought to Britain by the Secret Service on Beach's insistence). Beach gave evidence about the various terrorist activities of the American Clan-na-Gael. He had penetrated the inner circle of this organisation, and Anderson had incorporated the information his spy had obtained in the 'Parnellism and Crime' articles in *The Times*. Beach merely presented evidence of Fenian terrorist activities in an effort to try and build up some case against Parnell, but all this was undone when the celebrated trial lawyer Sir Charles Russell – the leading counsel for Parnell – cross-examined Pigott. Sir Charles asked Pigott to write down the words 'hesitancy' and 'likelihood' – and when the disgraceful journalist wrote those two words, he misspelt them in the very same way the forger of the letter had. Beads of perspiration formed on his forehead and dripped down his pug-nosed face into his long white beard as his breathing became rapid. The advocate grilled Pigott but still he refused to admit to forging the letter and other documents.

Few people outside the British Secret Service were aware of the machinations that had been going on behind the scene during the Special Commission. Soon after the Double Event Ripper murders of Eddowes and Stride (which took place on 30 September 1888), Anderson was recalled by Whitehall from a holiday (prescribed for exhaustion from overwork) in the Swiss Alps. Instead of returning straight to London, Anderson had embarked on a mysterious detour to Paris, and yet Home Secretary Henry Matthews had urged the Head of the CID to return without delay because of the latest Ripper murders. Anderson would not reveal why he had chosen to spend a week in Paris when he was urgently needed in London, but it is more than likely that the CID chief and intelligence expert had met with Fenian double-agent Francis Millen in the French Capital.

Millen was in Paris at that time, and so was Richard Pigott, the forger of the letters linking Parnell to the Phoenix Park murders. It is now thought that Anderson had attempted – unsuccessfully – to persuade Millen to give evidence against Parnell at the Special Commission. When Millen refused, Anderson had to make do with second best – Thomas Billis Beach. Furthermore, the day Anderson left Paris – 4 October 1888 – Pigott had also left the capital for Dublin.

On 26 February 1889, Pigott was summoned to the Royal Courts of Justice, but he failed to appear. It transpired that the main witness had absconded. Pigott had left the hotel he had been staying at in Fleet Street, and so the commissioners quickly applied for an arrest warrant.

Pigott had evaded two plain-clothed Royal Irish Constabulary men who had supposedly been guarding him at his hotel. The journalist fled to Charing Cross Station to catch the boat-train to Paris. Behind him, Pigott had left a signed confession with a Dublin solicitor named Shannon, and this affidavit was brought into court on the day Pigott had vanished.

Pigott remained in Paris for a matter of hours before travelling to Madrid by train. It may be a dark coincidence, but one Captain William O'Shea was in Madrid during this time. He was the husband of Charles Stewart Parnell's mistress, Katharine O'Shea, and the captain would later bring about something which Anderson and the British Secret Service had determinedly set out to achieve using the pawn Pigott – the instant downfall of the Irish leader. More on that shortly.

The Times was forced to withdraw the infamous 'facsimile letter', Parnell sued the newspaper for libel – and won, receiving an out-of-court settlement of £5,000. When Parnell entered the Commons after the lengthy trial, he received a standing ovation from most of the Members of the House, and yet the Irish leader did not react in the slightest to the warm reception; that was an idiosyncrasy of Parnell – he never said "thank you" to anyone, and on this momentous day in the House of Commons, the so-called 'pride of Erin's Isle' remained indifferent to the cheers and applause directed to him. By then, Richard Pigott was dead. After the police had tracked him down to the Madrid hotel, he told the officers: "Wait until I go to my room for some things I want." While the police waited, they heard a single pistol shot. Pigott had blown his brains out.

Coincidentally (or perhaps not) as the Pigott letter was being proven as a forgery in court, a Dr Maguire, Professor of

Moral Philosophy at Dublin's Trinity College and a devout Unionist, suddenly died at his London lodgings. Maguire – one of the men who had been in Paris with Pigott when he had 'received' the letter, had been summoned to give evidence against Parnell at the time of his sudden death. The Unionist was to have sworn as to the authenticity of the Pigott letter, but died in suspicious circumstances instead. There were rumours of poison, and the first reports of Maguire's demise maintained that he had choked to death, but doctors later claimed that 'fatty degeneration of the heart' had been the cause of death. And so ended one of the Establishment's black operations to discredit the only man who had come closer than anyone before, to achieving self-government for Ireland, but I believe there were other black operations going on to prevent the Home Rulers, the Fenians, the Anarchists, and the Socialists from bringing about a British revolution – and one of these black operatives was none other than Jack the Ripper. In the following chapter I will present this theory in detail.

Ironically, Parnell survived the reprehensible underhand attempts made by the Secret Service to destroy his career, only to meet his end in the divorce court. Captain William O'Shea, a former member of Parnell's party and one of the Irish leader's most loyal supporters, sued for divorce from his wife Katharine on the grounds of her adultery with Parnell. Captain O'Shea – a JP in County Clare – played the part of the injured Catholic husband, but in reality, he wasn't bothered by his wife's infidelity at all. Captain O'Shea entered a petition of divorce from his wife on the grounds of adultery, dating from April 1886 to December 1889. During the divorce trial, Katharine accused her husband (who was impotent) of cruelty and neglect and put on record statements implying that he had himself once committed adultery with her sister Anna.

Mrs O'Shea had first met Parnell in 1880, and was at that time separated from her husband. She bore Parnell three children during her marriage to Captain O'Shea. The first child died in 1882, she gave birth to Claire in the following year and Katharine in 1884. According to Mrs O'Shea, her husband learnt about the affair in 1881, and although he challenged Parnell to a duel, he later encouraged her to continue the adulterous affair. Why then, had he resorted to bringing his wife and Parnell to the divorce court in 1889? There was a rather weak theory that the captain had hoped to benefit from an inheritance from Anna Maria Wood, the 98-year-old aunt of Katharine O'Shea, who died in May 1889, leaving property valued at over £140,000. After the old woman had died, and Captain O'Shea had learned that Katharine's aunt had left him nothing, he supposedly decided, in bitterness, to sue his wife for divorce.

The facts of the matter paint a different picture. Sinister plotters in high places were at work, conspiring once again to disgrace Parnell. One of these schemers was Joseph Chamberlain, a ruthless breakaway Liberal Unionist and one-time supporter of Parnell who had become a vicious opponent of Home Rule. Chamberlain, a strong supporter of British Imperialism, had resigned from Gladstone's Cabinet over the hot issue of Irish Home Rule, an action which was to prove instrumental in bringing down the Liberal Government. He became the leader of the Liberal Unionists, and by 1886, had formed an alliance with the Conservative Party. His vision was to transform the British Empire into a united trading block to rival Russia and America – two nations who would be subjected to trading tariffs and restrictions, whereas Gladstone was an advocate of Free Trade.

As early as 2 November 1885 – almost four years before he filed for divorce, Captain O'Shea mentioned his friend and mentor Chamberlain in a letter to his wife Katharine. Embittered by his humiliating rejection from his Home Rule constituency in County Clare (because of his failure to take the party oath, which bound members to united action) and his failure to secure a seat in the general election as a Liberal agent for Liverpool, O'Shea wrote to his adulterous wife from Dublin, promising to 'hit back with a stunner'. In this intriguing missive, the captain assures Katharine O'Shea: 'I have packed my shell with dynamite' and in another part of the letter he states his intentions of blowing Parnell's reputation 'into smithereens'.

Joseph Chamberlain was undoubtedly just one of the arch-plotters who egged on Captain O'Shea to take his wife and Charles Stewart Parnell to the divorce court. Given Robert Anderson's record in attempting to smear Parnell's image by devious means, it would take no leap of the imagination to consider his involvement in the machinations behind the O'Shea-Parnell scandal. The British Intelligence Service of the day certainly knew about Parnell's liaisons with Captain O'Shea's wife and was ready to use the information as the trump card if the Pigott forgeries scheme fell through, which, of course, it did. Furthermore, it is now known that Captain O'Shea was having clandestine meetings with Richard Pigott and Robert Anderson's long-term informer George Mulqueeny in a room above the Golden Lion pub in Wardour Street, Soho in 1885.

The decree nisi was granted for the separation of Captain O'Shea and his wife. In Ireland, the Nationalist Press printed the general belief prevalent amongst Parnell's followers: that the trumped-up divorce case had been nothing more than a wicked reprisal for the Irish leader's triumph over the disgraceful affair of the Pigott forgeries. Parnell married Katharine in secret on the Thursday morning of 25 June 1891, at the office of the Superintendent Registrar at Steyning, near Brighton. Mary Gladstone, the wife of the Prime Minister, wrote of Parnell in her diary: 'Blot out his name!'

The Irish Catholic clergy issued and circulated a printed condemnation of Parnell, signed by priests and bishops, and only the Bishop of Limerick withheld his signature from the list. Although Parnell was a Protestant, Katharine O'Shea was a Catholic, and Catholics regarded the new marriage of a divorced woman of their faith as immoral. Close friends and associates of Parnell – people like Michael Davitt, Timothy Healy, John Dillon and William O'Brien – deserted him for splitting the Irish Party and wreaking irreparable damage to the cause. William Gladstone made it clear that he would only continue to fight for Home Rule if Parnell resigned immediately, and Queen Victoria branded Parnell a dishonest liar who was devoid of all civilised principles.

At 11.30pm on Tuesday 6 October, Parnell died at his Aldrington residence near Brighton. His sudden demise caused widespread astonishment, as no one had even known Parnell had been ill. The leader had recently returned from Ireland, where he had addressed a crowd in a freezing downpour at Creggs on the Galway-Roscommon border. It was believed Parnell had contracted pneumonia at the meeting. When he returned home to his beloved Katharine he complained of severe headaches and acute rheumatism. He died in the arms of his wife.

Upon hearing of his death in Paris, a scathing editorial in the *Catholic Universe* insensitively stated: 'How much better for Parnell to have died two years ago. What a fine reputation he would have left.'

All of the dirty, underhand tricks to prevent Parnell from making Home Rule for Ireland a reality had occurred before, during and after the Whitechapel Murders. The campaign to smear Parnell by exposing his illicit liaisons with Katharine O'Shea dated back to 1885, but the Pigott letters forgeries – linking Parnell with the Phoenix Park murderers – were produced in early 1887. The Special Commission, which was set up to investigate the shocking charges *The Times* had made against Parnell, as well as the claims of the smear letters – first sat on 17 September 1888 – nine days after the murder of the second canonical Ripper victim Annie Chapman, and ran parallel to the Whitechapel Murders case, with its proceedings often sharing the same page as the Ripper crimes reports. I believe that the same cadre of secret service agents attempting to bring down the 'Uncrowned King of Ireland' (as Parnell was widely regarded) were also involved in planning the murders of six women in the East and West End of London for purely political reasons. This cabal may have met, amongst other places, in Room 56, on the first floor of the Home Office, where the Jubilee Plot was hatched and coordinated. The Home Office is of course, the government department responsible for protecting the public from terrorism and serious crime, but the Jubilee Plot was what is known as a 'black operation' – a covert action carried out without the knowledge of the people, or even the Government, because it is unethical and almost always illegal. Black operatives entrapped the Fenians to try and blow up Queen Victoria and the Tory Cabinet at Westminster Abbey in 1887, solely to discredit the Home Rule movement. This is only one of the black operations carried out by the British Secret Service, and was only declassified in the year 2000. How many more astonishing revelations of this type will come to light in the near future?

In 1985, Paul Begg and Martin Fido, two respected authors and researchers into the Whitechapel Murders, finally traced the whereabouts of James Monro's memoirs in Edinburgh. For over a decade, Begg and Fido had searched for the memoirs of Monro, Assistant Metropolitan Police Commissioner to Colonel Henderson (until resigning in August 1888) and the head of his Secret (Intelligence) Department, which operated in Whitechapel throughout 1888. When Sir Charles Warren resigned in November 1888, Monro took up his post. Begg and Fido imagined that Monro's handwritten memoirs would surely throw some new light on the hoary Jack the Ripper enigma, but they were sorely disappointed, because there wasn't a single mention of the Whitechapel Murders within the bundle of papers. Why was this so?

Monro's son Charles, once cryptically stated that his father had referred to the Ripper murders as a very "hot potato", but Charles never elaborated further on this intriguing remark. Monro's peculiar silence regarding the greatest criminological mystery in history speaks volumes. Monro was a senior police official who had the most in-depth knowledge of the Ripper murders, yet he never wrote a word about the mysterious killer, nor did Monro ever pen a sentence about Robert Anderson, his closest colleague in Whitehall and the man who worked alongside him when they deceived the Fenians with the Jubilee Plot. All of Monro's papers and memoirs concerning the Whitechapel Murders were burnt, either by Monro himself or by his eldest son Charles. Why resort to burning material that could have been used in a best-selling book of memoirs?

Abberline and other police officials involved in the hunt

for Jack the Ripper were eagerly sought by publishers and journalists after the Whitechapel Murders case was closed in 1892. Monro, known in confidential circles as the 'Secret Agent of State', now sought anonymity and travelled 5,000 miles to India in 1890, where he set up the Dayabari medical mission at Ranaghat, West Bengal. This was a world away from Monro's life in Whitehall. Like Sir Charles Warren, who was now stationed in Singapore, Monro was unreachable, and free from accountability.

By 1892, the police had given up their search for the most mysterious killer in history. Monro returned to British shores in 1905 – 17 years after the Ripper's Autumn of Terror – and retired to Cheltenham. He died at Chiswick in January 1920, aged 81, and some (including the journalist George Simms) believed he took the secret of Jack the Ripper's identity to the grave.

10

TOWARDS A SOLUTION

In a report to the Secretary of State on 17 October 1888, Sir Charles Warren succinctly summed up Jack the Ripper's handiwork when he wrote: 'I look upon this series of murders as unique in the history of our country ... and so far the case is in a totally different category [when compared to the usual murders in the East End].'

The Whitechapel Murders certainly were unique, and remain unique and unequalled to this day. Jack the Ripper worked mostly in a specific area of London – Whitechapel and Spitalfields – one of the most densely populated districts of the capital, where there were people constantly milling about after dark, yet it seems he was never seen nor heard by anyone while he was at work. We have wildly varying descriptions of the killer from several 'witnesses' but in all likelihood, these people did not see Jack, and some reported sightings were undoubtedly invented, such as George Hutchinson's fanciful tale, detailed in the chapter on Marie Jeanette Kelly, and the far-fetched accounts of Matthew Packer's observations of Jack, which I covered in the chapter on Elizabeth Stride.

All of the descriptions of the Ripper given by witnesses are at odds with each other: he had a beard, he was clean-shaven, he was tall, he was short, he was fair-skinned, he was dark and Jewish-looking, he wore a deerstalker, he wore a black cap with a peak and so on. Most of these alleged sightings were simply lies spun by people hopeful of cashing in on the number of (unofficial) rewards being offered for the Ripper's capture. Some bogus witnesses were criminals themselves who believed a sighting of the Ripper would perhaps mitigate the seriousness of their own offences. Other false witnesses simply craved global publicity. The Socialist *Star* newspaper of 2 October 1888, criticised the false witnesses who concocted sightings of Jack:

> *There are many people in that district [of Whitechapel] who volunteer information to the police on the principle of securing lenient treatment for their own offences, and there are others who turn in descriptions on the chance of coming near enough the mark to claim a portion of the reward if the man should be caught, just as one buys a ticket in a lottery.*

Jack the Ripper was evidently an expert in stealth – that much we do know. He also seems to have had an uncanny knowledge about the whereabouts of patrolling policemen on their beat, so he knew when to strike and how long he had to kill and mutilate before the PC completed his circuit of the locality. When he struck, the victim made no noise, and in the first four canonical killings, the victims were incapacitated swiftly and laid on to the ground without a struggle before having their throats cut. The final victim, Kelly, was of course already lying down when she was killed on her bed, for there was an arterial blood spray evident on the wall to the right of the mattress at pillow level.

How did the Ripper silence his victims and lay them down without them making a noise or putting up a struggle? The answer seems to be through the skilful application of force to specific pressure points on the victim's body.

Besides his knife-work and the mysterious chalked message he scrawled on the wall, Jack the Ripper left evidence in the form of small bruises on the necks and collar-bones of his victims which doctors noticed and recorded in their notes and autopsies. The first Ripper victim, Mary Ann Nicholls, had such tell-tale bruises. Surgeon Dr Rees Llewellyn, in his post-mortem examination of Nichols' body, stated: 'There was a bruise running along the lower part of the jaw on the right side of the face.' What had caused this bruise, along with a circular one on the left side of the victim's face? Llewellyn states that pressure exerted by the fingers and thumb of the killer were undoubtedly the cause.

Next we come to Annie Chapman, the Ripper's second victim, and once again we learn of intriguing bruises. Dr George Bagster Phillips states that 'There were two distinct bruises, each of the size of the top of a man's thumb, on the forepart of the top of the chest.'

Elizabeth Stride, the next victim, also had the same type of bruises. Dr George Bagster Phillips immediately noticed something he had seen before, in Chapman and now in Stride: bluish discolourations over both shoulders, and these marks were under the collar-bones and in front of the chest. Phillips could see they were not caused by abrasions and he believed that they were not bruises but pressure marks; in other words, the bruises were not caused by the Ripper striking his victim but the result of the killer's firm finger pressure at that spot. It seems that the same pressure marks were also evident on Catharine Eddowes, who died at the hands of the Ripper the same night he killed Stride, because Dr Bagster Phillips, who observed Dr Frederick Gordon Brown's post-mortem of Eddowes with Drs George Sequeira and Sedgwick Saunders, stated at the Stride inquest, that he had seen the bluish discolourations 'on two occasions since' – not including the bruises on Stride. Dr Brown states: 'We looked for superficial bruises [on the body of Eddowes] and saw none.' However, after washing the left hand of Eddowes, Brown discovered 'a bruise the size of a sixpence, recent and red, on the back of the left hand between the thumb and first finger.' Dr Brown also found several small old bruises on the victim's right shin which had existed before the murder.

The body of Marie Jeanette Kelly was so extensively mutilated and stripped of flesh, any evidence of pressure point bruises around her neck and collar-bone was almost certainly obliterated by the murderer's knife-work.

What type of killer, in 1888, had the knowledge to render a person unconscious by exerting firm pressure on the twin pressure points behind the collar-bone to cut off the carotid blood supply to the brain or the deoxygenated blood flow from the brain to the heart? Today, such knowledge would be known to martial arts experts and members of elite military forces such as the Special Air Service, but even though some of the secrets of pressure points have been leaked via the Internet, most responsible martial arts instructors have largely kept that type of information from the general public, for obvious reasons.

In 1888, martial arts in Victorian England were virtually non-existent. Between 1893 and 1897, the British civil engineer Edward William Barton-Wright, who had been building railways in Japan, studied several forms of judo in that country, and upon his return to England in 1898 decided to teach an eclectic form of self-defence, based on Japanese martial arts – French kickboxing, British pugilism, and stick-fighting (similar to the French Canne de Combat – fighting with a cane). Barton-Wright named his hybrid martial art 'Bartitsu' a portmanteau word taken from the first four letters of his hyphenated surname and the last four letters of jiu-jitsu – a Japanese form of self-defence.

When the former American President Ulysses S Grant visited Japan in 1879, the art of Jiu-jitsu was demonstrated to him by Professor Kano Jigaro, the founder of Judo. Kano was one of the martial arts experts in Japan who later corresponded with Barton-Wright, but this was a decade after the Whitechapel Murders, and although it is possible that a 28-year-old Kano Jigaro communicated his skills regarding pressure points to an Occidental, it is unlikely. Kano's first European trip, to Paris, did not take place until 1889, and Barton-Wright's Bartitsu did not utilise pressure points anyway.

On 23 October 1868, Japan entered the Meiji era, named after the Emperor Meiji, who would reign for 45 years. During his reign, Japan rose to become a world power and strengthened the foundations of its imperial rule through an international search for the latest knowledge in the spheres of science, commerce and architecture, and naturally they looked to the West for inspiration. In 1876, a 24-year-old architect and artist, Josiah Conder signed a contract with the Japanese government to teach Western architectural techniques to the new Engineering College in Tokyo. Conder would also serve as an architect in Japan's Ministry of Public Works. Just why the Japanese government chose Conder, and why the latter accepted such a demanding position remains a mystery. Conder had recently received the highly prestigious Soane Medallion award from the Royal Institute of British Architects and a golden career awaited him in Britain, yet he chose to go to Japan instead. The Japanese found young Conder an inspiring architect and a great teacher. He designed 70 major buildings in Japan that stretched from Tokyo to

Josiah Conder in Japanse attire.

Nagasaki, and after marrying local beauty, Kumeko Mayeba, in 1880, Conder stayed in Japan for 44 years, until his death in 1920.

From 1878, the 'Father of Western Architecture in Japan', as Conder would ultimately become known, began to correspond with a number of people in England, including relatives and members of the Royal Institute of British Architects. Josiah also corresponded with his cousin, Colonel Claude Reignier Conder of the Royal Engineers, a close friend of Kitchener and Sir Charles Warren, and a man who had worked for the War Office as a military intelligence agent in Ireland and the Middle East. He is a man I have alluded to before in this book, and I will refer to him again later in this chapter, because I believe Jack the Ripper was a military man and a British Intelligence operative. I believe he was chosen by a cabal in Whitehall for several reasons: he had killed for his country before, under the clandestine circumstances of black operations and also in military conflicts such as the Battles of Kassassin and Tel el-Kebir. Conder was commanding troops at Weymouth until 1900, and was known as a highly intelligent, resilient but very arrogant man. He was a fluent speaker of Yiddish (a common language among the Jews of the East End and a language Elizabeth Stride was well-versed in), Arabic, several other European languages, and a first-class expert on the Altaic languages – especially Manchu.

'Juwe' – that enigmatic word chalked by the Ripper on the wall on the night of his double slaying – is a Manchu word meaning 'two'. Sir Charles Warren, the man who had that word and the rest of the cryptic message washed off the wall, certainly knew its meaning, yet pretended he was baffled. Like his good friend Conder, Warren was, in addition to being the Commissioner of the Metropolitan Police and a Major General in the Royal Engineers, a first-rate Biblical archaeologist and also a student of the Altaic languages. He would have immediately recognised the word 'Juwe', and he would have also recognised the glyphs etched on the face of Catharine Eddowes on that night of the 'Double Event' – because those inverted V's and other angular inscriptions drawn on the victim's face by the Ripper, were letters from the ancient Moabite language – a language Warren and Conder understood in great depth. Both could certainly read and write the glyphs of the language.

Claude Reignier Conder was also a respected expert on China and Japan, and may have been one of the few people in the West who studied the ancient martial arts from those parts of the world. Josiah Conder worked and lived in Japan long before the Whitechapel Murders, and may have sent information about these arcane arts of self-defence to his military cousin Claude in England. A thorough knowledge of pressure points on the human body is a highly significant part of the higher martial arts, and as we have seen, most of the victims of the Ripper were subdued by the application of skilful force to their pressure points.

Jack the Ripper then, possessed specialist knowledge of pressure points; something which, in 1888, was known only to a minority of people in China and the Far East, and he applied that deadly knowledge to subdue his victims. After cutting their throats, he did not always mutilate – Jack searched the pockets of at least two victims first (Chapman and Eddowes) – but what was he looking for?

If we accept that the Ripper was a military intelligence man, we obviously have to establish his motive; why did he do what he did? Well, as we learned in the previous chapter, Revolution was certainly in the air in 1888. Queen Victoria and the monarchy system were under constant criticism and soon to be rocked by the Cleveland Street Scandal (which curiously, was Chief Inspector Abberline's next case). Irish Home Rule was looking increasingly feasible, and the Socialists and Anarchists were set to join forces with the Fenians and Home Rulers. Things were looking very grim for the Establishment. It is known that there were various Fenian agents of both sexes in London who were willing to kill and maim with bombs and bullets for the cause.

In the chapter on the Lusk Kidney, I described how Liverpool Irishman and Fenian Frank Byrne, who was involved in the gory murders of Thomas Henry Burke and Lord Frederick Cavendish at Dublin's Phoenix Park in 1882, was aided by his 28-year-old wife Mary (who was seven months' pregnant) and several other women who acted as couriers by hiding the surgical knives used in the assassination along with guns and ammunition in rope scabbards which were secreted under their clothing. These women were then allowed into Ireland without being searched by the authorities. Mary Byrne was just one of many female couriers dedicated to the Fenian cause, and she used many aliases, including the surname Kelly. Mary was subsequently arrested in London in 1883, and was even put on an identity parade, but informer James Carey failed to pick her out from the line-up, and Mary was lucky enough to escape the gallows and travel to America with her husband. By February 1888, Mr and Mrs Byrne had even opened a liquor store in New York, on the south-west corner of 51st Street and Third Avenue, where O'Donovan Rossa and several Fenian bombers (all wanted in England) drank a toast to the cause.

Earlier, in October 1881, the *Birmingham Daily Post* reported what was initially dismissed as an alarmist story in circulation about a dangerous 'Fenian woman' in London who was distributing incendiary Fenian literature and despatches that had arrived from the United States. There was more than a grain of truth in these reports. In response to the British Government's Coercion Act of 1881, which allowed people to be imprisoned without a trial, the Ladies' Irish National Land League was formed. Because of a legal technicality, women fell outside of the terms of the Coercion Act, and so many Fenian women were able to fight evictions of Irish tenants and continue the No Rent Manifesto Campaign. Of course, at that time in history, most Victorian men regarded the 'fairer sex' as second-class citizens, and a majority of men were incensed by the activities of these outrageous militant women. The Suffragette movement and votes for women lay many years away in the future, so reports in the Press about female Fenians, such as the fanatical young Irishwoman found in

300

possession of two-hundredweight of dynamite who was arrested at a hotel in the Strand in April 1883, were greeted with horror by men and women alike.

Mary Jane O'Donovan Rossa, wife of prominent Fenian leader Jeremiah O'Donovan Rossa, is a prime example of a militant Irish female rebel. Mary Jane toured the length and breadth of America on a grand fund-raising campaign for the Fenian cause, and later co-edited the Irish Nationalist one-man newspaper *United Irishman* with her husband. Earlier in time, in 1866, we have a record of one Catherine Tracey, who made pikes and pike staves for the Fenians and also acted as a courier for them. Then in May 1878, Mrs Carroll, another female Fenian courier was active. She was accused of smuggling rifles and revolvers along with the beef she imported into Ireland, and sure enough, when police searched Mrs Carroll's home, they found many firearms under her bed.

As early as 1865, a Fenian informer had warned the British Consul in Philadelphia, Charles Kortright, about the thousands of Irish-born women who were returning home from America with guns – both dismantled and intact – hidden on their persons. On 23 April 1888, a suspicious American woman with three well-maintained rifles tried to board a ship to Liverpool at Deepwater Quay, in the Irish port of Queenstown, when she was immediately arrested on suspicion of being a Fenian man disguised as a woman. She was in fact Birdie Grover, a professional rifle crack-shot. She had recently fallen out with Buffalo Bill, who had been giving a show at Liverpool, and had intended to sail to New York on the Arizona, but had a change of mind as she sailed down St George's Channel, and had decided to return to Liverpool by ship from Queenstown. What is peculiar about the latter comedy of errors is the entrenched mindset of the Irish police in 1888. The Royal Irish Constabulary and Customs officials at Queenstown were more readily inclined to consider Ms Grover as being a Fenian man disguised as a woman, rather than a woman who just happened to be a Fenian.

In all probability, Marie Jeanette Kelly – the last known victim of the Ripper, was a Fenian agent who had been sent from Ireland to London as a 'sleeper'; a spy with no immediate mission, who would loyally stand by for further orders from Ireland. Her landlord McCarthy and his wife both stated that Kelly had indeed received letters from Ireland, but there is not a single mention in the Press or the police reports of these letters being found at 13 Miller's Court after Kelly was killed by the Ripper. The letters stopped coming after her murder – as if the senders knew she was dead – but if her parents and many purported brothers knew Marie Jeanette was dead, why didn't they come to London to bury her? The Royal Irish Constabulary made concerted efforts to trace Kelly's large family over in Ireland, but never found a single relative of the murdered girl. If Kelly's real family knew she was a Fenian agent, they would probably share her views towards the British, and would never have come forward to help 'the enemy'. It would be both dangerous and disloyal to do so. There is a remote possibility that there is a family of Irish descent somewhere in the world today that harbours vague but dark rumours concerning Marie Jeanette Kelly.

Kelly probably never had a child before she came to London, but she may have had a sister and/or brother, and their descendants living today may have heard fragmented stories, passed down from generation to generation, about the enigmatic tenant of Miller's Court. Perhaps this skeleton will remain in the family cupboard because there is some stigma attached to the deeds of Kelly in her role as an

Irish terrorist, which are better left buried in a dark episode of the past that deserves to be forgotten. Then again, perhaps Kelly's relatives and friends never mentioned Marie Jeanette's fate to their sons and daughters because it would have scared them away from fighting for the cause. I admit this is all hypothetical, but bear in mind that for decades, the world's greatest genealogists have been unable to trace any records pertaining to a Marie Jeanette, or Mary Jane Kelly, who was born around 1863 in Limerick. A search for Kelly's marriage in South Wales to a man surnamed Davis or Davies, circa 1879 has also drawn a blank. I believe this is because no such ever marriage took place, that Kelly never lived in Wales, and that her surname was not even Kelly, but some other Irish surname.

If Kelly was an agent, she'd have concocted a false history to cover her real origins, and strangely enough, people who had known 'Marie Jeanette' during her ill-fated time in London had remarked upon her contradictory accounts of her background; she maintained she was Welsh but had an Irish accent; she said her parents lived in South Wales but then at Miller's Court she received letters from her family in Ireland. In the wake of her horrific murder in November 1888, the newspaper reports touched on the problem of establishing her nationality, and a Swansea journalist even visited the main Police Station at Cardiff – the city where Kelly had supposedly been arrested for prostitution with a cousin circa 1882-1883, but Walter Hemingway, the Chief Constable of Cardiff (since 1876), was adamant that none of his men had known anyone answering Marie Jeanette's description or name during that time. Other enquiries were made. Perhaps Kelly had been known by her married name of Davies or Davis, but once again, all investigations drew a blank, and it was firmly established that Marie Jeanette Kelly had never come under the notice of the police in Cardiff.

Kelly told Barnett and a former landlady Mr Carthy that she had been a tenant of a landlady named Buki, who had a lodging house in one of the roads off St George's Street in the tough St George's-in-the-East area of the East End. If Mrs Buki existed, she would have read or heard of the horrendous murder at Miller's Court, and someone who knew Buki would certainly have spotted her surname mentioned in the press articles on Kelly, which were syndicated across the world. The Press were desperate to find out more about the victim of the Ripper's most brutal murder, and would have paid good money to talk to Mrs Buki, but the elusive landlady was never heard from.

Why was Kelly targeted by the Ripper, and why did the Whitechapel Murders end after her murder? Jack the Ripper took enormous, unnecessary risks when he chose Marie Jeanette as a victim. If Jack had been merely some misogynistic psychopath, he could have killed any one of a thousand or more prostitutes of Kelly's age in places where he would not have to endanger himself as he did in the busy cul-de-sac of Miller's Court. People were coming and going to and from the court until the early hours of the morning, so there was a real risk of being seen. Dorset Street was a fairly well-illuminated thoroughfare, with hundreds of people inhabiting the doss-houses on both sides of the street.

On one side of the entrance to Miller's Court, at Number 27, John McCarthy had his shop, which was still open at 1.20am on the morning of the Kelly murder. From 1am till around 1.20am, Elizabeth Prater, a tenant of the court, had been standing at the arched entrance to the court, and at one point she even went into McCarthy's shop to talk with Kelly's landlord. Then we have the comings and goings of hard-up prostitute Mary Ann Cox, another resident of Miller's Court, who finally returned to the court at 3am. Half an hour before this we have Sarah Lewis arriving at Miller's Court from Great Pearl Street after a heated argument with her husband. Around the same time a couple of drinkers were walking up Dorset Street, possibly from one of the local public houses – the Horn of Plenty or Blue Coat Boy. On top of this, we have policemen such as PC George Blunden H38 on the beat around Dorset Street.

Jack the Ripper then, had a lot to contend with when he set out to kill Kelly in her bed. He obviously knew his victim was alone, and that no one would be calling on her later in the early hours of the morning. Jack had certainly done his homework, and may have observed Kelly's movements for some time prior to the killing. When the time came, the Ripper was able to go about his ghastly work safe in the knowledge that he would never be disturbed by a visitor. Why take all this trouble and run so many risks just to kill the girl from Limerick when Jack could have found dozens of similar victims roaming the darkest streets and loneliest alleyways of Whitechapel that night?

I believe Kelly was specifically marked out for death because she was a Fenian agent who was planning to take part some act of terrorism in the near future – possibly on the day she was murdered – the day of the Lord Mayor's Parade. In 1883, extensive precautions were taken by Scotland Yard after the Lord Mayor received an anonymous letter, claiming that the Fenians were ready to blow up London Bridge. A special corps of policemen – many of whom spoke Irish Gaelic – was placed on guard at Government buildings around Westminster. Armed members of this special corps also guarded Mr Gladstone's residence at Hawarden Castle. Sir Charles Warren was only too aware of the possibility of the Lord Mayor's Parade of 9 November being hijacked by Fenians, Socialists and Anarchists, and on 5 November he had issued, in the Press, a stern notice prohibiting any processions and speeches by these 'dissidents' at any thoroughfare through which the Lord Mayor's procession was to pass. Marie Jeanette Kelly was said to have made regular trips to see a person in the Elephant and Castle area of London – and in the 1880s, an Irish ghetto existed there. The district was also a haven for Fenians like Joseph Moroney, a highly devious Clan-na-Gael member from Philadelphia who was later involved in the revolting murder of Philip Patrick Cronin in Chicago, in 1889. Cronin, a physician and Irish Nationalist, had publicly accused certain members of the Clan-na-Gael of embezzling many thousands of dollars in funds collected for the party. Dr Cronin's corpse was afterwards found as a blockage in a sewer. He had been bludgeoned to death.

Perhaps Kelly had met up to be briefed with Fenians like Moroney during her mysterious trips to the Elephant and Castle district. As we have seen, Warren was very concerned about the Lord Mayor's Day parade on 9 November, and Kelly herself had told several people she was looking forward to attending the pageant herself. Was Kelly due to play some part in a Fenian attack on the Lord Mayor's Parade? What better time to strike, when the police have their hands full supervising the hundreds of thousands of Londoners thronging the streets of the capital as the Lord Mayor travels from Mansion House to the Royal Courts of Justice? All it would take is for one person to throw a bomb into the Mayor's carriage, and that, perhaps would be the starting shot for a premeditated uprising, coordinated by Fenians, Anarchists and hard-line Socialists.

This almost happened in November 1909, when Sir

John Knill was elected the Lord Mayor of London. Rudolf Rocker, a prominent German-born Anarchist (and one-time editor of the *Arbeter Fraint*, printed at 40 Berner Street, Whitechapel, adjoining the Liz Stride murder scene) was approached by a young Russian Anarchist who stated that he belonged to a small group of like-minded people, and that he had formulated a plan to throw a bomb at the Lord Mayor during the parade. Rocker talked the young Anarchist out of committing the atrocity by telling him that such an act would not only kill many innocent bystanders, it could also result in the revoking of the right to political asylum in England for many Russian and Polish refugees. The group of fanatics (which included a young cherubic-looking girl) regarded the Lord Mayor as a symbol of oppression and despotism, but fortunately, after considering Rocker's views, the bomb was never thrown and the group eventually disbanded.

If Kelly was involved with the Fenians, could it be possible that she had even kept explosives or incendiary devices at Miller's Court prior to her death? Abberline and the other detectives who surveyed the scene of the Kelly murder at 13 Miller's Court were intrigued to see that a fire in the grate had been so fierce, it had melted the spout and handle of the old kettle. Some reports say that there was some warmth emanating from the vestiges of what had been an unusually intense fire when a forced entry was made into the room. It was surmised at one point that the Ripper had perhaps burnt his own bloodstained clothes on the fire to get rid of incriminating evidence, but there were only remnants of female clothing (none of them Kelly's), burnt velvet and the carbonised wire frame and rim of what seems to have been a woman's hat. Some wondered if the Ripper had fed the fire to provide himself with a good light to work by, but he had worked in much feebler light in Mitre Square on the last occasion, and if he had needed illumination, why didn't he simply light the 'penny dip' candle in the room? The light of a single candle, filtering through a gap in the improvised curtain would have been less suspicious to anyone in the court passing Kelly's window, than a roaring inferno in the grate, which would be sure to attract attention. Clothes slung on a fire tend to smoulder, but the fire in Kelly's grate was intense enough to melt the tin solder of her kettle. The melting point of tin is 449 degrees Fahrenheit (231 degrees Centigrade). There were no bellows present in Kelly's room to concentrate air on to the combustible materials of the fire, yet the heat damaged a kettle that could normally withstand prolonged high temperatures. Coal and coke could not have generated sufficient heat to melt the kettle spout, so what was responsible?

One possibility is 'Fenian Fire' – an extremely highly inflammable solution of phosphorous and bisulphide of carbon, which gained its name because the Fenians used it in various incendiary devices during their campaign of terror in Britain. The same dangerous chemical compound was later used in British grenades in World War One, and in the darkest days of World War Two, when a Nazi invasion seemed imminent, Albright and Wilson, the UK's manufacturer of phosphorous for matches and the compound potassium chlorate, suggested an incendiary grenade to the War Cabinet which was little more than a bottle of Fenian Fire. Furthermore, the United States Army's 87th Chemical Mortar Battalion fired almost 12,000 shells of Fenian Fire during the liberation of Cherbourg in the 1944 Normandy campaign.

In December 1888, an Anarchist printing press in the neighbourhood of Leicester Square began to produce and circulate copies of *The Dynamiter's Guide*. This volume of dangerous knowledge supplied the reader with all of the technical details and formulae needed to create dynamite, nitro-glycerine, 'Lorraine Fire' (an inflammable explosive), 'Sudden-death grenades', and Fenian Fire: 'excellent for throwing amongst policemen and cavalry' according to the text of the anarchic guide.

At the beginning of that memorable year, in January 1888, another remarkable explosive was being developed – flameless dynamite. The Coal Mines Regulation Act of 1887 had prohibited the use of flaming explosives down mines. After a number of mine explosions in Wales, the miners in the Rhonda Colliery went on strike. The Government quickly came to a compromise and rendered 'Flameless Explosives' compulsory. These explosives were absolutely safe to be used down the mines in the presence of fire-damp and coal dust. They could not be ignited by being struck with force, even by hammers, yet they were four times as powerful as conventional dynamite. The manufacturers of this new explosive, named 'Securite', were the Flameless Explosives Company Limited, and one of their chief directors was Edward Horner, of Horner & Co, the chemical warehouse in Mitre Square, the place where Catharine Eddowes had been murdered by the Ripper.

Of course, Mitre Square has another Ripper connection, which I have referenced before in the chapter on Catharine Eddowes. In 1885, Inspector Frederick Abberline, the man in charge of detectives on the ground in the Whitechapel Murders case, went to Mrs Whittridge's lodging house at 5 Mitre Square to arrest Harry Burton, one of the Fenians responsible for the explosions at the Tower of London, Westminster Hall and the House of Commons. Whilst under police supervision, Burton went to the John Wright coffee rooms at 23 Aldgate High Street, close to the spot where Eddowes was found drunk on the eve of her murder.

When Jack the Ripper killed Catharine Eddowes on the morning of 30 September 1888, her body was found in the south-west corner of Mitre Square, 35 feet from the entrance to Horner's chemical warehouse. Perhaps Eddowes had been sent to collect a message or parcel from someone at Horner & Co. who had dealings with the Fenians and/or Anarchists, and she may have met her death at the hands of the Ripper soon after she collected something from that factory. When Eddowes woke from her drunken stupor at Bishopsgate police station on what was to be the night of her murder, she repeatedly asked the jailer, "What time is it?", as if she was worried about a prearranged rendezvous. That same night at 1.30am, an unidentified, respectably-dressed man came into St James' Place (also known as the Orange Market) from the adjacent Mitre Square, to ask a night-watchman who was overseeing road works a very curious question. "Have you seen a man and a woman go through here?" the stranger asked watchman James Blenkinsop. Blenkinsop said he had seen a few people pass, but hadn't really taken that much notice of them. If the night watchman was right, and there is no reason to suppose that he was lying, an unidentified man was in Mitre Square around 15 minutes before Eddowes was found dead. This well-dressed stranger was widely reported in the newspapers in the aftermath of the double murder of 30 September, but he never came forward and was never traced.

Was this unknown person supposed to meet Eddowes at her rendezvous? If Eddowes and an unidentified male had passed through St James' Place to get into Mitre Square, it could mean that the victim had met the Ripper on Duke Street or Houndsditch, and had assumed he was the man she was told to meet that morning – the man who would take her to Mitre Square to give her something; possibly a document or parcel. Instead, he took her to that dark corner, maybe under the pretence of opening the locked gate there to get something, and instead he subdued Eddowes in his expert way, then laid her down to cut her throat before rifling through her pockets. This searching of Eddowes' pockets must have been essential, because the Ripper only had a few minutes to carry out his macabre operation before PC Watkins returned to the square.

The same night Eddowes was murdered, Elizabeth Stride was mysteriously laid down in Dutfield's Yard before her throat was cut. She had been wearing a red rose backed with maidenhead fern in the lapel of her coat when she was found. People like Charles Preston, Catherine Lane and Elizabeth Tanner, who had seen Stride earlier in the evening at the lodging house in Flower and Dean Street said she had not been wearing the rose then. Around five hours after she leaves that lodging house, Stride turns up murdered in the yard of a club used by known Anarchists, agitators and radicals with a red rose pinned to her lapel. Was she wearing that rose because she had to meet someone that night who she had never seen before and the rose was a way of identifying her? Stride was highly secretive about her movements that night. She spoke fluent Yiddish and was found in the yard of a Socialist Club frequented mostly by Jews. As we have seen in previous chapters, the Fenians were also meeting up at this same club. Stride was also a visitor to the Swedish Church at Prince's Square, in the district of St George in the East, and in this same square there was an Anarchist club that was under investigation from early summer that year. The club, at number 23a, was being used for an organised smuggling operation. Hundreds of gallons of spirits where smuggled into the club until the police and a detective from the Inland Revenue confronted the gang in May 1888. Stride visited the Swedish Church, which was close to the Anarchists' club, whenever she needed alms, and it was just 400 yards (365 metres) from the International Workingmen's Educational Club on Berner Street. On her person when she was found murdered, Stride had a pencil and an amount of paper in her pockets. Is it possible that they were used to take down messages that were to be passed on to Anarchists and Fenians? Edward Spooner and Abraham Ashbrigh, two of the first people who arrived at the murder scene in Dutfield's Yard, stated that they had seen the cachous in the tissue paper in Stride's left hand, but Spooner also saw a piece of paper doubled up in the victim's right hand. If Spooner is not mistaken, what happened to the piece of paper and what was written or printed upon it?

Getting back to Eddowes, and her mysterious rendezvous that fateful morning in Mitre Square; the Ripper incapacitated her in his usual skilful way, laid her on the floor, cut her throat, then searched her pockets, for the items belonging to the murdered woman were laid out beside her when she was found. The silent slaughterer then mutilated Eddowes, leaving her 'all ripped open like a pig in the market', as PC Watkins, the policeman who found her, later told a newspaper. I am sure the Ripper left Eddowes in such a state in order to terrorise the Fenians and Anarchists – in the same way that the Zulus disembowelled soldiers with their assegai as a shock tactic. The Ripper took organs from Chapman and Eddowes, and I am sure there were several reasons for this.

When George Lusk, president of the Mile End Vigilance Committee wrote to *The Times* after the Double Event, not only to complain about the lack of a reward being offered for the capture of Jack the Ripper, but to mention in passing that a reward (of £10,000) was given for information leading to the capture of the Phoenix Park murderers, this must have sent alarm bells ringing in the upper echelons of Whitehall, for it would have seemed that Lusk had spotted a connection between the Ripper murders and the Fenians. As I described in the chapter on the so-called Lusk Kidney, a mysterious man, with an Irish accent, visited a shop near to Lusk's Mile End Road home, asking for his address. That was undoubtedly a scare tactic, and on the following day, half of a human kidney was posted to Lusk. This seems to have been an act of postal terrorism, and at some point, Lusk must have deduced that he had come close to hitting on a truth when he mentioned the Phoenix Park murders and the Whitechapel murders in *The Times* letter. The note accompanying the boxed kidney was written with words such as 'Sor' and 'Mishter' – traditionally used by hack writers in the press when portraying stereotypical Irish people – to give the impression that the author was Irish, thus implying that the Whitechapel Murderer was an Irishman, just to confuse Lusk, who seems to have suspected the Ripper's real motives: to slaughter a network of couriers working for the Fenians and Anarchists.

Lusk reported the bisected kidney he received to the police and newspapers, but I wonder if anyone received the other half of the Lusk kidney? Perhaps a Fenian or Anarchist who had dealings with Eddowes had received a gruesome parcel containing the other half of her excised kidney or even her womb. There is also a possibility that the Ripper took the wombs from Chapman and Eddowes in case someone attempted to track him down with a bloodhound. Bloodhounds had been mentioned during the Whitechapel Murders, and yet when Marie Jeanette Kelly was killed, they

313

never arrived to take up the scent at Miller's Court because Sir Charles Warren had countermanded the decision to use them. And on that occasion, Kelly's womb was not taken by the Ripper, and the story of her heart being taken away by the killer seems to be a misunderstanding of Dr Thomas Bond's post-mortem report.

The night the Ripper killed Eddowes, he wrote a message on a wall that has baffled generations of criminologists and armchair detectives. The message is undoubtedly a code to someone, but to those hopeful of decoding its meaning, the syntax has always been a stumbling block to speakers of the English tongue, because of the double-negative. The person who wrote the message was, I believe, a Gentile pretending to be a Jew. Yiddish commonly uses double-negatives. One example of a double-negative, given in a Yiddish text book, is the phrase: 'Ich hob nit kein feder'. This translates as 'I don't have no pens'.

This graffito, then, was written in letters three quarters of an inch-tall on the jamb of a doorway to a tenement inhabited principally by Jews, and it was written in such a way as to suggest the writer was Jewish, by its use of a common Yiddish double-negative:

The Juwes are
The men that
Will not
be Blamed
for nothing

It seems the peculiar spacing of the chalked words may be due to the available space of the bricks on the jamb of the doorway in Goulston Street. Now, would it not have made more sense if the Ripper had written this on a wall close to the body of Eddowes in Mitre Square, instead of walking 516 yards (471 metres) to Goulston Street and chalking it in small letters? Furthermore, the Ripper could have sent the piece of apron to the Central News Agency, along with the Juwes message. That would have guaranteed maximum publicity for him. How could the Ripper have been sure that anyone would have even found the piece of cloth torn from Eddowes' apron in that dark entrance to the stairway of Wentworth Model Dwellings, let alone connect it with the murder in Mitre Square?

One criminologist seriously suggested that, because of earlier rain, the walls might have been too damp in Mitre Square for the Ripper to chalk a message there, but the exposed brick jamb of the Goulston Street doorway was just as wet from the rain showers that night. It is possible that even if PC Long hadn't noticed the blood-stained apron and graffito, then had bloodhounds been deployed at the murder scene in Mitre Square, they might have tracked the scent of the blood on the apron to that doorway. Of course, bloodhounds were never used, and Warren later countermanded the decision to use them at Miller's Court, but why did the Ripper go to that specific doorway and what was behind the peculiar idea of writing on a wall?

I believe that he knew there was a connection with Eddowes and certain Anarchist Jews who lived in the tenement where the message was scrawled. The doorway led to numbers 108 to 119, and, as I mentioned in the chapter on Eddowes, one Israel Sunshine, a Jewish teenager, lived at 109 Wentworth Model Dwellings. In January he and several agitators, Anarchists and Socialists were involved in a fight with Louis Diemschutz, Isaacs Kozebrodsky and several of their comrades on Berner Street. Diemschutz, the 27-year-old steward of the

315

International Workingmen's Educational Club, was the man who found Elizabeth Stride dead outside that club on the very night Jack the Ripper wrote his cryptic message on the doorway leading to Israel Sunshine's dwelling. You may recall how, in the Eddowes chapter I related that PC Long – discoverer of the apron and chalked graffito in the doorway of the Wentworth Model Dwellings – had never walked that beat before that night, for he had been sent from A Division, the Westminster district of the capital in which Whitehall lies. Could it be possible that Long was planted on that beat, knowing full well that the Wentworth Model Dwellings, like the International Workingmen's Educational Club and other hotbeds of Anarchy and Socialism, was under observation? The presence of the graffito and apron on the stairways to the Jewish dwellings also gave the police (and British Intelligence agents) a legitimate reason to search every room in the tenement, which was a justifiable way of snooping for subversive literature, anarchic plans and even bombs. Likewise, the International Workingmen's Educational Club at 40 Berner Street was also thoroughly searched by the authorities in the wake of the Stride murder.

The Ripper's act of writing a message on the wall was eerily preceded by the numerous mentions throughout 1888 of the phrases 'the handwriting on the wall' and 'writing on the wall' in newspaper columns and articles. The idiom 'the writing's on the wall' means, of course, that there is a likelihood that something bad will soon happen to someone or something – a portent of approaching doom – and it comes from the Biblical story of Daniel, who reads mysterious writing on a wall which foretells the end of Babylon.

On 14 January 1888, Oscar Wilde is quoted in the *Manchester Times* on the subject of female poets as saying:

'They leave the triviality of triolets to men, and try to read the writing on the wall, and solve the last secret of the Sphinx.' Here are more examples of this idiom, which is to be abundantly found in Press articles throughout that fateful year. One relevant example is to be found in *Freeman's Journal*, 20 February 1888, when Alderman John Hooper, a supporter of Parnell, and an MP for Cork, was released. Hooper said the 'writing was on the wall' for the English people who opposed Home Rule for Ireland. Hooper had been sentenced to two months' hard labour in Christmas 1887 for publishing information relating to the meeting places and times of suppressed branches of the Irish National League. This phrase is to be found again and again within the newspapers of Britain and Ireland, whenever someone warns Salisbury's Government about the inevitability of Home Rule. On 16 March then, in *Reynold's Newspaper* for 16 September 1888, we have an article about Lord John Manners, the 7th Duke of Rutland, apparently misusing the idiom:

> *"Order reigns in Warsaw," was the brief message of the brutal Paskiewitch to his master, the Czar, after he had exterminated the Poles and laid the cities of Poland in ashes. Order will reign in Ireland under this coercion Ministry only when preceded by similar enormities; and cynical and cold-blooded as Mr. Balfour is, he values too much his own neck to try the extreme measures of the tyrant proper upon the country which today is cursed by his rule. Of course the 'old nobility' oddity went in for the deification of the Irish Secretary. "All the merit of our victories in Ireland is due to the man whose name is written on the wall."*
> *There is only one writing on the wall that lives in history*

317

– 'Mene, mene, tekel, upharsin', and unless the Duke of Rutland meant to convey his conviction that Mr. Balfour and his policy were weighed in the balance, and found wanting, and that he and his colleagues are politically doomed to perdition, the words have no meaning in their historical association.

Then, on the 22 September 1888, just over a week before the Ripper wrote his message on the wall, an Irishman Hugh Murphy wrote a letter to the *Freeman's Journal* newspaper in Ireland, condemning the way *The Times* was slandering Parnell. He enclosed a cheque for £23 with the letter, his donation towards The National Indemnity Fund, set up to defray the costs of Mr Parnell and his colleagues in their costly contest against *The Times* and the Tory Government. Mr Murphy included this phrase in his letter: '*The Times* has already read the writing of its fate upon the wall.'

Less than two weeks after Jack the Ripper had written his cryptic five-liner on the wall, a Fleet Street journalist saw a connection between the Biblical writing on the wall and the Goulston Street graffito. The following appeared in the pages of the *Belfast News-Letter*, on 13 October 1888:

OUR LONDON LETTER

The critics of Sir Charles Warren in the Press are making the most of his supposed order to have 'the writing on the wall' obliterated before it could be photographed by the city police. He is reminded of the Scriptural writing on the wall, and informed that it may, before long, prove fatal to his continuance in his present responsible position.

The article then goes on to describe how mischievous children and adults are chalking sanguinary messages and threats from Jack the Ripper on pavements and walls across the metropolis.

It is my hypothesis that Jack the Ripper was a trained killer and British intelligence agent carrying out the blackest of black operations: the brutal and terrifying murder and mutilation of female couriers working for the Anarchists and the Fenians. The Ripper's job was to strike terror into the hearts of the agitators and radicals who wanted to overthrow the order of things, and that is why he disembowelled, disfigured and mutilated his victims (with the exception of Elizabeth Stride, because of a lack of time). His gruesome and shocking work was unprecedented, and it sent messages to those who would dare to challenge and try to change the Establishment. The murders warned Louis Diemschutz, William Wess, as well as the Fenian associates of 'Marie Jeanette Kelly' that the plotting of a revolution, a regicide or an armed uprising in the United Kingdom would be met with severe, unthinkable consequences. I believe some of the Fenians, Anarchists and Socialists began to realise the truth behind the Jack the Ripper murders after the killing of Stride and Eddowes. George Lusk seems to have suspected a conspiracy in high places around the time of the Double Event on 30 September, when he wrote to the Home Secretary, pointing out that there was no official offer of a reward for the apprehension of the Ripper, whereas a substantial reward had been put up for the capture of the Phoenix Park murderers of 1882. Not long afterwards Lusk was stalked by a mysterious Irish-speaking man in black, and half a kidney was posted to him, along with a letter written in ersatz Irish. These scare tactics worked, and Lusk backed down and gave up trying to take over the East End with his private army of vigilantes.

With this hypothesis in mind, let us go back to what is generally thought to have been the first killing in the series: the murder of Mary Ann Nichols.

Nichols left her lodging house in Thrawl Street around 1.20am. She was penniless, but had recently acquired a hat no one had seen before. Where she obtained that black straw hat trimmed with black velvet remains a mystery to this day; had she received it as payment, having done someone a favour? She was seen by her friend Ellen Holland at about 2.30am on the corner of Osborn Street and the Whitechapel Road in an extremely drunken state. No one recalled seeing Mary Ann in an hour stretching from her departure from the Thrawl Street lodging house to the meeting with her friend at 2.30am on the corner of Osborn Street, yet in that period she had evidently been drinking, even though she didn't have the money to buy a drink. One hour and ten minutes later, Nichols is found dead in Buck's Row. Bucks Row was something of a political venue in those days. Socialists and Anarchists often gave firebrand speeches each Sunday in front of Buck's Row and Winthrop Street; people like George Bernard Shaw and William Morris (who associated with the radical members of the International Workingmen's Educational Club in Berner Street) delivered stinging attacks upon the ruling classes and the hypocrisy of capitalism. In later years, Anarchists such as Rudolf Rocker gave speeches in Bucks Row, and the history-changing architects of the Soviet Union's Communist Party – Lenin, Trotsky, Litinov, Gorky and even Josef Stalin – all came to Whitechapel in the early days of the twentieth century in an effort to cause a working class uprising amongst the poor of the East End.

By 1891, William Wess, the writer and printer of subversive Socialist literature who worked as the Secretary of the International Workingmen's Educational Club, a man who had been in the very yard – Dutfield's Yard – on the night Elizabeth Stride's body was found there – was living at 108 Brady Dwellings – Buck's Row. Many of the Jews living in Buck's Row in 1888 had connections with the Berner Street Club. I believe that Nichols was going to meet somebody that night, perhaps acting as a courier. I believe that she was silently intercepted, incapacitated and laid down by a military-trained killer in Buck's Row before she could reach her destination. The killer, who has only been unsatisfactorily known as Jack the Ripper for generations, cut Mary Ann's throat and perhaps searched her, as he is known to have done with Chapman and Eddowes. The abdominal mutilations were then inflicted as an act of 'terrorism', to instil fear in the minds of all who would later read about this shocking but grotesquely distinctive murder in the newspapers. I believe that a minute or so after the slaying, the military-trained Ripper made a casual and silent escape into the useful darkness of Buck's Row with the stealth of a modern-day SAS soldier. I believe the people who were meant to meet Nichols that morning were deeply shocked when they came upon her body. Harriet Lilley lived just two doors away from the spot where Mary Ann Nichols was found on Buck's Row. She heard noises on the morning of the murder. Her intriguing story was told in many newspapers, including *Lloyd's Weekly Newspaper*, 9 September, 1888:

An important statement, throwing considerable light on a point hitherto surrounded with some uncertainty – the time the crime was committed in Buck's Row – was

*made on Thursday by Mrs Harriet Lilley, who lives two
doors from the spot where the deceased was discovered.
Mrs Lilley said: I slept in the front of the house, and
could hear everything that occurred in the street. On that
Thursday night I was somehow restless. Well, I heard
something I mentioned to my husband in the morning. It
was a painful moan – two or three faint gasps – and
then it passed away. It was dark, but a luggage train
went by as I heard the sounds. There was, too, a sound
as of whispers underneath the window. I distinctly heard
voices, but cannot say what was said – it was too faint.
I then woke my husband, and said to him, "I don't know
what possesses me, but I cannot sleep tonight." Mrs
Lilley added that as soon as she heard of the murder she
came to the conclusion that the voices she heard were in
some way connected with it. The cries were very different
from those of an ordinary street brawl. It has been
ascertained that on the morning of the date of the murder
a goods train passed on the East London railway at
about half-past three – the 3.7 out from New-cross –
which was probably the time Mary Ann Nichols was
killed in Buck's Row.*

None of the Ripper's victims was thought to have been able
to call out or scream for help before they were murdered, as
the killer seems to have applied expert pressure to nerve
points in the neck and clavicle areas which caused instant
unconsciousness in the victim. He then cut their throats,
severing the vocal cords and carotid artery, so death was
instantaneous. If what Harriet Lilley said was true, then
whose voices and gasps did she hear at 3.30am on Buck's
Row on the morning of the murder? The men who came
upon the body first – Charles Cross and Robert Paul – did

not arrive at the murder scene until 3.40am, and they did not emit gasps, as they were not even sure if Nichols was dead. It is as if other individuals had turned up at Buck's Row before Cross and Paul, but never came forward to notify the police of the murder, perhaps because they had something to hide. Were these unknown people Anarchists from the nearby Brady Dwellings?

As we have seen, Buck's Row was a popular meeting place where Jewish radicals and Socialist reformers would give open-air speeches. At midnight on 2 May 1891, a midnight meeting of the East End tailors was staged at Buck's Row, with 2,500 people attending, many of them from the International Workingmen's Educational Club in Berner Street. The chair was occupied by Lewis Lyons, who condemned the sweatshop system and asked the working classes of Great Britain and Ireland to back him in his condemnation.

The next victim of the Ripper, Annie Chapman, was also killed close to a location where Socialists and radicals were giving talks – Christ Church Parish Hall at 22 Hanbury Street. In July 1888 Princess Beatrice and Prince Henry of Battenberg visited this hall in Spitalfields for the purpose of inaugurating a bazaar held to raise money to pay off a debt of £750 which had been hanging over the place for some time. The hall was not only a venue for lectures and concerts; it was also home to a workingman's club with 160 members.

Annie Besant gave speeches at this hall during the London Match Girls' Strike of 1888, and as a consequence, one thousand match girls downed tools, and within a fortnight the strikers won and Besant became head of the executive committee of the Match Maker's Union. Up to that point the girls who manufactured matches were receiving very low pay, working 14-hour days in poor working conditions, and many of them were suffering from 'phossy jaw' – a medical condition in which the white and yellow phosphor used to make the matches would infiltrate the jawbones of the workers, causing painful gum swelling, disfiguring necrosis of the jaw and brain damage. Abscesses smelt foul when they began to drain and if the jaw was not removed, death was the almost certain outcome. Thanks to the work of Besant and other, an act was passed by the Commons in 1908 which prohibited the use of white phosphorous in matches. This act was an implementation of the terms outlined in the Berne Convention of 1906, regarding white phosphorous.

Sharing her office with Annie Besant in Hanbury Street's Christ Church Parish Hall, was Eleanor Marx Aveling, youngest daughter of Karl Marx. She was also instrumental in the success of the Match Girls' Strike and collaborated with Besant. Annie Besant is also connected to another site where a Ripper victim died – 40 Berner Street, the address of the workingmen's club. Not only did she give speeches there, she also entered into regular correspondence with the club's secretary, William Wess.

The Sugar Loaf pub on Hanbury Street was a popular meeting place for Anarchists and radicals, and Anarchist Rudolf Rocker not only attended meetings there, he also gave speeches in front of the Board School and Schneider's factory on Buck's Row. Some meetings of the oppressed and those of the sweatshops took place in cellars and available spare rooms, and I cannot help but suspect that the room at 29 Hanbury Street which Mrs Richardson claimed she used for 'prayer meetings', was one such room.

In the first four locations where Jack the Ripper killed his victims; Buck's Row, Hanbury Street, 40 Berner Street and Mitre Square, there are connections with Anarchy, radical Socialism and Fenianism. In the first murder, whispers and gasps were heard in Buck's Row, and I believe they were made by people who had arranged to meet Nichols. In the second murder, that of Annie Chapman, at 29 Hanbury Street, unidentified voices were heard in the backyard where she was killed before the 'official' discovery of the body. Carpenter Albert Cadosch heard these voices as he returned from his toilet in the neighbouring backyard at number 27. One of these unknown people in the yard of number 29 exclaimed "No!" – perhaps in shock at finding Annie Chapman mutilated and disembowelled on the floor with her intestines over her shoulder and her belongings in an orderly pile beside her, left by the Ripper after he had searched her pockets. In the third canonical murder, that of Elizabeth Stride, we see that she is wearing a red rose in her lapel, as if she is ready to go and meet someone who will recognise her by that flower – but instead she meets the Ripper. In the fourth murder we have Eddowes asking the jailor at Bishopsgate police station: "What time is it?" to which the jailor sarcastically replies, "Too late for you to get any more drink."

"Well, what time is it?" she asks him again.

"It's just on one," he tells her, and Eddowes pretends she's concerned about the lateness of the hour because she fears her common-law husband John Kelly will give her "a damned fine hiding" when she gets home – but from all accounts we learn that Kelly, who is not in the best of health, is not that sort of violent chap, and anyway, when Eddowes leaves the police station she is seen to go in the opposite direction to that of her home. As I mentioned earlier, before the body of Catharine Eddowes was found, a well-dressed stranger appears near to the scene of the crime and asks a night watchman if he has seen a man and a woman in the vicinity. After Eddowes was murdered, her sister, Eliza Gold remarked of her: "She would never do anything wrong. I cannot imagine what she was doing in Mitre Square."

If we take the testimony of one of the witnesses at the inquest into the murder of Marie Jeanette Kelly into consideration, it seems there may have also been a rendezvous arrangement at Miller's Court. The laundress Sarah Lewis arrived at Miller's Court at 2.30am on the morning of the Kelly murder. Sarah had just had an argument with her husband, and had decided to stay at Mrs Keyler's at 2 Miller's Court. As Sarah was about to go into the court she noticed a man on the other side of Dorset Street, at the arched passageway that led into Miller's Court. Sarah saw that this stranger was not tall, but stout, and he wore a black 'wide-awake' hat. "The man standing in the street was looking up the court as if waiting for someone to come out," Sarah Lewis told the coroner at the inquest. This individual might have simply been someone who was lodging at Crossingham's doss houses, which faced the entrance to Miller's Court, or he could have been a Fenian who was waiting for Marie Jeanette to come out of her room so he could pass on information to her, or take information from her regarding the planned act of terrorism on Lord Mayor's Day. On seeing Sarah Lewis enter the court, as well as the comings and goings of Mrs Cox, this Fenian might have waited a while until the coast was clear.

I believe at this time, at 2.30am, when Sarah Lewis entered Miller's Court, Marie Jeanette Kelly was already dead, and in all probability, Jack the Ripper was still in the room of his final victim, calmly listening to the footsteps outside as he mutilated Kelly's corpse. Not long after Mary Ann Cox returned to her home in Miller's Court at 3am, the Ripper must have left the scene of the crime. Perhaps the small stout man Sarah Lewis had seen outside Crossinghams had become suspicious by Marie Jeanette's absence and rather than venture into what could have been a trap by the Special Irish Branch, instead sent someone else to determine Marie Jeanette's whereabouts. When the man with the wide-awake hat went to fetch this someone, the Ripper casually left Miller's Court and vanished into the rainy night.

By this time, when Nichols, Chapman, Stride, Eddowes, and possibly the unknown woman, whose torso was found at Whitehall, had been killed by the Ripper, those in the know, the Fenians and Anarchists, would have expected Kelly's life to be at risk as well, but the Ripper's month of inactivity (October) might have lulled these terrorists and revolutionaries into a false sense of security. The Fenians, Socialists and Anarchists must have wondered if the distinctive series of killings had been halted by the Cabal in Whitehall. Had the murders stopped? Had the Establishment's ruling elite – who undoubtedly had a hand in hiring some inhuman monster to slaughter these penniless female messengers and couriers – possessed a modicum of decency and given up perpetrating these atrocities just to protect the flawed British way of life, and the continuation of the Royal Family? The answer to these questions, was of course – no. At Buckingham Palace in 1997, in the aftermath of the tragic death of the Princess of Wales, Queen Elizabeth II, in a three-hour meeting with Paul Burrell, Diana's former butler, warned him to be vigilant, as he had been very close to the Royal Family. She warned Burrell: "There are powers at work in this country about which we have no knowledge."

Those unknown forces were just as prevalent in 1888, the year in which the future of the monarchy hung in the balance, and revolution and Irish Home Rule seemed imminent. I believe that if Elizabeth Prater and Sarah Lewis were not lying, or mistaken, about the cries of "Oh murder!" that they both claimed to hear around 4am, they may have heard a female associate of Marie Jeanette Kelly who had just entered 13 Miller's Court to see the grossly mutilated corpse. By then, of course, the Ripper had left the room, and the intense blaze would have been roaring in the fireplace, illuminating the entire grotesque and shocking scene.

Once the Fenians learned about the death of their agent in Miller's Court, they would have aborted their campaign of terror for 9 November and realised that the Whitehall conspirators had not given up their most secret and terrifying black operation. After Marie Jeanette Kelly was killed, the Whitechapel Murderer stopped for good. Sir Charles Warren, a man who was certainly not a quitter, resigned; as if he knew the black operation was now over. He returned to the War Office. 'If' is a small word with a big meaning, and all of this hangs on that word, but it's a possibility that's worth considering, as it seems to fit the facts surrounding the murders, where the first four victims seemed to have been on their way to, or from, a rendezvous.

Mary Ann Nichols spent an hour off the streets in the company of someone who got her drunk after she left her Thrawl Street lodging house on 31 August 1888. Not a soul set eyes on her until her friend Ellen Holland saw her drunk on the corner of Osborn Street and Whitechapel Road at 2.30am. From that time until 3.40am, Nichols was not seen by anyone. Who was she with?

Annie Chapman went missing for over three hours after she left Crossingham's Lodging House at 1.45am on 8 September 1888. Not a soul saw her on the streets of Whitechapel or Spitalfields. She was found dead in the back yard of 29 Hanbury Street at 5.30am. Where had Annie been for over three hours?

Elizabeth Stride left her lodging house on Flower and Dean Street sometime between 7pm and 8pm on the Saturday night of 29 September 1888, and there were no reliable sightings of her after that time. Charles Preston, who lived in the same lodging house as Stride, said the latter was 'dressed to go out', but she didn't tell him where she was going. She wanted to look smart as she asked Preston if he had a clothes brush. Stride's body was found at 1am the next morning in the yard of a club frequented by Fenians, Anarchists and Socialists, six hours after she left her lodging house.

Catharine Eddowes disappeared off the face of the earth twice – turning up insensibly drunk on Aldgate High Street on the eve of her murder, on Saturday 29 September 1888, before spending over 40 minutes somewhere unknown after she was released at 1am from Bishopsgate Police Station – before she was found dead in Mitre Square at 1.45am.

Marie Jeanette Kelly also vanished, seemingly into thin air, hours before she died at the hands of the Ripper. After her ex-boyfriend Joseph Barnett visited her around 8pm on Thursday 8 November, four hours elapsed before Mrs Cox saw her coming into Dorset Street, apparently the worse for drink, with a red-haired blotchy-faced man in his thirties who wore a billycock hat and carried a quart pail of beer. Police later made enquiries in all of the pubs in the district and not one pub landlord or landlady could recall seeing Marie Jeanette Kelly on their premises.

We now come to the suspect who may have been the legendary killer generations have attempted to identify – Jack the Ripper.

Claude Reignier Conder was born in Cheltenham on

Friday, 29 December 1848, the son of 33-year-old civil engineer and railway contractor Francis Roubiliac Conder and Anne Matilda (nee Colt), aged 25. Claude's grandfather was the famous London bookseller and editor Josiah Conder, the non-conformist writer of many great hymns, including, amongst others, 'Bread of Heaven, On thee we Feed' (1824). Josiah is said to have married a granddaughter of the eighteenth century French sculptor, Louis Francois Roubiliac, but recent genealogical research has cast doubt on this. It is now thought that Claude's great-grandfather was one Samuel Conder, a surveyor, cabinet maker, and estate agent from Bedfordshire. Claude had a sister, Anne, born at Cork, Ireland in 1850, and two brothers – Louis, born at Everton, Liverpool in 1847, and Rene Francois Reignier Conder, born at Naples in 1859. Claude's London-born bohemian cousin, Charles Conder, was an artist of note who painted on silk fans and later became associated with the so-called Heidelberg school in Australia. He befriended Oscar Wilde, Aubrey Beardsley and Henri de Toulouse-Lautrec, and died from syphilis, aged 40, in 1909.

Whereas Charles was unconventional, decadent and debauched, his cousin Claude was highly religious, serious and mentally and physically disciplined. Claude's early years were spent in Italy, where his father worked for eight years on the construction of a railway network, but after his family had returned to England to settle down, Claude attended University College London, where his brilliance in most subjects, especially drawing and water-colour painting, became instantly noticeable. Claude entered the Royal Military Academy at Woolwich where he excelled as a surveyor, draughtsman and military engineer. In 1870, Conder was commissioned as a lieutenant in the Royal Engineers, a versatile corps of multi-skilled soldiers he felt he was made for.

Kitchener as a young cadet at Woolwich.

Two years before he became a lieutenant, Conder struck up a friendship with another young man who, like him, held a profound interest in the Bible. His name was Horatio Herbert Kitchener, whose moustached face would one day be seen on tens of thousands of 'Your country needs you' recruitment posters in World War One. The two youths had met in 1868 at 28 Kensington Square, the London home of a well-known Army crammer, the Reverend Frost.

Kitchener's father had wanted his son to join the cavalry, but Kitchener had set his heart on becoming an officer in the Royal Engineers. Sitting side by side at a desk in Frost's study, Conder and Kitchener bonded and became the best of friends. They both learned Hebrew and spoke in that language to one another. The two students were also interested in the rituals and ceremonies of High Church Anglican theology. When the Army exam came, Claude and

331

Horatio did well and entered the Royal Academy, a place where they had been preceded by such luminaries as Charles George Gordon (of Khartoum) and Sir Charles Warren, who would one day be the Commissioner of Police of the Metropolis during the Whitechapel Murders.

Conder was an able fighter, despite his small but stout frame (he was 5 feet 5 inches tall) whereas Kitchener was imposingly taller at 6 feet 2 inches, but a rather shy person. Conder, on the other hand, was very arrogant, and although he was unquestionably a highly intelligent cadet, many found him cold, blunt, unapproachable and something of a loner. Conder started to attend the Military Academy of Engineering after his initial period at Woolwich, and on 8 January 1870 he was commissioned lieutenant in the Royal Engineers. Kitchener went on to a greater career and international fame, of course, but the path of his life would cross Conder's once again.

In May 1872, the military authorities at the War Office unanimously suggested Conder as a leader of the Western Survey of Palestine party. In 1865, under the patronage of Queen Victoria, the Palestine Exploration Fund (PEF) was established by distinguished academics and clergymen – for a dual purpose. To the public and the Church, the PEF was a noble organisation that endeavoured to scientifically discover villages and natural landmarks mentioned in the Bible and map and measure them. In essence, the PEF was to bring back photographs, maps, plant specimens and etchings to back up the Bible's Old and New Testament stories with hard evidence, to repel the growing army of sceptical scientists who were being converted to Darwinism.

The War Office was not at all interested in the theological value of any surveys of Palestine; all they wanted were detailed maps – for future military use – of a country that formed part of the Turkish Ottoman Empire. It was thought that the Ottoman Empire would be part of some future military theatre and it was certainly eyed by the 'Great Powers' of Europe. In the Crimean War, the Ottomans had joined forces with Britain, France and other nations in the conflict with Russia, Britain's main rival in the near-East. In the 1870s, Britain and France were determined to prevent Russia encroaching in the Mediterranean in order to establish a foothold in south-western Asia. From 1874 to 1880, Britain's strategy was to secure, at all costs, its routes of commerce and communication with the Far East and India. Bismarck would later propose, in 1878, that the Ottoman Empire should be broken up, with France occupying Tunis and Britain annexing Egypt. Britain flatly refused to even consider this outrageous suggestion. A little knowledge is a dangerous thing, and to acquire knowledge that would be highly advantageous in the event of a conflict, the War Office needed highly accurate maps of Palestine, so they loaned Royal Engineers to the PEF to carry out this Herculean intelligence-gathering task. Over six thousand square miles would be surveyed, and this assignment was given to one Captain R W Stewart in July 1871, but he became seriously ill by the following January, and he was ultimately forced to return home.

At the War Office in May 1872, the urgent question of finding an able successor to Captain Stewart was raised and mooted, and everyone agreed that the best man to take his place was 25-year-old Claude Reignier Conder. He was duly summoned to the War Office to be interviewed by captains Charles Warren and Charles Wilson, and they were very impressed with Conder's vast archaeological knowledge and surveying skills. Warren admired the young lieutenant and

333

struck up a friendship with him that would endure for decades.

On 9 July, 1872, the War Office announced that Lt Conder RE would be seconded to the PEF from 11 July, and from that date, Conder became the leader of the survey. He and the party worked under a firman of the Sultan, and the Turkish government fully consented to the project – as long as the survey confined its work within mutually agreed borders. Conder's first important task was to draw up the 400 mile-long baseline from which the entire survey of Palestine would work. Assisting Conder was a tall, likeable fair-haired civilian named Charles Tyrwhitt-Drake, a member of the PEF and a Fellow of the Royal Geographic Society. Tyrwhitt-Drake had joined the survey at the outset, and had taken command of the party when Captain Stewart had been compelled by his illness to return to England.

In July and August 1872, Conder and Tyrwhitt-Drake came into the possession of a number of highly controversial and largely pornographic artefacts. They were obtained from Moses Wilhelm Shapira, a Jew who had been converted to Christianity. Shapira was the proprietor of a shop on Jerusalem's Christian Street, which specialised in Levantine artefacts and ancient scrolls and documents that Shapira had allegedly unearthed in the hills of Moab. Conder was fascinated by one of the first artefacts from Shapira's collection – a life-size copy of a woman's womb, engraved with a strange glyph. Conder sketched the earthenware womb and shaded it with his water colour paints. On the same parchment page he sketched and painted other sexual organs – all male, including a horse's penis. In Conder's distinctive and idiosyncratic shadow font, he titled the painting, 'Phallic Emblems' (PEF Archives, reference: PEF/DA/WS/425/5).

Another detailed watercolour by Conder depicts a

Conder's watercolour of a womb.

naked woman holding a large erect penis, but the most intriguing of these pornographic paintings and drawings is of a naked woman with an oversized vagina with her left arm bent so her left hand is resting on her upper abdomen just under the breasts (PEF Archives, reference: PEF/DA/WS/425/9). Conder has written the word 'Ashtaroth' (the Demon Prince of Hell) next to this illustration. The Moabite figure's left arm, bent so the forearm lies across the upper abdomen, is eerily reminiscent of the position Marie Jeanette Kelly was left in by the Ripper after he had murdered and mutilated her. Kelly's forearm had been positioned over her (hollowed out) abdomen. Annie Chapman's left arm was laid across her left breast. Dr George Bagster Phillips said it had been 'placed' in that position. Elizabeth Stride's right forearm was also placed in this position. The body of Mary Ann Nichols was moved by the two men who found her – Charles Cross and

335

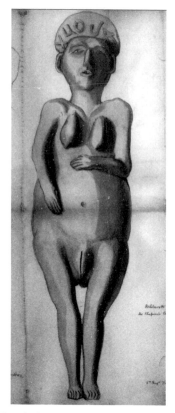

Conder's watercolour of a woman.

Robert Paul – so we do not know if her arm was positioned over her breast. Catharine Eddowes was found in a different position altogether, although, as I mentioned in the chapter dedicated to this victim, there were glyphs carved into her face that bear a strong similarity to the letters of the Moabite script.

The drawings and watercolours of the supposed ancient pornographic artefacts were sent back to the PEF in London, and most of the illustrations bore the phrase 'Not to be published' written by Conder in the corner of the sheet. As you can imagine, in the late Victorian period, the illustrations of wombs, naked women in strange positions and phallic symbols were deemed highly distasteful, if not downright offensive. They were an embarrassment to the PEF members, and were quickly filed away in the organisation's archives. Tyrwhitt-Drake hadn't been keen on having anything to do with the peculiar pornographic artefacts, but Claude Reignier Conder had been highly intrigued by the erotic and sinister items of pottery.

That year, in Palestine, Conder visited the tomb of Phinehas on the Plain of Mukhnah. Phinehas was the grandson of Aaron the High Priest, and is something of a controversial figure in the Old Testament. In the Book of Numbers (25: 1-8) Phinehas ended a plague visited upon the Israelites by God, by throwing a spear through the belly of a Midianite prostitute named Cozbi and her 'client' Zimri – Prince of the Tribe of Simeon. The Israelites had gone with the Moabite prostitutes to join in fertility rites to the god Baal, and so 24,000 lay dead from the plague sent by God. Oblivious to the weeping Israelites at the Tabernacle entrance, Zimri insensitively paraded the prostitute Cozbi past the mourners and went into his tent with her to have sexual intercourse. Phinehas was so enraged by this shocking act of gross immorality, he grabbed a spear and impaled Zimri and Cozbi (penetrating her womb), killing them both. The double slaying stopped the plague that had been killing tens of thousands of Israelites, and God, pleased by the zeal of Phinehas, decreed that he would receive divine recognition. Conder sketched the tomb of the Biblical prostitute-slayer in some detail and his drawing was later used to illustrate his highly successful book about the surveying expedition, *Tent Work in Palestine* (1878).

Not long after the illustrations of Shapira's controversial artefacts had been completed, Tyrwhitt-Drake contracted a severe malarious fever, which he seemed to shake off at one point, but he remained in ill health until he died on 23 June 1874 at Jerusalem, aged just 28. Conder had one person in mind to replace the late Tyrwhitt-Drake - his old friend Kitchener. He wrote to him suggesting that he might be interested in working in Palestine, and Kitchener, who was only too keen to escape humdrum peacetime duties at Aldershot military camp, eagerly accepted Conder's offer.

On 19 November of that year, Kitchener arrived in the Holy Land. He joined Conder at the survey camp at El Dhoheriyeh on the Plain of Philistia (land of the Philistines), on the south-west coast of Palestine. Kitchener found the men of the survey party in a down-hearted state when he arrived, for the Palestinian climate subjected the soldiers and officers to extremes of searing heat and glacial cold, and hauling heavy equipment over the rough terrain in such temperatures as they surveyed many square miles was very fatiguing. Kitchener, who had up to that point, been a rather reserved and introverted man, came out of his shell in Palestine. The survey party really took to him and his relationship with Conder was strengthened by the many trials and tribulations of their Middle Eastern adventure. Conder, a fluent multi-linguist, taught Kitchener how to speak basic phrases in Arabic. Kitchener duly became even more interested in the language of the local Bedouins and studied their speech and written glyphs. Kitchener also became fascinated with two other subjects at this time; practical archaeology, and photography.

Early in January 1875, Kitchener developed a dangerous fever that inflamed his bowels and made him extremely ill for almost two months. The symptoms of the long fever were similar to dysentery, but Kitchener's strong constitution pulled him through, and not long after his recovery, it was Conder's turn for a brush with death. This took place in April of that year, when the Sirocco wind from the Sahara was unusually strong and Conder and Kitchener decided to go for a morning swim in the Mediterranean. Conder swam too far from the shore and found himself being dragged by a strong current into the huge waves of the rough sea. He shouted for help at the top of his voice and Kitchener came to the rescue. The two men made it back to the shore of Israel and Conder thanked Kitchener for saving his life.

Eight weeks later, in the summer of 1875, Kitchener once again saved the life of his close friend. In July of that year, Conder, Kitchener, and the other 13 members of the survey party had just pitched their tents in an olive grove near Safed, in the Upper Galilee area, when a group of Arabs came upon the scene and began to make offensive remarks about Christianity to the foreigners. A pistol belonging to Conder's servant went missing, and was found hanging from a tree branch. The local fanatical Moslem sheikh knew very well that the so-called 'archaeologists' had a hidden agenda. He knew officers when he saw them, and he had heard the worrying rumours: Whitehall wanted maps of the area we know today as the West Bank for a great war that was looming. There were darker rumours too; some Arabs not only believed that the outsiders would try to impose Christianity upon the Moslems, they imagined that the British would take over the Arab lands of the Middle East and hand it to the Jews – after all, wasn't the British Prime Minister Disraeli a Jew?

The sheikh, incensed at the presence of the survey party on his land, marched into the camp, pushed aside a servant, and began to rifle through the bags and cases containing the party's equipment and belongings. Conder was resting in his tent recovering from a bout of fever when he heard the sheikh loudly cursing Christ with obscene words as he rummaged about. A deeply religious man such as Conder was gravely offended by the blasphemies. He rushed from the tent and was immediately set upon by the sheikh, who tried to grab his throat, but Conder, who had excelled at hand-to-hand combat at the Royal Military Academy at Woolwich, knocked him down with one swift punch to the chin. The Moslem came to his senses moments later and, seething after the humiliating put-down, he launched a second attack. Once again as he lunged at Conder, he was knocked to the ground, this time with a combination of punches. The sheikh, bleeding from the mouth and nose, drew a knife, but Conder's servant wrenched it from his grasp, and several other members of the party easily subdued the bellicose Arab and tied him up. However, the sheikh let out a cry for help. "Where are my young men?" he yelled, and around two hundred men, armed with clubs, knives and stones, poured into the camp. With two hundred men against five Englishmen and ten native servants, the odds looked very bleak indeed, although the five English surveyors were armed – but they only had intentions of opening fire as a last resort. In the face of certain death, Conder released the sheikh in an attempt to appease the mob, but as soon as he was unbound, the sheikh yelled: "Kill the Christian dogs!"

Conder was warning the Arab crowd that they would pay with their lives if they harmed an Englishman when a member of the mob suddenly rushed out and delivered a furious blow to his forehead with a large club. Blood flowed down Conder's face, and when his attacker attempted to strike again, he butted him in the chest, winding the Arab, but the club still struck Conder's neck, inflicting a serious injury. Conder staggered away, and the crowd surged forward, but Kitchener stood between them and Conder. He bravely shielded his best friend, and Conder joined the rest of the search party for a hasty retreat up a hill, from where they saw, to their immense relief, the local Turkish garrison coming their way by pure chance. Seventeen of the attackers were later given prison sentences of varying lengths and the PEF was awarded £112 in compensation (which disappointed them as they had put in a damages claim for £400). Conder later gave details of the incredible retreat from what seemed like certain death in a report to the PEF:

> *I must inevitably have been murdered but for the cool and prompt assistance of Lieutenant Kitchener, who managed to get to me and engaged one of the club-men, covering my retreat. A blow descending upon the top of his head, he parried it with a cane, which was broken by the force of the blow. Having retired a few paces from the thick of the fray, I saw the Arabs were gradually surrounding us, stealing behind trees and through vineyards ... I gave the order to leave the tents and fly round the hill. Lieutenant Kitchener was the last to obey this order, being engaged in front. He retreated to his tent, and whilst running he was fired at, and heard the bullet whistle by his head.*

In October 1875, Kitchener and Conder returned home after concerns of a cholera epidemic in northern Palestine. Both had also deemed it wise to suspend the Survey's work until the perpetrators of the Safed incident had been dealt with. By now, Conder had become seriously ill from an attack of malaria contracted on the Plains of Samaria. He was not expected to live long, and at home, as he shivered in his bed, his fiancee, Myra Rachel Foord, the feisty, eldest daughter of a prominent army general, broke off her engagement to him. Conder felt crushed and betrayed by this heartless abandonment, and although he became engaged to Myra again when he was well, and subsequently married her at Guildford, Surrey, on 12 June 1877, his attitude towards Myra, and women in general, changed for the worse after that awful time when his fiancee had deserted him in his hour of need, as he hovered between life and death. Conder's army life and intelligence work kept him from home for days, often weeks and months, and although Claude and Myra never divorced, they lived separate lives.

In 1901, Conder visited Clare and Limerick to carry out a map-making survey (a thinly-disguised excuse to spy on Irish Nationalists). His officers brought their wives and children to Ireland, but Conder chose to leave his own wife and two children at home. The only woman he seemed close to was his mother Anne Matilda, and he had written to her regularly when he was in Palestine. When she died in 1890, Claude was devastated and was given a fortnight's compassionate leave.

In the days prior to the Safed incident, the Survey had been facing a funding crisis. Charles Warren was making plans to request extra funding for the Survey from the United Grand Lodge of Free and Accepted Masons (for they had given substantial amounts to the cash-strapped PEF in the past) when suddenly, the Safed attack was reported in the press and was seen by readers at home as a classic example of the 'Christian soldier' being assailed by Moslem Arabs on the grounds of religion. This propaganda was expected to motivate British Christians to fill the coffers of the PEF, but the public were not roused at all.

The War Office came to the short-term rescue, paying for rented rooms in South Kensington Museum, where Kitchener and Conder (when he had recovered from malaria) would draw up two maps (on different scales) of the vast territories of Palestine. With a Russian-Turkish war becoming an increasing possibility, the maps being painstakingly produced by Conder and Kitchener were eagerly awaited by British military intelligence. If Russia occupied the Turkish provinces (including Palestine), then Britain's interests in India would be threatened, and Russian ships would undoubtedly control the Persian Gulf – an extension of the Indian Ocean.

For twelve months, Conder and Kitchener worked on the maps, but Conder soon found himself cold-shouldered out of an inner circle of military men (which included Kitchener) during the management of map compilation. Moreover, Kitchener insisted that his name should appear on the maps – as the main compiler. Conder felt Kitchener had blatantly cheated him out of his epic work, and the matter resulted in the break-up of what had been a long friendship.

It is said that Conder's personality was abominable at times. He has been described as fiercely arrogant, egotistical, outspoken and prone to react viciously to criticism. "What an impossible fellow Conder is," complained Sir Charles Wilson, War Office and Intelligence Department bigwig, in a letter to Walter Besant, PEF treasurer, in 1877. Others found Conder impossible as well. Sir Charles Warren, one of Conder's closest friends, and one of the most accomplished and respected Masons in the world, did not invite him into the Brotherhood. Conder condescendingly dismissed the

Masons as just some clique of deluded individuals, and yet he had a vast knowledge of Masonry rituals and their Biblical origins, particularly those linked to the Temple of Solomon. In his military career, Conder rose no further than a brevet Colonel, despite his many years of distinguished service and heroic achievements in Palestine. Promotion never came his way because he was something of a loose cannon, who vehemently stood up to senior officers if he thought they were wrong, almost to the point of insubordination.

Conder was also a fierce royalist, and in 1881, he was delighted and honoured to be appointed to take the 18-year-old Prince Albert Victor and 16-year-old Prince George of Wales (the future King George V) on a tour of the Holy Land. Conder later noted, rather romantically, in his book *Heth and Moab* (1883), that no royal personages had ventured into the country beyond the Jordan since the twelfth century. Their Royal Highnesses were captivated by Conder's exotic tales of the Druzes, the superstitions and folklore of the Oriental Jews, the nomadic life of the Arabs, and of course, stories from the Old Testament, told in the very settings where they had taken place many centuries before. Conder took the princes throughout the whole of Palestine and went with them to a sacred harem and also into the Mosque at Hebron, before travelling into the country east of Jordan. Prince 'Albert V' (as the future Duke of Clarence would be nicknamed), was given an ancient Phoenician seal with a human figure holding a disc, flanked by a hawk-headed cherub on one side, and a scarabaeus on the other. Conder told him how the hawk on the seal was the emblem of Horus, Egyptian god of the sky and a highly important deity. The scarabaeus beetle was a symbol of birth and renewal. Prince Albert treasured the

Phoenician seal until his death at Norfolk – at the age of 28 – during the great influenza pandemic, in January 1892.

On 8 May 1894, two years after the death of the Duke of Clarence, his younger brother, George, the Duke of York, presided at a meeting by the PEF in the Westminster Town Hall, introducing Claude Reignier Conder's talk on 'Future Researches in Palestine'. Before and after the talk, the Duke heaped praise on Conder, who he now regarded as a great friend.

Conder was in the thick of the action at some of the bloodiest conflicts of the 1880s, most notably the fierce battles at Kassassin and Tel-el-Kebir, both fought during 1882 in Egypt. At this time, Conder was serving in the Headquarters Staff of the Intelligence Department at Egypt. The Battle of Kasassin was the scene of great confusion and slaughter, with the Egyptians fleeing from British troops in great disorder. Then, just a fortnight later came the Battle of Tel-el-Kebir. Lieutenant General Wolseley and his officers coordinated an incredible stealthy attack under the cover of darkness which lasted around half an hour, yet in that short space of time, the battle against Arabi Pasha was won. The 60,000-strong Egyptian army slept, armed, behind earthwork fortifications, but they were still taken by surprise. Arabi was still in bed when the attack took place and he later complained that because the British had not warned him of the attack, he had not even time to put on his boots.

Conder was one of the soldiers who took part in the silent attack by starlight. He and the other troops had awaited orders in complete silence that night, and earlier in the evening, no soldier had been allowed to smoke in case the enemy saw their Lucifer matches lighting pipes and cigarettes. Conder seemed particularly suited to night-time operations in Egypt. Today, it is known that rhodopsin – a chemical found in the retina of the eye – is responsible for good night vision, and Conder may have been one of those people who have higher rhodopsin levels than the average person. It is also known that large pupils aid night vision, and Conder's eyes, described by many who knew him as unusual, had large pupils. In Buck's Row, Berner Street and Mitre Square, Jack the Ripper operated in darkness that would hinder the work of an average killer. When Charles Cross and Robert Paul came across the body of Mary Ann Nichols, it was so dark in Buck's Row, they couldn't tell whether the victim was alive or dead, and neither of them could even see that the corpse had wide open eyes and a cut throat. In Dutfield's Yard on Berner Street, Louis Diemschutz couldn't see Elizabeth Stride's body on the ground and had to feel for it with his whip before striking a match. The corner of Mitre Square where Catharine Eddowes met her fate was very dark indeed, and in all probability, when PC James Harvey glanced in at the square on the night of the murder, he was unable to see the Ripper crouching in the shadows because of the lack of illumination. And yet, in this darkness, the Ripper expertly extracted a womb and kidney from Eddowes – after he had drawn a series of mysterious glyphs on the face of the corpse.

Conder was an expert in unarmed combat, and up to 1900 he was instructing the troops at Weymouth in self-defence. Kitchener was surprised at Conder's self-defence skills when his friend fought off several Arab attackers at Safed in 1875. One of these Arabs hurled himself at Conder, who calmly crouched down so that the Arab went straight over his shoulders, and Kitchener watched as his colleague slowly rose with split-second timing, and threw the attacker off balance at his body's centre of gravity. Conder's hand-to-hand fighting skills seemed a world away from the clumsy John L Sullivan style of fisticuffs of the day, and it is likely that Conder, being an outstanding student of Orientalism, as well as being a cousin to Josiah Conder, the first Western architect in Japan, would have studied Eastern martial arts.

As Conder's career in the army and the secret military intelligence service progressed, Sir Charles Warren became his closest friend, and in 1884 the two men wrote a best-selling book, 'Jerusalem', about their joint archaeological work and discoveries in that ancient capital city. Conder then enjoyed a stint as a senior officer in Bechuanaland till 1885, before he was appointed British Commissioner on the Transvaal border in the following year.

In 1867, rich diamond mines had been discovered in Griqualand West, Central South Africa, and this area, being bordered by the Transvaal (which was colonised by Boer settlers) and the British Cape Colony, led to a conflict of interests about the vast source of wealth that was there for the taking. Both the British and the Boers wanted to take control of the mines. By 1871 Griqualand West had been annexed by Britain, but the Boers remained antagonistic towards the British, and some of them began to appropriate areas of land (along with cattle) from the local Tswana tribes by force. An enforcer for the Government, who could assert British Sovereignty, was needed in Griqualand West, and Warren was chosen for the post. In the autumn of 1884, Warren and Conder were sent to Bechuanaland with an army of regulars and volunteers to 'clear' the country. Their mission was a resounding success without a shot being fired. The freebooters were removed from the territories and Bechuanaland was pacified.

In April 1886, Warren returned to London to take up the post of Chief Commissioner of the Metropolitan Police. A

347

writer in the Royal Engineers' Journal proudly reported the appointment, and the idea of appointing such a distinguished army general as the head of the Met was received with warm enthusiasm by the editors of the right-wing newspapers, but T P O'Connor, the Irish Home Ruler and editor of the radical *Star* newspaper, knew the real reason behind the appointment of Warren, as did William T Stead, the Socialist editor of the equally radical (and sensationalist) *Pall Mall Gazette*.

The previous Commissioner of the Metropolitan Police, Sir Edmund Henderson, had failed to prevent a serious demonstration against unemployment in London. This demonstration, which had taken place weeks before Warren's appointment, on 8 February, had been held in Trafalgar Square. The mass-meeting to draw the authorities' attention to the plight of the outcast poor was addressed by speakers of a very inflammatory character, and revolutionary doctrines of a violent kind were loudly voiced by them. When the meeting ended, the mob did not disperse peacefully, but went on the rampage instead, and in the ensuing riot, a number of ministerial club windows on Pall Mall were smashed. The rioters broke into the premises of wine sellers, bakers and jewellers in the vicinity of Piccadilly and South Audley Street. Stores such as Peter Robinson and Marshall & Snelgrove were looted, and the rioters also attacked and robbed innocent bystanders as well as the passengers of passing carriages.

The police, outnumbered and disorganised, were powerless to stop the march of the rioting mobs as they passed through Oxford Street and Regent Street, smashing the windows of various shops. Metropolitan Police Commissioner Sir Edmund Henderson was heavily criticised for allowing the Trafalgar Square demonstrations to get out of hand and promptly tendered his resignation. Hardliner Warren replaced the inefficient, almost spineless Henderson. The radicals knew hard times lay ahead with a new, uncompromising adversary placed in such a position of power. From that moment on, all plans for a Socialist revolution needed more than stones and inflammatory speeches. The Fenians, Socialists and Anarchists joined forces against the Establishment.

Later that year, Sir Charles Warren visited Limerick – Marie Jeanette Kelly's alleged home county – supposedly to give a talk to the Scientific Society there, but also to give backing to his military colleague Sir Redvers Buller, who was soon to become the Under Secretary at the Irish Office in 1886. Buller was in Ireland at this time on a mission to confront militant Fenians. Whilst staying at a Kerry residence close to Lake Killarney, Warren received an audacious request; a group of locals had invited him into a barn to talk about his detection of the murderers of Professor Edward Palmer in Egypt. Buller immediately smelt a rat and strongly advised Warren not to accept the sinister invitation, but Warren decided to go, and was taken by boat across Lake Killarney to the barn, where 25 men waited. The men were probably Fenians, but they treated Warren to a meal and fine whiskey. One of those assembled asked him about his "detective work" regarding the detection and apprehension of the killers of Professor Palmer, who had been murdered during an intelligence-gathering mission in Egypt in 1882.

Palmer had brought a vast amount of gold to bribe the sheikhs and purchase camels for his reconnaissance mission, and during his trip to Jaffa, he happened to meet Meter abu Sofieh, an old Arab, who pretended to be sheikh of the Lehewat tribe. Palmer naively believed Sofieh. By 23

August that year, it was obvious to the War Office and the PEF that something had gone wrong. Palmer's party was not heard from, even though the telegraph they used to relay back information was still working. Sir Charles Warren was immediately chosen as the man who could hunt for Palmer and his expedition. Warren took command of the search on 6 October, and quickly discovered books, clothes and other personal effects of the missing men in the desert dust. On Friday 27 October, the search ended when bodies were discovered. The five members of the expedition had been almost stripped naked before being led by 25 Bedouins along high precipices for about a mile to the edge of a plateau. Sixty feet below there was a stream. Professor Palmer was executed first and his body fell into the gully. The four others made a run for it but each was shot in the back, and one was finished off by a sword. Within eight weeks, Warren had tracked down the guilty party, which included the impostor Meter abu Sofieh. He gave himself up after hiding in the desert because, he maintained, Palmer had chillingly cursed him before he died. Strangely enough, Sofieh later died in a Suez hospital suffering from an extraordinary persecution complex. Three of the murderers were executed and the Bedouins who aided them were given prison sentences.

The Irishmen at the barn near Lake Killarney asked Warren if he would be able to track down their own countrymen, should they commit a murder of the type perpetrated by the Bedouins. Warren calmly replied that he could, and that he would undoubtedly be able to bring the hypothetical Irish killers to justice just as easily as the Bedouin murderers, as the Irish tribal customs would be as helpful to him as the traditions of the desert-dwelling Bedouins. The Irishmen agreed after a tense pause in the conversation. Warren finished his meal, and the whiskey, and after a few handshakes he was ushered from the barn and taken back across the lake.

From 1887 to 1894, Claude Reignier Conder spent periods in London at the War Office, and Southampton, where he had a relatively undemanding job as a supervisor of map engravings at the Ordnance Survey. He also visited Fort Elson, Gosport on several occasions – where Ted Stanley, Annie Chapman's enigmatic 'lover' was stationed. During the year the Ripper murders took place, 1888, 39-year-old Conder's exact whereabouts and activities are a little fuzzy. He was a prolific writer, with books being published each year, but in 1888 he wrote nothing. Two days after the murder of Annie Chapman, on 10 September, Conder was asked to read a short paper on his theories for the British Association lectures, held at Bath. He mentioned his theories about the origins of the early races of Western Asia, maintaining that the Turkish River Sangarius was connected to the Manchurian river Sangari, and he discussed the many Manchu words that were related to similar words in the West. At the end of that month, a Manchu word 'Juwes' would be chalked on a wall over a piece of bloody apron torn from Ripper victim Catharine Eddowes.

The mysterious symbols carefully cut into Eddowes' face are identical to the glyphs read and written by Conder and Warren. Warren had the Ripper's 'Juwes' message erased from the wall, and Juwe is a Manchu word known to Conder and Warren (who were both renowned authorities on the Altaic languages), yet Warren unashamedly lied to the public and his own police force when he stated that he was not familiar with that word. Some years later, Warren presided at a Caxton Hall lecture delivered by Conder on the origin of the Chinese, and during that lecture, Conder drew the audience's attention to words such as duo, dual, deux and duet – which all pertained to two. Conder believed these words were connected by etymology to the Manchu word Juwe, which means 'two'. Did the duality symbolised by this word have any relevance to the Jews? A lot of the speculation expressed by Conder was hotly criticised in his lifetime, but he vehemently believed that the Chinese and the Jews shared the same ancestors, by way of the Babylonians, Hittites, Moabites and so on. Conder's Juwes would be a unification of the two families of Jew – the Jews of Israel (Middle East) and the Jews of Manchuria (Far East). The Juwes message was chalked by the Ripper on the doorway to 108-119 Wentworth Dwellings tenement, which was inhabited mostly by Jews, and the address on which the cryptic message was chalked was the entrance leading to the home of Israel Sunshine, a young Russian Jew who would later be involved in a fight in Berner Street with Louis Diemschutz – the Socialist Jew who found Elizabeth Stride's body on the night of the Double Event. Not only was the address at the Wentworth Dwellings marked with a chalked message, it was also marked with a piece of bloody apron taken from Catharine Eddowes, a woman who, according to her partner John Kelly, had been making a living by running errands for the Jews.

During research for this book, in 2001, it was leaked out that Claude Reignier Conder was the man we suspected of being Jack the Ripper, and an article subsequently appeared in the *Gloucester Citizen*. We afterwards received a letter from a man in Cheltenham who had read the newspaper article, and who said he was a distant relative of Claude Conder. This man had heard a strange story many years before in his youth from an aunt, that Conder's younger brother, Rene Francois Reignier Conder, who was born at Naples in 1859, had been involved in the British intelligence service in Victorian and Edwardian times. His cover had been a librarian and peripatetic schoolteacher, and in later years he had been an associate of one Frederick Abberline, the police inspector in charge of the detectives on the ground during the Whitechapel Murders case. Rene Francois was said to have also been a friend to Abberline's brother Edward, but in what capacity is not known. Facts to substantiate the link between Conder and Abberline are exceedingly scarce, but there is one intriguing piece of information to be found in the 1901 census of England and Wales. In 1901, Inspector Frederick Abberline is listed as living at 313 Clapham Road, Lambeth, with his wife Emma. Living next door to Abberline, in the house of William Knight, is Rene Francois Reignier Conder. It is also known that Rene Conder often visited his uncle, the Reverend Rene FR Conder at St George's, Botolph Lane, in the Billingsgate ward of London (where Marie Jeanette Kelly's boyfriend Joe Barnett worked) in 1888.

Conder's penultimate book *The Rise of Man*, written in 1908, was not well-received by academia. Within this uneven work, Conder ambitiously attempted to condense nothing less than the 'social history of mankind' into 400 pages. Critics branded Conder as a naive writer who, while unquestionably a world expert in Biblical archaeology, was clearly out of his depth as a social historian. In *The Rise of Man* Conder presented this peculiar parable to illustrate his concept of 'necessary evil':

In the American plains there grows a poisonous shrub, covering great spaces which neither man nor beast of prey can pass. What use could good being have intended to result from such an evil growth? The answer is that

*the antelope stamps with her armoured hoofs a nest in
the midst, where she may safely lay her young.*

Was the slaughter of six women (including the Whitehall
Torso victim) another example of Conder's necessary evil?

After the murder of Marie Jeanette Kelly, the Ripper
killings stopped. The Anarchists, Fenians and Socialists
began to fragment into impotent factions once more, and
any attempts to regroup into their once formidable alliance
would be doomed, because the Establishment had a few
new and unlikely weapons in its armoury. One was the
'tanner' – a silver coin worth sixpence. That was the hourly
wage finally paid to the London Dockers after the success
of the Great Dock Strike of 1889. This strike had been
preceded by the landmark Gas Workers' Dispute and the
Bryant & May match strike. Running parallel with the Great
Dock Strike of 1889, was the Tailors' Strike, which lasted
until the end of September.

One of the many Socialists making donations to the
Strike Fund for the East End Tailors during this time was
one Louis Diemschutz, the man who found Elizabeth
Stride's body outside his club. Diemschutz donated over
eight shillings to the strike fund, so the families of the
strikers could afford food during the prolonged stoppage. In
an act of grand solidarity, the Dockers Strike Committee
donated £100 to the striking tailors, even though the
committee were struggling to attract funds for their own
cause. William Wess, the overseer of the radical printing
office in Dutfield's Yard (who had been called to give
evidence at the inquest into Stride's death) was acting as a
secretary to the tailors' strike organisers and also audited
the balance sheet of the strike fund. All of the posters and
printed handbills that incited the tailors' to strike were

printed by the Worker's Friend at 40 Berner Street, the scene of the Stride murder. Diemschutz and Wess, of the Berner Street workingmen's club, no doubt hoped the tailors' strike would escalate into a violent mass demonstration of ten thousand strikers, but fortunately, the striker's terms were accepted. Government contractors paid decent wages at trade-union rates, hours of work were reduced to no more than 12 per day, meals would be taken outside factory premises, with one hour given for dinner, and a half hour given for tea. Government contractors also agreed not to give out work to be done at home at night after working hours.

Louis Diemschutz had been, from all accounts, unjustly sentenced to three months behind bars that year, supposedly for assaulting a policeman (who kicked Mrs Diemschutz) during a Socialist riot in Berner Street. Israel Sunshine, who had allegedly been attacked by Diemschutz and other Socialists in that street fight between the Anarchists and undercover police, was from the Wentworth Dwellings. Jack the Ripper had written his controversial Juwes graffito on the very doorway that led to Sunshine's tenement apartment. At the court hearing into the fracas, Sunshine said he had been innocently walking down Berner Street (but did not say why he was there, three quarters of a mile from his home, or where he was going) when he was set upon by Diemschutz and Isaacs Kozebrodsky. The Assistant Judge of the London Session, Sir Peter Edlin, refused to accept the Not Guilty verdict of the Jury twice, and sent them back to deliberate in a room that was locked until the Jury decided on the verdict Sir Peter wanted to hear. Diemschutz was sentenced to three months' imprisonment with hard labour.

When the police stormed the workingmen's club during

that planned fight in January, they not only tore down pictures of Karl Marx, smashed the windows, and ransacked the premises, they even broke open the loft door of 40 Berner Street in their search for bombs and inflammatory literature. Police batons and fists battered club members, and even women who were present. After this, Whitehall kept Diemschutz's Berner Street Club under constant observation until the Anarchists and Socialists had had enough. The club closed and the staff of the Worker's Friend held their business meetings in the Sugar Loaf public house on Hanbury Street. Marie Jeanette Kelly's landlord, John McCarthy, often met the famous music hall singer Marie Lloyd at this same pub. Marie helped to get McCarthy's children on to the stage years later.

Throughout the early 1890s, Diemschutz found himself flogging the dead horse of Anarchism. He visited working men's clubs in northern England, and spoke on matters that seemed increasingly irrelevant and quaint in the days of the new trade unionism, such as pointless debates on the failed Paris Commune of 1871 (which always ended with the comrades singing 'La Marseillaise'). Eventually, Louis Diemschutz disappeared into obscurity.

Near the top of Whitechapel's New Road, close to Commercial Road, in a quiet corner of the East End, the new headquarters of the Worker's Friend stood for a while, hidden down a dark narrow passage. Admittance through a door devoid of any knocker, bell, or handle was only allowed to those who knew the passwords, but in the end, nobody came. The trade union movement would soon give birth to the Labour Party, and Socialism would no longer be a sinister word. Philip Krantz, who edited the radical publication *The Worker's Friend* at Berner Street, eventually gave up trying to convert the oppressed masses and went to

356

the United States, where he ended his days in disillusionment in the Bronx. He died of heart disease at his American home at 2008 Hughes Avenue, aged 65, on 28 November 1922.

In the aftermath of the Ripper murders, there was, as we have seen, a wave of strikes, but all of them ended peacefully with the strikers having their demands met. There was one incident that year which could have supplied the ailing radicals, dissidents and Fenians with propaganda on a plate, but it was quickly hushed up by the authorities. This was the Cleveland Street Scandal. In November 1889, the following article appeared in syndicated newspapers across Australia:

A LONDON CLUB SCANDAL

THE AFFAIR SUPPRESSED
[United Press Association]
London, November 9

A horrible scandal in connection with a private West End Club is reported. Ninety-eight members in all are implicated. Thirty-one warrants have been issued, but will not be executed on the understanding that the persons connected with it leave the United Kingdom. The list of offenders includes future dukes, the sons of dukes, peers, Hebrew financiers, many honourable persons, and several officers of the Imperial Army. All the latter have suddenly resigned their commissions. The offenders have fled. The newspapers have suppressed reference to the scandal, but there is no doubt to its having taken place.

Was this tantalisingly short article penned by a

sensationalist reporter, or was there a grain of truth in it? Well, there was much more than a grain of truth in it, and the origin of the story undoubtedly stemmed from the Cleveland Street Scandal, which unfolded in the infernal summer of 1889.

The scandal was uncovered by accident. There had been a number of petty postal order thefts at the London Central Telegraph Office in St Martin-le-Grand, and early in July, a diligent policeman, Constable Luke Hanks, discovered that 15-year-old Charles Thomas Swinscow, one of the telegraph delivery boys at the office had 18 shillings upon his person. This amounted to several weeks' wages for a messenger boy of that age, so the police were keen to know where he had obtained such a sum. Swinscow's reply was to send shockwaves through Victorian society. The boy said that he had earned the money from sleeping with men at a house in Cleveland Street, in the well-to-do Fitzrovia district of London. Number 19 Cleveland Street, the house in question, turned out to be a homosexual brothel catering for aristocratic and other upper-class clients, run by 35-year-old Charles Hammond and his intimate live-in acquaintance, 40-year-old George Veck, a former Post Office employee who often impersonated a clergyman, often going out bedecked in clerical robes. Veck had been dismissed from his position at the Post Office because of improper conduct towards the messenger boys. He often went out bedecked in clerical robes, even though he had never been in holy orders. Swinscow alleged that he had been introduced to Charles Hammond by an 18-year-old Post Office Clerk named Henry Horace Newlove. Swinscow named two other telegraph boys, both aged 17, who also worked at the brothel: Charles Ernest Thickbroom and George Alma Wright.

Hanks lost no time in obtaining statements from Thickbroom and Wright, and reported his findings to his superiors. On the Saturday morning of 6 July, Inspector Frederick Abberline arrived at the male brothel on Cleveland Street with a warrant to arrest Hammond and Newlove for violation of Section 11 of the 1885 Criminal Law Amendment Act – an act that effectively branded all homosexual acts between men (along with procurement and attempted procurement of such acts) punishable by up to two years' imprisonment. Abberline discovered that Number 19 was locked, and Hammond had fled.

The teenager Newlove was subsequently apprehended at his mother's house in Camden Town by Abberline. It transpired that Newlove had warned Hammond, and he had gone to hide at his brother's Gravesend house. On the way to the police station, Henry Newlove began to name some of the illustrious clients at the male bordello. Lord Arthur Somerset (known to his close friends as 'Podge'), the son of the Duke of Beaufort and assistant equerry to the Prince of Wales, was a frequent visitor to the brothel, as was divorcee Henry James Fitzroy, Earl of Euston, and a prominent Army Colonel named Jervois.

Lord Somerset was duly interviewed by the police, yet no immediate action was taken against him. It soon became clear that a cover-up was under way. Why had Abberline, who had been in charge of the detectives on the ground in the Whitechapel Murders case in the impoverished East End, now been assigned to a scandal case in the affluent West End? These cases were surely worlds apart – or were they? Apparently not, because it was revealed that someone much closer to the throne than Somerset had also been visiting the Cleveland Street brothel – Prince Albert Victor – soon to become the Duke of Clarence, the Prince of

Wales' eldest son and heir.

Prince Albert Victor was called 'Victoria' in homosexual circles, and the Prime Minister Lord Salisbury and other members of the Government feared it would only be a matter of time before the prince's sexual orientation would become known to the public, and worse still, the radicals, who would use the scandalous information to undermine the Monarchy and rock the British Empire to its foundations.

Abberline had undoubtedly been brought in to deal with the potentially dangerous scandal because a Royal was involved. He had protected the Royal family and the Establishment before, in his capacity as a Fenian hunter and also as an intelligence officer placed in the Whitechapel Murders case to investigate a Fenian, Socialist and Anarchist network which was prepared to resort to a violent programme to start a British Revolution.

Lord Somerset fled the country, and later wrote to his closest friends, telling them that he had been forced to go abroad, rather than be made to give evidence against Prince Albert Victor in the ensuing trial. There were allegations of a cover-up in high places, made by Henry Labouchere, the Liberal MP who had been responsible for bringing in the amendment bearing his name in the Criminal Law Amendment Bill of 1885, which made all homosexual behaviour (short of buggery) a misdemeanour. Labouchere stated in the House of Commons that the Prime Minister, the Marquis of Salisbury, had deliberately let Charles Hammond escape from England to hide in the United States. Salisbury was also blamed for allowing Somerset to leave the country. Labouchere was temporarily suspended from Parliament because of his allegations. There were even whispers about Abberline's strange actions during the whole affair.

Abberline and his men kept watch on 19 Cleveland Street after the 'Reverend' Veck was seen, on 9 July, to offer Henry Newlove money to pervert the course of the impending trial, yet Abberline waited six weeks until Veck was arrested, and in that period, the former Ripper detective even watched the guilty parties remove furniture belonging to Charles Hammond from the brothel, yet Abberline still took no action. Hammond left the country with that furniture and went to France (with a boy), never to return to British shores.

Another unsavoury fact later emerged which added credence to Labouchere's allegations of a conspiracy in high places. Lord Salisbury had met Sir Dighton Probyn, senior aide to the Prince of Wales, at King's Cross Station, and the Prime Minister had imparted a warning to him: a warrant was about to be issued for the arrest of Lord Somerset. Sir Dighton then tipped off Somerset, who left the country immediately. Labouchere, again risking suspension from the House of Commons, said he was disgusted with this criminal behaviour "by the very guardians of public morality and law, with the Prime Minister at their head, to defeat the ends of justice."

Abberline and the Cabal at Whitehall which orchestrated so many of these black operations, once again saved the necks of the Royal Family by misleading and confusing the public, the Press and even the House of Commons, with devious lies, delayed legal action, and the abuse of the power invested in certain elected ministers by the people.

George Veck was jailed for four months, while Henry Newlove, a teenaged victim, corrupted by the self-styled bogus reverend, received a prison term of nine months. The other young men involved in the scandal were offered a regular income for the next three years, on the condition that they went to Australia and remained there. And what became of Prince Albert Victor? He was referred to as 'P.A.V.' in the Director of Public Prosecutions file on the Cleveland Street Scandal, which was kept under lock and key for 86 years, until the papers were opened to public inspection in 1975. The prince was hastily sent on a seven-month tour of India in October of that year, and it was widely rumoured at the time that Queen Victoria had sent her grandson abroad to avoid the aftermath of the Cleveland Street Scandal. Upon his return from India, the Queen made Prince Albert Victor the Duke of Clarence and Avondale, and Earl of Athlone. The Press in Britain had hardly mentioned the Cleveland Street Scandal. One publication, *The North London Press*, dared to name a few of those involved in the disgraceful affair, and its brave editorial stated:

> *These men have been allowed to leave the country, and thus defeat the ends of justice, because their prosecution would disclose the fact that a far more distinguished and more highly placed personage than themselves was inculpated in these disgusting crimes.*

The American Press freely reported on the scandal. *The Daily Northwestern* reported in May 1890:

> *Cable reports from England announce that Prince Albert Victor, eldest son of the Prince of Wales and heir presumptive to the throne, has returned from India, where he had gone to escape the smoke of the Cleveland Street Scandal, in which he was mixed up … Victor seems to inherit his father's vices without retaining any of his virtues, and his connection with the Cleveland Street*

*scandal is only another indication of the debauchery
which too conspicuously tinctures European royalty. The
inbred crowd of royal stock of all Europe is becoming
sadly deteriorated, both bodily and mentally, and cannot
long, in any event, survive the strength of higher order of
governmental civilisation which the common people are
attaining. Whether England will ever have a king after
the Prince of Wales is a matter of speculation, and some
prophets have even gone so far as to predict that
England will never have another king.*

Upon the death of King Edward VII – the father of the Duke of Clarence – all of his Royal Highness's private papers were burnt, in accordance with specific instructions in the monarch's will. Lord Knollys, the King's Private Secretary, and Lord Esher, the historian and Governor of Windsor Castle, personally incinerated the late king's documents, which were said to have detailed many dark secrets that could have seriously undermined the future of the Monarchy.

The Cleveland Street Scandal is just another example of the powers in Whitehall obstructing, perverting and defeating the course of justice in order to preserve and protect the Monarchy and maintain the status quo. The 'Jubilee Plot' – the British Government's shocking black operation to discredit the Home Rule movement in 1887, was not discovered until the files were declassified in the Public Record Office at Kew in the year 2000. Are there other secret files relevant to the Jack the Ripper murders that are awaiting declassification in the Public Record Office?

I believe that most of the documents directly relating to the truth behind the Whitechapel Murders were burnt long ago. We know that the handwritten memoirs of James Monro, Head of the Secret Department of intelligence-gathering agents (many of whom operated in Whitechapel in 1888) never once mention Jack the Ripper, and the silence speaks volumes. Monro cryptically remarked that the whole Jack the Ripper affair was a political 'hot potato' – but never elaborated any further on that comment, and in this book I have presented strong political connections between the Fenians, Anarchists and Socialists and the scenes of the Ripper crimes. It is my belief that in 1888, someone in Whitehall sanctioned the murders of six women: an unidentified female in her twenties, whose torso was found at Whitehall, Mary Ann Nichols, Annie Chapman, Elizabeth Stride, Catharine Eddowes and Marie Jeanette Kelly. I believe the torso woman and Kelly were Fenian agents (and possibly sisters), and Nichols, Chapman, Stride and Eddowes were merely couriers.

Claude Reignier Conder remained one of Sir Charles Warren's closest friends until his death from a cerebral embolism at the age of 61, on 16 February 1910. Conder died at his home, St Oswalds, Tivoli Road, Cheltenham, in the presence of his 55-year-old wife Myra, his 30-year-old son, Archibald – a Captain in the Royal Army Medical Corps – and his married daughter, 31-year-old Maude Lousada. Conder was buried two days later in Cheltenham Cemetery. The distinctive tapering granite headstone marking his resting place is engraved with the Cross of Jerusalem – the symbol of the Crusaders. Myra was interred in the same grave, aged 80, in 1934. Conder left his beloved mother's gold wedding ring to his brother Rene (the neighbour of Frederick Abberline), and to his wife, he bequeathed the various stocks, shares and government securities he held. The gross value of Conder's estate was just one thousand and seventy pounds, thirteen shillings and one penny. In the following year, Myra Conder was awarded a Civil List pension of £75 to support her. This

Sir Charles Warren in his eighties.

was awarded 'in consideration of the important services' her husband had provided.

Before he passed on to the Great Architect above, at the age of 86 years and 11 months, that other sentinel of the British Empire, Sir Charles Warren, remained tight-lipped about the Whitechapel Murders, even to fellow Masons. In 1919, Warren's wife, Lady Fanny Margaretta, passed away at Ellenborough Hall, Weston-Super-Mare. For eight years, Warren carried on with the remainder of his life without his beloved wife. He would rise each day at 6am, chop firewood and even in the most inclement weather, he would often pick mushrooms for breakfast in the local park. He passed away at 3 Southside Mansions, Weston-Super-Mare, Somerset, on 21 January 1927. The funeral service was held at Canterbury Cathedral, and when Warren was interred at nearby Westbere, I believe he was buried along with one of the greatest secrets in history.

AFTERWORD

WHAT IF WE ARE WRONG?

M any theorists and authors have publicised their unshakeable 'final solutions' to the great conundrum of the Whitechapel Murders case, only to see their theories fall apart when some previously unknown fact about their suspect subsequently comes to light. Stephen Knight, author of *Jack the Ripper: The Final Solution*, was convinced that the Ripper was three men – Royal Physician, Sir William Gull, a social-climbing coachman named John Netley and the impressionist painter Walter Sickert. Gull was 72 years of age at the time of the Ripper murders and was partially paralysed down one side of his body because of a recent stroke. Sickert, who has been nominated as a Ripper suspect by a number of people over the years, was actually in France from August to October in 1888, which means he could not have been responsible for the first four canonical Ripper murders.

Today, Knight's conspiracy theory – that the Whitechapel Murders were perpetrated by his 'unholy trinity' as they went about killing Royal blackmailers – has been largely discredited. It would be arrogant for the authors of this book to say that Claude Reignier Conder was, without a doubt, Jack the Ripper. We have looked at strong possibilities, but solid proof is still required. If Conder wasn't the Ripper, I believe we were not far off the mark, and that a military-trained man still fits the bill; a man who was close to Warren, and a man of exceptional stealth; a specialist in silent killing who had assassinated many times before, in wars as well as peacetime. I would still maintain that the Ripper murders were carried out for the reasons given in this book – to terrorise the Fenians and radicals by horrifically slaughtering their couriers. Although I believe that any Whitehall files about the Whitechapel Murders black operation have long been burnt, there may still be some momentous surprise waiting in store for us all; some small scrap of incriminating information carelessly overlooked by the Mandarins of Victorian Whitehall and accidentally filed away by them in a dusty folder which might be released by the Public Records Office any day soon.

INDEX

Aarons, Joseph, 140, 144, 146, 150, 154

Abberline, Emma 353

Abberline, Edward 353

Abberline, Inspector Frederick George 9, 10, 27, 100, 168, 188, 208, 212, 222, 223, 224, 228, 236, 238, 252, 253, 299, 307, 309, 353, 359, 360, 361

Abercarn (Newport) 184

Abergeldie (Scotland) 226

Abraham 177

Act of Treason (1351) 170

Adam Street (Adelphi, London) 107, 131, 175, 177,

Adler, Chief Rabbi Hermann Marcus 137

Al-Aqsa Mosque 123

Albert Victor Christian Edward, Prince (see Clarence, Duke of)

Albright and Wilson 308

Albrook, Lizzie 183, 200, 241, 242

Alderney Road 140, 145, 146, 149, 158

Aldgate 99, 102, 106, 159,

Aldgate High Street 85, 96, 97, 159, 161, 329

Alexander II, Tsar 118-119

Alexander III, Tsar 119

All Sorts and Conditions of Men 107

Altaic languages 125, 130, 134, 178, 298, 351

Alti Mountains 125

American Declaration of Independence 254

Anarchists 120, 122, 137, 138, 163, 165, 166, 169, 180, 182, 198, 199, 204, 225, 272, 285, 299, 306, 307, 308, 310, 311, 312, 315, 316, 319, 323, 327, 329, 349, 354, 355, 356, 360, 364

Anderson, Sir Robert 121, 122, 182, 230, 231, 282, 283, 287

Andrews, Keith 4, 6, 7

Andrews, PC Walter 249

Argent, Charles 19

Arnold, Superintendent Thomas 69, 127, 129, 224, 227

Arscott, Inspector 192

Ashbrigh, Abraham 312

Ashtaroth 335

Asquith, Herbert 156

At the Back of the North Wind (serialised 1868) 156

A Vindication of the Rights of Man, 256

A Violet from Mother's Grave 202

Baal 179

Bachert, Albert 275

'Backchurch End' 73

Backchurch Lane 81, 82

Baden-Powell, Sir Robert 132-133

Badham, Sergeant E 208, 220

Baker Street 72

Balfour, Arthur 317

Balmoral 226

Bank of England 257, 258

Barnaby and Burgho (see Bloodhounds)

Barnett, Joseph 92, 182,183, 184,187, 188, 189, 197, 198, 200,201, 209, 228, 229, 240, 243, 244, 329, 353

Barnett, Reverend Samuel 145

Bartitsu 295, 296

Barton-Wright, Edward William 295, 296

Bastille 254

Batchelor, J.H. 71, 72, 74, 75, 76

Bates, Ralph 8

Baxter, Wynne E 41, 43, 47, 107, 237, 238

Beach, Thomas Billis 282, 283

Beardsley, Aubrey 330

Beatrice, Princess 323

Bechuanaland 347

Beck, Inspector Walter 220

Bee Hive (public house) 65

Begg, Paul 290

Bell, William Edwin 54

Berkeley Square 30

Berkshire 30
Berlin 169
Bermondsey 95
Bermondsey Workhouse 86
Berner Street 60, 64, 65, 66, 67, 70, 71, 72, 74, 75, 77, 78, 79, 81, 82, 83, 108, 118, 127, 135, 136, 137, 166, 199, 212, 250, 321, 324, 346, 355, 356
Berners Hall (Islington) 203
Besant, Annie 107, 272, 273, 323, 324
Besant, Walter 107, 108,
Bethnal Green 30, 142, 187, 210
Bethnal Green Police Station 23
Bethnal Green Road, 113, 186
Bill, Buffalo 301
Birke, Alexander 100
Birmingham 86, 222, 262
Birmingham Daily Post 300
Bishopsgate 216
Bishopsgate Police Station 85, 97, 98, 106, 114, 164, 310, 329
Blackwell, Dr Frederick William 67, 68, 69, 77
Black Eagle Brewery 43
Black Swan (public house) 34, 36
Blair, Tony 266
Blairfindy 255
Blenkinsop, James 310
Bloodhounds 222, 224, 227, 313
Bloody Sunday Riots 132, 199, 226, 227, 272-275
Bluecoat Boy (public house) 216, 305
Blunden, PC George 305
Boer War 138
Boleyn, Anne 169
Bolshevik Revolution 254
Bond, Dr Thomas 172, 174, 231, 232, 233, 235, 236, 249, 313
Bow Street Police Court 191
Bow Street Runners 259
Bowyer, Thomas 216, 217, 218, 219, 220
Bradford 51, 172
Brady, Joseph 142
Brady Street 23
Brady Dwellings 323
Breezer's Hill 187
Brick Lane 17, 42, 191
Bright's Disease 150, 152

Britannia (public house) 31, 201, 214, 216
British Army's Centre of Excellence for Military Engineering 89
British Intelligence 91, 132, 204, 316, 319, 353
British Labour Party 138, 199, 356
British Law 170
British Museum 124
British Revolution 169, 275, 285, 360
British Secret Service 255, 281, 283, 289
Brittain, Charles 25
Broad Street 20
Brown, Dr Frederick Gordon 107, 108, 111, 112, 115, 134, 151, 162, 231, 294, 295
Brown, James 78
Brown's stable yard 21, 22
Brushfield Street 34
Buck's Row 20, 21, 22, 23, 24, 27, 28, 36, 39, 103, 134, 320, 321, 322, 323, 346
Buckingham Palace 90, 265, 327
Buckle, George Earl 281
Buki, Mrs 187, 304
Buller, Sir Redvers 349
Burckhardt, Johan Ludwig 130
Burgess, Anthony 11
Burke, Thomas 141, 142, 168, 278, 280, 299
Burns, John 273
Burrell, Emily 89, 91, 110, 114,
Burrell, Paul 327
Burton, Harry 100, 168, 309
Bury, William Henry, 5
Byfield, Sergeant James 97
Byrne, Frank 143, 144, 299
Byrne, Mary 143, 144, 299, 300
Bywell Castle 54

Cable Street 61
Cachous 63, 66, 68, 70, 135, 136
Cadosch, Albert, 44, 45, 325
Cardiff Infirmary 186
Caernarvonshire 186
Caine, Michael 9, 10
Callan, Thomas 89, 91
Cambridge Road (Bethnal Green) 202

Cambridge University 124
Cannon Street 223
Carey, James 140, 300
Carmichael Bruce, Assistant
    Commissioner Alexander 76
Caron, Henry Le 282
Carroll, Mrs 301
Carthy, Mrs Mary 187-188
Carttar, C J 54
Cassells Saturday Journal 253
Castle Alley 249
Castle, John 258
Castle Street 159
Cater, Christopher 112
Cater, Frank 112, 113, 136
Cater, Frank (junior) 112
Cater, Lydia 112
Catholic Universe 288
Cato Street Conspiracy 259-260
Cavendish, Lord Frederick 141, 142,
    168, 278, 299
Cavendish Square 121
Caxton Hall 126, 351
Central News Agency, 47, 50, 153,
    177, 179, 315
Central Vigilance Agency, 145
Chamberlain, Joseph 286
Chandler, Inspector Joseph 37, 45,
    46, 184
Chaplin, W. Knight 265
Chapman, Annie 19, 20, 29, 30, 31,
    32, 34, 36, 37, 38, 39, 40, 42, 45,
    46, 47, 107, 108, 110, 120, 134,
    155, 163, 164, 171, 181, 184, 212,
    237, 250, 268, 289, 294, 299, 312,
    321, 323, 327, 328, 329, 335, 351,
    364
Chapman, Annie Georgina 30
Chapman, Emily Ruth 30
Chapman. George 5
Chapman, John 29, 30
Chapman John (junior) 30
Charing Cross Station 284
Chatham 89, 91, 92
Chatham Jail 90, 91
Chatham, Lord 255
Cheapside 223
Chelsea 87, 183
Cheltenham 364
Chicago 306

'Chinese Fire' 100
Christ and Criticism 123
Christian Street 79
Chronicle newspaper 172
Church Passage 98, 99, 102, 160, 161,
    162, 164
Church Row (Bethnal Green) 42
Church Street (Spitalfields) 89, 95,
    199
City of Chester, SS 90
City of London Police 6, 117
Clan-na-Gael, 282, 306
Clapham Road (Lambeth) 353
Clarence, Duke of 5, 10, 226, 344,
    359, 360, 362
Clark, Mr 250
Clerkenwell Green 199
Cleveland Street Scandal 252, 299,
    357-363
Clockwork Orange, A 11
Clewer 30
Coal Mines Regulation Act (1887)
    309
Coercion Act (1881) 300
Cohen & Lavy 100
Coldstream Guards 183
Coles, Frances 251, 252
Collard, Inspector Edward 106, 107,
    110,
Collins, Maurice 142
Columbant, Father 243, 244
Commercial Road 63, 66, 67, 76, 77,
    81, 82, 136, 166, 252
Commercial Road Police Station 167
Commercial Street 58, 182, 199, 201,
    205, 206, 208,
Commercial Street Police Station
    127, 210, 217, 219, 220, 239, 244
Conder, Ann (Claude Conder's sister)
    330
Conder, Anne Matilda 330, 342
Conder, Archibald 364
Conder, Charles 330
Conder, Claude Reignier 119, 120,
    123, 124, 125, 126, 130,
    176, 177, 178, 297, 298, 299, 329,
    330, 331, 333, 334, 337, 338, 339,
    340, 341, 342, 343, 344, 345, 346,
    347, 351, 352, 366
Conder, Francis Roubiliac 330

Conder, Josiah (grandfather of
Claude Conder) 330
Conder, Josiah 296, 297, 298, 347
Conder, Louis 330
Conder, Maude 364
Conder, Myra Rachel (Claude
Conder's wife) 342, 364
Conder, Rene Francois Reignier 330,
352-353, 364
Conder, Reverend Rene 353
Conder, Samuel 330
Conway, Annie 87
Conway Catharine 86, 87
Conway, Thomas 86, 87
Conway, Thomas (junior) 86
Cooney's Lodging House 87-88, 92,
93, 95, 96, 98, 113, 114,
Cork 191
Cormack, John 146
Corn Laws 258
Coroner, Maria 51
County Mayo 86
Courts of Public Inquiry 157
Cowdry, Samuel and Sarah, 16-17
Cox, Mary Ann 201, 202, 204, 205,
212-213, 237, 246, 305, 326, 329
Crime and Disorder Act (1998) 169
Criminal Investigation Department
(CID) 168, 222
Criminal Law Amendment Act 359
Crispin Street 206
Cronin, Philip Patrick 306
Cross, Charles 20-21, 322, 323, 335,
346
Crossingham's Lodging House 31, 32,
38, 45, 46, 205, 210, 328
Crowley, Aleister 27
Crystal Palace 61
Cunningham, John Gilbert 100, 168
Cunninghame Graham, Robert 273,
275
'Czar' 222

Daily Mirror 52
Daily News 106
Daily Northwestern 362
Daily Telegraph 146
Daily Universal Register, The 280
Dale, Mr 56
Dalmatia 132

Dalston 159
Damascus 176
Davis or Davies (alleged husband of
Marie Jeanette Kelly) 184, 186,
303
Davis, John 34, 39
Davis, Thomas 192
Davies, Thomas 185
Davitt, Michael 138, 139, 166, 199,
288
Dear Boss Letter, 48, 50, 153
Declaration of the Rights of Man 254
Depp, Johnny 10
Der Arbeter Fraint (see Worker's
Friend, The)
Despard, Edward Marcus 257
Devonshire Street 56
Dew, Chief Inspector Walter 181,
220, 248
Dhiban 125
Diana, Princess of Wales 170, 327
Diemschutz, Louis 60-63, 65, 66, 78,
84, 118, 135, 136, 163, 315, 319,
346, 354, 355
Diemschutz, Mrs 62, 63, 77, 83, 352,
355
Dieppe 191
Dillon, John 288
DNA of Ripper 5, 51, 53
Dockers Strike Committee
Donovan, Timothy 31, 32, 34
Dorset Street 19, 30, 31, 34, 45, 46,
47, 56, 92, 95, 188, 190, 191, 196,
199, 201, 204, 205, 206, 207, 209,
210, 211, 212, 213, 214, 215, 219,
222, 223, 230, 232-235, 236, 237,
241, 243, 244, 304, 305, 326, 329
Douglas, Harry 71
Double Event murders 49, 50, 134,
140, 141, 144, 165, 226, 283, 298,
312, 319, 352
Doveton Street, 20
Dr Jekyll and Sister Hyde(1971) 8
Dr Jekyll and Mr Hyde (1932 and 1941
films)
Druitt, Montague John 5
Dublin 183, 283
Duke Street 98, 99, 102, 159, 160,
165, 310
Dunbar, Archdeacon 192

Dutfield's Yard 60, 63, 65, 66, 71, 74, 77, 78, 80, 81, 84, 85, 118, 135, 311, 312, 321, 346, 354
Dynamiter's Guide, The 308

Eagle, Morris 63, 65, 66
East End Underworld: Chapters in the Life of Arthur Harding 189
Easter Rising 156-157
East India Dock Road 56
East London Advertiser 101
Ecclesiastes 4
Echo newspaper 172
Eddowes, Catharine, 49, 50, 56, 85, 86-87, 92, 93, 94, 95, 96, 97, 98, 100, 104, 105,106, 108, 111, 112, 113, 114, 116, 118, 134, 135, 136, 140, 150, 151-152, 159, 161, 162, 163, 164, 165, 170, 178, 181, 224, 226, 277, 282, 294, 295, 298, 299, 309, 310, 311, 312, 314, 315, 316, 319, 321, 325, 327, 329, 336, 346, 351, 352, 364
Eddowes, Emma 86
Eddowes, George 86
Eddowes, Thomas 86
Edmett & Son 93
Edward VII, King 363
Edwards, George 259, 260
Elephant and Castle district 204, 306
Elephant and Castle Theatre 203
Ellen Street 82
Elliot, John George 192, 194
Elizabeth II, Her Majesty Queen 327
Ellisdon, Inspector 208
Engels, Friedrich 264
English Civil War 254
Esher, Lord 363
Essex Wharf 21, 23
Euston, Earl of 359
Euston Road, 195
Evans, John 34
Evening Express 94
Evening News 76, 77, 113, 161

Factory Act (1833) 262
Fairclough Street 78
Farmer, Annie 245, 246
Farnborough 45, 46, 184
Fashion Street 56, 58

Fawkes, Guy 170
Fenians 91, 100, 104, 120, 121, 122, 138, 139, 142, 143, 144, 154, 156, 165, 166, 168, 169, 180, 182, 184, 191, 204, 225, 278, 281, 285, 289, 299, 300, 305, 306, 313, 319, 327, 328, 329, 349, 354, 357, 360, 364, 366
'Fenian Fire' incendiary 308
Fenchurch Street 159, 223
Fetter Lane 15
Fido, Martin 290
Finsbury Circus 107
Finsbury Square 192
Flag of Ireland, The 281
Flameless Explosives Company Limited – Mitre Square 309
Fleet Street 51, 223, 283, 318
Fleming, Jospeh 186, 187
Flower and Dean Street 15, 17, 56, 59, 88, 95, 98, 113, 163, 206, 208, 311, 329
Foord, Myra Rachel 342
Fort Elson 19, 120, 351
Foster, Superintendent Alfred 137
Foster, Elizabeth 199
Foster, Frederick William 134, 135
Fox, Will 202
Francis, James 203
Francis, Williams 203
Freemason's Hall 247
French Revolution 254, 255
Friar's-Mount Gang 210
From Hell Letter 147-149, 152-153, 155
From Hell (2001 film) 10
Frost, Reverend 331
Frying Pan public house 17

George Yard 61
Genesis, Book of 126, 131
George III, King 256, 257, 259
George V, King 344, 345
George Street (Spitalfields) 245
Gestapo 11
Gandhi, Mohandas Karamchand 139
Gerrald, Joseph 256
Gilbert, Monsignor 276
Gilleman 63
Gladstone Street

372

Gladstone, Mary 288
Gladstone, William Ewart 5, 271, 279, 286, 288, 305
Glaisher, James 130, 131
Globe Road 146, 149, 158
Glorious Revolution of 1688 255
Gloucester Citizen 352
Glyphs on face of Eddowes 134, 135, 298
Golden Jubilee 90
Golden Lane Mortuary 110
Golden Lion (public house) 287
Goldstein, Leon 79
Goldstein & Son 79
Goodson, Henry 191, 193, 195
Gordon of Khartoum 332
Gorky, Maxim 320
Gospel and its Ministry, The 230
Gosport 19, 120,
Gothenburg, Sweden 55
Goulston Street 115, 116, 118, 127, 128
Goulston Street Graffito 116, 117, 132, 165, 178-179, 224, 227, 314-315, 355
Grand, Charles Le 71, 72, 74, 75, 76
Grand Lodge of England 107
Grant, Colonel 255
Grant, Ulysses S 296
Great Assembly Hall 138
Great Dock Strike 354
Great Eastern Railway 24
Great Pearl Street 205, 305
Great Synagogue (Duke Street) 98, 136
Great Tower Street 223
Green Gate Gang 210
Green, Mrs Emma 24
Green, James 36
Greenfield Street 76
Grenadier Guards 275
Gresham Street West 223
Grey, Lord 262
Grossmith, George 9
Grosvenor Square 270
Grove Street 66
Grover, Birdie 301, 302
Guildford 342
Guildhall 100

Gulf of Aqaba 176
Gull, Sir William Withey 5, 10, 366
Gwent 184, 185

Hackney 159
Halse, Detective Constable Daniel 117,
Hamburg 169
Hammer House of Horror 8
Hammond, Charles 358, 359, 360
Hampshire Militia, 20, 120
Hanbury Street 22, 34, 36, 37, 40, 42, 43, 44, 45, 52, 108, 129, 134, 171, 212, 244, 268, 323, 324, 325, 329, 356
Hanks, Constable Luke 358
Harding, Arthur 188
Harkins, Michael 89, 91
Harper's New Monthly Magazine 196
Harris, (Gaoler) 101
Harris, Harry 159, 160, 161, 164
Harrison, Sarah 71
Harrison, Barber & Co 25
Harrowby, Lord 259
Harvey, Maria 241, 243, 244
Harvey, PC James 80, 98, 102, 103, 106, 111, 162, 164, 346
Havering 209
Hayman, William 100
Healy, Timothy 288
Hejaz Railway 176
Hemingway, Cardiff Chief Constable Walter 303
Henderson, Sir Edward 89, 348
Henry of Battenberg, Prince 323
Heth and Moab 179, 344
Hewitt, Major James 170
Hibbert, Dr Charles 250
Hickey, Christopher 157
Hickey, Thomas 157
High Treason 256, 257, 260
Hill, Roland 30
Himmler, Heinrich 11-12
Hindustani 134
Hitchcock, Alfred 9
Hittite 125, 130
Holland, Ellen 17, 18-19, 20, 27, 328
Holland, PC James Thomas 106
Holland, Henry 36

373

Holmes, Sherlock 6
Home Office 6, 130, 156, 226, 258, 259, 289
Home Rule Bill 279
Hooper, MP John 317
Horn of Plenty (public house) 31, 216, 305
Horne & Co. 309, 310
Horner, Edward 309
Houndsditch 96, 98, 115, 310
House of Commons 204, 309
Howard, Catherine 169-170
Howells, Miriam 51
Humble, John Samuel 52
Huntley (Aberdeen) 156
Hunton 89
Hutchinson, George 206-212, 239, 292
Hutchison Street 159
Hutt, PC George Henry 97, 98
Hyde Park 55, 222, 265, 271

Ilford Cemetery 28
Imperial Club 159, 160, 161, 164
Indian Cavalry 90
Ings, James 259
International Workingmen's Educational Club 60, 70, 77, 79, 80, 81, 84, 118, 135, 136, 137, 139, 164, 166, 199, 312, 316, 321, 323, 324, 356
Invincibles, The 141, 169, 278, 281, 320
Ionian Revolts 254
Irish Home Rule 91, 166, 272, 276, 277, 278, 279, 285, 286, 287, 289, 299, 317, 328
Irishman, The 281
Irish National Land League 138, 281, 300
Irish Republican Brotherhood 138, 169
Isle of Wight 271
Ives, Mrs 202

Jack the Ripper (1959)
Jack the Ripper (1988 TV series) 9
Jack the Ripper: The Final Solution (1976 book) 10, 366
Jaffa 176

Japan, 295, 296, 298
'Jacqueline' (unnamed midwife) 5
Jekyll and Hyde (1888 play) 12-14
Jenkinson, Sir Edward 165, 166
Jerusalem 124, 177, 347
Jervois, Colonel 359
Jewish Chronicle 136, 137
Jewish Restoration campaign 120
Jewry Street 106
Jigaro, Professor Kano 296
Johnston, Edward 67
John Wright Coffee Rooms (Aldgate High Street) 309-310
Jones, Joseph 89, 92, 95
Jordan River 125, 176, 344
Joyce, William 169
Jubilee Day (1887) 90, 156
Jubilee Plot 91, 156, 277, 278, 289, 363
Jubilee Plotters 89, 91
Jubilee Street 146, 149
'Julia' 197
Juwes graffito, (see Goulston Street Graffito)
Juwes, Manchu word 126, 178, 298, 351, 352

Kassassin, Battle of 298, 345
Kearley and Tonge, 100, 101, 103, 105
Kelly, Mary Ann 97
'Kelly, Jane' 95
Kelly, John (common-law husband of Catharine Eddowes) 87, 88, 92, 93, 94, 95, 96, 110, 113, 114, 115, 325
Kelly, Henry 'Johnto' 183, 186
Kelly, John (father of Marie Jeanette) 182, 186
Kelly, Marie Jeanette 31, 56, 92, 158, 172, 175, 180, 181, 182, 183, 184, 185-187, 188, 189, 196, 197, 198, 199, 200, 201, 202, 203, 204, 205, 206, 207, 208, 209, 210, 211, 212, 213, 214, 215, 216, 217, 218, 219, 220, 221, 222, 223, 224, 226, 227, 228, 229-230, 231, 232, 233-235, 236, 237, 238, 239, 240, 241, 242, 243, 244, 246, 252, 253, 292, 295, 302, 303, 304, 305, 306, 307, 313, 314, 319, 326, 327, 328, 329, 335, 349, 353, 354, 364

Kelly, Timothy 140, 142
'Kennedy, Mrs' 212
Kent 89, 94, 96
Kent, James 36
Keturah 177
Keylers 205, 206, 220, 326
Kidney, Michael 55, 57
Kilgever 86
King Mesha 125
Kingston, Lady 272
Kinski, Klaus 9
Kirby, Madge 222
Kitchener, Lord Horatio Herbert 119, 120, 177, 331, 332, 338, 341, 343, 346
Knollys, Lord 262
Korean Peninsula 125
Kirby, Sergeant 23, 26
Knight, Stephen 10, 366
Knightsbridge 29, 187
Knightsbridge brothel 186, 187
Knill, Sir John 307
Kortright, Charles 301
Kozebrodski, Isaacs 62, 63, 65, 66, 315, 355
Krantz, Philip 65, 137, 356-357
Kray, Charlie 189
Kray, Reggie 189
Kray, Ronnie 189

La Marseillaise 137, 356
Labouchere, MP Henry 360, 361
Lamb, PC Henry 66, 67, 81
Lambeth Workhouse 27
Lander, Albert 87
Land of Promise 119
Lane, Catherine 58-59, 311
Lane, Patrick 59
Lave, Joseph 65
Lawende, Joseph 159, 160, 161, 164
Leadenhall Market 35
Leadenhall Street 223
Leather Apron, 48
Leeds 262
Leeds Mercury 166
Leman Street Police Station 79, 82, 127
Lenin, Vladimir 320
Letters from Hell (1868) 155

Leviticus, Book of 230
Levy, Joseph Hyam 159, 160, 161, 164
Lewis, George 192, 193
Lewis, Maurice 214, 215
Lewis, Sarah 205, 206, 211, 213, 214, 220, 237, 305, 326, 328
Leytonstone 5, 199
Lieven, Countess Dorothy 260-262
Life Guards 275
Lilley, Harriet 321, 322
Lilly, Joseph 192
Limerick 182, 186, 199, 239, 303, 305, 342, 349
Lindsay, James Ludovic 121
Lindsay, Lord Alexander William Crawford 120
Linnell, Alfred 275
Little Paternoster Row 34, 206, 214
Liverpool 90, 222, 287, 301
Liverpool Docks 91
Liverpool, Lord 260
Llewellyn, Dr Rees 25, 26, 38, 231, 294
Lloyd, Marie 190, 356
Lloyd's Magazine 113
Lloyd's Weekly Newspaper 321
Lodger, The (1926 film) 8
Lodger, The (novel) 8-9
London, Jack 267
London Correspondent Society 255, 256
London Echo 175
London Fire Brigade 18
London Hospital (Whitechapel Road) 44, 150, 265
London Labour 266
London Poor 266
Long, PC Alfred 115, 116, 315, 316
Long, Mrs Elizabeth 42-43, 45, 212
'Lord Haw Haw' 169
Lord Mayor's Show 198, 199, 219, 240, 241, 305, 306, 307, 326
'Lorraine Fire' 309
Lower George Street (Chelsea) 87
Lowndes, Marie Belloc 8-9
Ludgate Circus, 47
Ludgate Hill 223
Lushington, Sir Godfrey 130

Lusk Kidney 147-148, 150-152, 279, 299, 313
Lusk, Sir Andrew 100, 101
Lusk, George 71, 72, 140, 144, 145, 146, 147, 148, 149, 150, 153, 154, 155, 157, 168, 275, 312, 313, 319
Lusk, Susannah 145-146
Luxembourg 169
Lyceum Theatre 12
Lynchford Road Post Office, 46
Lyons, Lewis 323

Macarthur, Danny 190
Macluish, Dr David 269
Macdonald, Dr Roderick 235, 236, 237, 238
MacDonald, Winifred Louise 156
MacDonald, George 155, 156
Macguire, Billy 190
Maguire, Dr 284, 285
Mackay, John Henry 267
Madame Tussauds 227
'Mad Monk of Mitre Square' 99
Madrid 284
Maidstone 89
Maidstone High Street 92-93
Mallon, Superintendent John 144
Manchester 262
Manchu language 125, 126, 130, 134, 298, 351
Manhattan Minstrels 202
Manifesto of the Communist Party 264
Mann, Thomas J 152
Manners, Lord John 317
Manning, Cardinal 270
Mansfield, Richard 12-13
Mansion House 306
Mansion House Street 223
Maragot, Maurice 256
Marsh, Emily 146,149, 154
Marsh, Mr 146, 147
Marshall, William 78
Martin, Brother 99
Martin, Joseph 223, 224
Marx Aveling, Eleanor 138, 324
Marx, Karl 138, 264, 356
Match Girls' Strike 107, 323, 324, 354
Matters, Leonard 5

Matthews, Home Secretary Henry 127, 140, 227, 248, 283
Maxwell, Caroline 215, 216, 236, 237
Maybrick, James 5
Mayeba, Kumeko 297
Mayhew, Henry 266
McCarthy, Daniel 191
McCarthy, Elizabeth 191, 242
McCarthy, John 31, 47, 56, 188, 190, 191, 194, 195, 196, 200, 205, 216, 217, 218, 219, 220, 221, 224, 228, 242, 243, 252, 302, 304, 356
McCarthy, Margaret 191
McCormick, Donald 5
McKenzie, Alice 249, 250, 251
Meiji, Emperor 296
Metropolitan Board of Works 146
Metropolitan Police Force 89
'Mick Malone's Letters' 149
Midian 177
Mile End 92, 93, 140
Mile End Road 107, 137, 146, 150, 313
Mile End Vigilance Committee 71, 312
Millen, General Francis 278, 283
Miller's Court 31, 47, 56, 185, 188, 189, 196, 198, 201, 204, 206, 208, 210, 211, 213, 214, 215, 217, 220, 222, 223, 224, 227, 228, 230, 235, 236, 239, 240, 241, 242, 246, 302, 304, 305, 307, 313, 326, 328
Mincing Lane 223
Mitochondrial DNA, 51, 52
Mitre Square 85, 86, 98, 99, 100, 103, 104, 105, 106, 107, 108, 112, 115, 116, 127, 134, 137, 150, 151, 159, 160, 161, 162, 163, 164, 168, 199-200, 309, 310, 311, 312, 324, 329, 346
Mitre Street 100, 106
Mizen, PC Jonas 22, 23, 26
'Moab and Midian' Ripper Letter 177-178
Moabite Stone 125
Mohawk Minstrels 202-203
Molly Maguires 191
Monk, Mary Ann 27
Monro, Charles 290

Monro, James 156, 165, 204, 225, 247, 248, 249, 250-251, 290, 291, 363, 364
Montagu, MP Samuel 129
Montpelier Place (Brompton) 29
Moore, Inspector Henry 251, 252
Morganstone 186, 187
Moroney, Joseph 306
Morris, George 100, 101, 105, 106
Morris, William 138, 272, 273, 320
Mortimer, Fanny 77, 78, 79, 80, 83, 84
Mortimer, William 83
Moses 179
Moss, Aaron 191
Moss, Thomas 192
Mulqueeny, George 287
Mulshaw, Patrick 24-25
Mumford, James 25
Murder By Decree (1979 film) 10
Murphy, Hugh 318
My Adventures as a Spy 132

Neil, PC John 22, 23, 26
Nelson, Christian 72
Nelson, Lord 257
Netley, John 366
New Rhenish Newspaper, The 264
New Scotland Yard 81, 172
New Bridge Street, 47
New Court, 241
Newgate 260
Newlove, Henry Horace 358, 359, 361
New Road (Whitechapel) 356
New Street (Bishopsgate) 185
New York 90, 165, 300, 301
Nichols, Mary Ann 15-18, 20, 22, 24, 25, 26, 27, 31, 38, 47, 92, 107, 134, 175, 181, 225, 237, 294, 320, 321, 322, 323, 327, 328, 335, 364
Nichols, William 15, 27
'Nick Carter' 222
Norfolk 86
Norfolk Road 159
Northern California 103
North London Press 362
Notting Hill 30
Novello, Ivor 9

O'Brien, MP William 272, 288
O'Connor, T. P. 348
O'Shea, Katharine 284, 285, 286, 287, 288, 289
O'Shea, Captain William 284, 285, 286, 287
Old Bailey 275
Old Montague Street 22,
Oldfield, Assistant Chief Constable George 52
Old Nichols Gang 210
Olofsson, Lars Fredrik 55
Olsson, Sven 55
Openshaw, Dr Thomas 150, 152
Oram, Jane 17,
Osborn Place 19
Osborn Street 18, 19, 320, 328
Oxford Street 142
Oxford University 124

Packer, Matthew 70, 71, 72, 73, 74, 75, 76, 77, 212, 292
Packer, Mrs 71
Paine, Thomas 256
Pale of Settlement 119
Palestine 121, 332, 338, 341, 342, 343, 344, 345
Palestine Exploration Fund (PEF) 122, 130, 131, 175, 176, 177, 332, 333, 336, 337, 341, 342, 343, 345, 350
Pall Mall 225, 348
Pall Mall Gazette, The 238, 251, 253, 348
Palmer, Amelia 31, 32,
Palmer, Professor Edward 349-350
Palmerston, Lord 120,
Paris 165, 204, 283, 284, 296
Parnell, Charles Stewart 91, 278, 279, 280, 281, 282, 284, 285, 286, 287, 288, 317, 318
Pash, Arthur 93
Pasha, Mehmed Emin Aali 123, 345
Paul, Robert 21, 322, 323, 326, 346
Pearse, Grace 104
Pearse, PC Richard 104
Pedachenko, Dr Alexander 5
Peel, Sir Robert 266
Pennefather, Sir Richard 249
Pennett, PC William 250

Pennington Street 186, 187
Pennsylvania 191
Penygraig (Tonypandy) 185
People of the Abyss, The 267
People's Palace, 107, 265
People's Will, The 119
Peterloo Massacre 258, 259
'Phallic Emblems' 334
Philadelphia 301, 306
Phillips, Annie 95, 96, 97
Phillips, Dr George Bagster 37, 38, 39, 40, 42, 45, 69, 220, 222, 223, 229, 231, 232, 236, 239, 249, 250, 251, 294, 335
Phillips, Henry 97
Phinehas the Harlot-Slayer 337
Phoenix Park Murders 140, 141-144, 154, 168, 278, 279, 281, 289, 299, 313, 319
Picket, Catharine 204, 205, 214, 215
Pickfords 20
Pigott, Richard 281, 282, 283, 284, 285, 287
Pinchin Street, 250
Pinhorn, Inspector Charles 69
Polo, Marco 126
Ponsonby, Henry 227
Poplar High Street 55
Portman Square (Westminster) 187
Portpool Lane (Gray's Inn Road) 185
Portsoken Ward 99
Prater, Elizabeth 198, 199, 205, 210, 213, 237, 240, 242, 304, 328
Pressure points 294, 295, 296, 299
Preston, Charles 58, 163, 311, 329
Prince Charles 10
Prince's Square 55
Priory of the Holy Trinity 99
Princess Alice Disaster (1878) 54
Probyn, Sir Dighton 361
Public Records Office, 278, 363, 366
Punch 148
Purkiss, Walter 23
Purkiss, Mrs 23

Quatuor Coronati Lodge 107, 247
Queen Street, 86
Queen's Head (public house) 58, 59, 207
Queen's Royal Lancers 115-116

Queenstown 301, 302
Quinn, Thomas 87

Raffles 228
Raleigh, Sir Walter 170
Ranaghat (West Bengal) 248, 291
Ratcliff Highway 186, 187
Red Lion (public house) 204
Reed, Dr 150
Reform Act (1832) 262
Reid, Inspector Edmund 222
Reynold's Newspaper 113
Richardson, Mrs Amelia 40, 41, 42, 45
Richardson, John 40, 41
Rights of Man, The 256
Rise of Man, The 353-354
River Rom 209
Robarti, Francis 102
Robespierre, Maximilien 255
Robinson, PC Louis 96, 97
Rocker, Rudolf 307, 320
Romford 208
Room 56 289
Rosemary Lane 251
Rossa, Jeremiah O'Donovan 300
Rossa, Mary Jane O'Donovan 301
Roubliac, Louis Francois 330
Rowan, Sergeant 192, 194
Royal Army Medical Corps 364
Royal Courts of Justice 283, 306
Royal Engineers 89, 122, 176, 177, 297, 330, 331, 333
Royal Family 14, 90, 91, 327, 361
Royal Foresters' Music Hall 202
Royal Institute of British Architects 296
Royal Irish Constabulary 239, 240, 284, 302
Royal Irish Regiment 87
Royal Military Academy (Woolwich) 330, 332, 340
Royal Mint Street 251
Royal School of Military Engineering 89
Royal Sussex Regiment 33, 45, 46, 164, 184,
Ruffell, Frank 245
Russell, Lord 266
Russell, Sir Charles 282

St Andrew's Hall 191
St Bride's Church 15
St George's Road (SW London) 247
St George's Street 304
St James's Gazette 200
St James's Place (the Orange Market) 99, 162, 310
St Jude's committee 145
St Leonard's Church, 243
St Leonard's Hill 30
St Martin's-le-Grand 223
St Mary's (Spitalfields) 191
St Patrick's Roman Catholic Cemetery 5, 197, 239, 243
St Paul's Churchyard 223
Sadler, James Thomas 252
Sadler, MP Michael 263
Salisbury, Lord 91, 155, 156, 226-227, 277, 278, 317, 360
Salvation Army 268
Satchell, John 191, 194
Satchell's Lodging House 245
Saucy Jack postcard 49, 50, 51
Saunders, Dr William Sedgwick 294
Scandrell, Detective 192
Schwartz, Israel 82, 83
Scoll, William 191
Scotland Yard, 6, 49, 51, 76, 151, 170, 223, 235, 244, 253, 305
Scots Guards 183, 184
Seditious Meetings Act 257
Sequeira, Dr George William 106, 110, 162, 231, 294
Shadwell Dry Dock 18
Shaftesbury Avenue 273
Shakespeare, William 50, 51
Shamrock. The 281
Shapira, Moses Wilhelm 334
Shaw, George Bernard 272, 273, 275, 320
Shawcross, Sir Hartley 169
Shoe Lane (Mile End) 92, 93
Shoreditch 238
Shoreditch Town Hall 237
Sickert, Walter 366
Silva, Colvin R de 264
Simmonds, PC George 97
Singapore 247

'Sivvy', John 30, 31
Six Acts 259, 260
Slemen, Tom 4, 6, 7
Smith, Emma Elizabeth 225-226
Smith, Emily Latitia 29
Smith, George 29
Smith, R 192
Smith, PC William 79, 80, 81, 82, 84
Smith, Theresa 269
'Smoker' 172
Social Democratic federation 273
Society of Spencean Philanthropists 257
Sodeaux, John 52
Sodeaux, Mrs 53
Solomon's Temple 344
Somerset, Lord Arthur 359, 361
Son of Sam, The 103
South Saxon Lodge 107
South Staffordshire Regiment 157
Southwark 86
Spa Fields (Islington) 257
Special Air Service (SAS) 295, 321
Special Irish Branch 91, 137, 156, 165, 166, 327
Spectacle Alley 79
Spence, Thomas 257
Spitalfields Clock 35
Spitalfields Market 36, 40, 115
Spooner, Edward 65-66, 312
Spratling, Police Inspector John 26
Sri Lanka 264
Stalin, Josef 320
Standard newspaper 60
Stanley, Dr 5
Stanley, Ted 19-20, 29, 120, 351
Star newspaper 51, 60, 77, 83, 89, 105, 113, 114, 187, 212, 213, 244, 245, 293, 348
Stead, William T 348
Stepney Gas Works 186
Steeven's Hospital, Dublin 142
Stevens, George 192
Stevens, William 32, 33, 45, 46, 164
Stevenson, Robert Louis 9, 10,
Stewart, Captain 176, 333
Strand, The 71, 72
Strange Case of Dr Jekyll and Mr Hyde, The (1886 novel) 10

Stride, Elizabeth 54, 55, 56-60, 65, 66, 67, 68-69, 70, 71, 74, 77, 78, 80, 82, 83, 84, 85, 98, 100, 107, 108, 115, 118, 134, 135, 136, 140, 163, 166, 170, 181, 212, 224, 226, 237, 250, 283, 292, 294, 298, 307, 316, 319, 321, 327, 329, 335, 346, 352, 354, 355, 364

Stride, John Thomas 56

Sugar Loaf (public house) 324, 356

Sullivan, John L 347

Sullivan, Thomas Russell 12

Sullivan, William 245

Sumner, Henry 46

Sutcliffe, Peter 52

Sunshine, Israel 118, 315, 316, 352, 355

Survey of Western Palestine, The 124, 177

Swallow Gardens 251

Swanson, Chief Inspector Donald Sutherland 82

Swedish Church (Prince's Square) 311, 312

Sweeney, Inspector John 166

Swinscow, Charles Thomas 358

Tanner, Elizabeth 55, 57, 58, 59, 311

Telegraph, Daily 13, 51, 60, 76, 77, 83, 230

Tel el-Kebir, Battle of 298, 345

Temple Mount, Jerusalem 122, 123, 124

Temporary Regulations 119

Ten Bells (public house) 31, 199, 207, 216

Tent Work in Palestine 177, 337

Thain, PC John 23, 25

Thames 172, 175, 204

Thames Embankment 265

Thames Magistrates' Court 57, 252

Thickbroom, Charles Ernest 358, 359

Thirkettle, Henry James 46

Thistlewood, Arthur 257, 259

Thisted, Valdemar Adolph 156

Thompson, Mr 42

Thompson, PC Ernest 251, 252

Thomson, Superintendent 192

Thrawl Street 17, 20, 88, 206, 207, 208, 245, 319, 320, 328

Thugee and Dacoit Department 248

Times, The 51, 60, 83, 100, 112, 130, 140, 154, 155, 191, 208, 269, 279, 280, 281, 282, 289, 312, 318

Times, The Sunday 151

Tollit Street 145

Tomkins, Henry 25

Toulouse-Lautrec, Henri de 330

Tower of London 257, 258, 309

Tower of London bomb 100

Tracy, Spencer 9

Tracey, Catherine 301

Trafalgar Square 132, 199, 265, 271, 272, 275, 348

Treason Trials (1794) 256

Treasonable Practices Act 257

Tredegar (Blaenau Gwent) 185

Trotsky, Leon 320

Troup, Charles Edward 156-157

Troutbeck, Coroner John 173

Tyrwhitt-Drake, Charles 334, 337, 338

United Irishman 301

United Lodge of Free and Accepted Masons 342

United States 169

Upper North Street, Poplar

Vaughan, Judge 191, 193, 195

Vauxhall 32

Veck, George 358, 361

Venturney, Julia 198

Victoria, Queen 90, 91, 108, 156, 176, 225, 226, 243, 265, 266, 271, 277, 288, 299, 362

Victoria Embankment 107, 172, 177, 180

Victoria Workingmen's Home 206, 208, 223

Walker, Edward 15, 27

Walls, Rosetta 16

Wandsworth 16

Wandsworth Prison 169

War Office 6, 176, 225, 297, 328, 332, 334, 343, 351

Warren, Sir Charles 69, 72, 76, 89, 90, 107, 108, 119, 120, 122,123, 125, 126, 127, 129, 130, 131, 132, 134, 154, 177, 178, 198, 199, 221, 224, 225, 226, 227, 246, 272, 273, 275, 290, 291, 292, 297, 298, 305, 318, 332, 342, 343, 347, 348, 349, 350, 351, 364, 365, 366

Warren, Lady 365

Warren's Gate 124

Waterloo, 260

Watkins, PC Edward 101, 102, 103, 104, 105, 110, 162, 164, 311, 312

Watson, (John H) 6

Wearside Jack 52

Weeks, Josiah 30

Weiss surgical knives 142, 143, 144, 168

Wellington, Duke of 260, 261, 275

Wentworth Model Dwellings 115, 116, 117, 118, 127, 132, 136, 165, 315, 316, 352, 355

Wentworth Street 206

Wess, William 64, 65, 319, 321, 354, 355

West, Chief Inspector 69

West End 15, 71, 107, 180, 186, 269, 272, 289, 359

Westow Hill 61

Westminster 180, 305

Westminster Abbey 90, 91, 231, 278, 289

Westminster Division 172, 316

Westminster Bridge 259

Westminster Palace Chambers 142

West Yorkshire Police 52

Weymouth, 298, 346

White Sergeant Stephen 71, 72, 74, 75

Whitechapel Division 37

Whitechapel Murderer 12, 14, 38, 48, 49, 50, 51, 83, 94, 118, 149, 181, 182, 242, 313, 328

Whitechapel Road 18, 20, 23, 320, 328

Whitechapel Vigilance Committee 140, 145, 146, 150, 275

Whitehall 154, 169, 198, 222, 283, 313, 316, 327, 328, 339, 356, 363, 364, 366

Whitehall Division 115

Whitehall Place 223

Whitehall Review 270

Whitehall Torso 81, 172, 175, 177, 179, 180, 231, 354, 364

White House 17

White's Row 92

Whittridge, Mrs 309

Wickes, David 10

Wilde, Oscar 316, 330

Wilkinson, Fred 95

William Street 65

Wills, Dr 150

Wilson, Sir Charles 130, 131, 333, 343

Wilton, Henry 243

Windsor 30

Windsor castle 363

Wollstonecraft, Mary 256

Wolseley, General 345

Wolverhampton 86

Wood, Anna Maria 286

Wood, Matthew 260

Woolwich 183, 330, 331

Worker's Friend, The (Der Arbeiter Fraint) 64, 65, 137, 166, 355, 356

Workhouse Infirmary (Old Montague Street) 26

Workhouse Infirmary Mortuary, 43

World Association of Document Examiners (WADE) 152

Wright, George Alma 358, 359

'Writing on the wall' idiom 316-319

Yarmouth 86

York Place 72

Yorkshire 51

Yorkshire Ripper 52, 103

Young, Captain 46

Zodiac, The 103

Zulus 312

381